Essentials of
Elementary Reading

☐ *Essentials of Classroom Teaching Series* ☐

Essentials of
Elementary Reading

Second Edition

Michael F. Graves
University of Minnesota

Susan M. Watts-Taffe
University of Minnesota

Bonnie B. Graves
Minneapolis, Minnesota

Allyn and Bacon
Boston   London   Toronto   Sydney   Tokyo   Singapore

Vice President, Publisher, Education: Sean W. Wakely
Senior Editor: Virginia Lanigan
Editorial Assistant: Bridget Keane
Marketing Managers: Ellen Dolberg and Brad Parkins
Editorial Production Service: Chestnut Hill Enterprises, Inc.
Manufacturing Buyer: Suzanne Lareau
Cover Administrator: Jennifer Hart

Internet: www.abacon.com

Between the time Website information is gathered and published, it is not unusual for some
sites to have closed. Also, the transcription of URLs can result in typographical errors. The
publisher would appreciate notification where these occur so that they may be corrected.
Thank you.

Library of Congress Cataloging-in-Publication Data
Graves, Michael F.
    Essentials of elementary reading / Michael F. Graves,
Susan M. Watts-Taffe, Bonnie B. Graves. — 2nd ed.
        p. cm.
    Rev. ed. of: Elementary reading methods. c1994.
    Includes bibliographical references and indexes.
    ISBN 0-205-28034-X (pbk.)
    1. Reading (Elementary)—United States.   I. Watts-Taffe, Susan M.
II. Graves, Bonnie B.   III. Graves, Michael F.   Elementary reading
methods.   IV. Title.
LB1573.G65   1999
372.41—dc21   98-17391
                                                                  CIP

The Gradual Release of Responsibility Model on page 44 is taken with permission from
Pearson, P. D., and Gallagher, M. C. (1983). The instruction of reading comprehension.
Contemporary Educational Psychology, 8, 317–344.

The list of books on pages 103–105 is taken with permission from Trachtenburg, P. (1990).
Using children's literature to enhance phonic instruction. *The Reading Teacher, 43,* 648–654.

Portions of the text appearing on pages 106–130 were taken with permission from Lapp, D.,
Flood, J., and Farnin, N. (1996). *Content Area Reading and Learning: Instructional Strategies*
(2nd ed.). Needham Heights, MA: Allyn and Bacon.

Portions of the text appearing on pages 134–160 are reprinted with permission from Graves,
M. F. and Graves, B. B. (1994). *Scaffolding Experiences: Designs for Student Success.* Norwood,
MA: Christopher-Gordon.

The Two Phases of a Scaffolded Reading Experience on page 139 is taken with permission
from Graves, M. F., Palmer, R. J., and Furniss, D. W. (1976). *Structuring Reading Activities
for English Classes.* Urbana, IL: National Council of Teachers of English and from Graves,
M. F., and Graves, B. B. (1994) *Scaffolding Reading Experiences: Designs for Student Success.*
Norwood, MA: Christopher-Gordon.

Printed in the United States of America

10 9 8 7 6 5 4 3 2 1   03 02 01 00 99 98

To teachers everywhere and especially to
Wilma Watts
who is Susan's first and best teacher
and to
Helen Beecher
whose love and devotion to children is a model for us all

Contents

Preface

Writing a reading methods text such as this one is a tremendous learning experience. Doing so gave us the opportunity to review and consider carefully the rich knowledge base about reading that teachers, researchers, and scholars have amassed. Using a methods text that we had written in our classes and our work in public schools is an even better learning experience. It gave us myriad opportunities to share our ideas with preservice and practicing teachers, try them out in elementary schools, and observe as other teachers tried them out. Revising a methods text is a still better learning experience. It gave us the opportunity to use what we learned from teaching with the earlier edition to fine-tune the revised book. That is what we have done with this second edition of *Essentials of Elementary Reading,* and we believe that the result of our fine-tuning is a text that is uniquely clear, concise, and on target—a text extremely well suited to helping beginning teachers learn how to assist students as they become competent, inquiring, and avid readers.

How can teachers effectively teach children to read? How can they ensure that each and every student—those who learn almost automatically and those for whom reading is a challenge—gets the best possible start on the road to literacy? Over the past 100 years, and increasingly during the past 30 years, that question has been posed repeatedly. Answers have been sought by classroom teachers, educational researchers, linguists, psychologists, parents, and others concerned with the education of young people. Answers have been found, many of them. The research and scholarly dialogue on phonics alone would fill several hefty volumes. Why, then, is this volume you are holding, *Essentials of Elementary Reading,* just over 200 pages long?

This book is designed to be informative, helpful, and manageable. It is designed so that you can thoroughly study and understand its contents. Obviously, this book does not answer every question you might have about teaching reading. We have been very selective in what we have included. We have included only the information that research, classroom experience, and common sense have shown to be the most important information you need to set up and maintain an effective reading program.

Because we have been selective in choosing information to include, we have also been able to cover information quite thoroughly. We have included theories about effective instruction, procedures for implementing that instruction, and concrete examples to make those theories and procedures come to life. These thorough presentations give you the opportunity to learn the information well—to really understand it, remember it over time, put it in your own words, question it, discuss it with classmates, try it out, evaluate it, and ultimately make it a part of the strategies you use to lead students to become competent lifelong readers.

Technology

Leaders of professional organizations have become increasingly aware of the need to integrate technology instruction in all courses dealing with teaching methods. For this second edition, we have added an icon—shown at the left—to highlight places in the text where technology is discussed.

Finally, because the information presented here is not overwhelming, you have the option of further investigating topics you find particularly interesting or those that are likely to be especially important in your classroom. Carefully selected, annotated references at the end of each chapter facilitate such investigations.

Over the years, you will undoubtedly learn more about teaching reading and will add a number of insights and instructional techniques to your store. In the meantime, the information and techniques described here will prepare you to design and teach a powerful and effective reading program that you understand thoroughly and that will lead all students to the sophisticated literacy they will need in the new millennium.

ACKNOWLEDGMENTS

No book is written alone, or in this case, with just three authors. We want to extend our heartfelt thanks to our colleagues, friends, and family who have supported this endeavor. Without their patience and encouragement, this book would never have become a reality.

We also want to thank the students we've had in our classrooms, from whom we've learned a lot about what works and what doesn't and what it is that elementary school teachers need to know in order to be successful in their own classrooms. We extend heartfelt appreciation to our own teachers at Stanford University, the State University of New York at Buffalo, and California State University at Long Beach, whose knowledge, expertise, and example inspired and encouraged us. Susan extends particular gratitude to Michael W. Kibby for his continual support, guidance, and wisdom.

We thank our colleagues, both known and unknown, who took the time to review the first edition of this book and provide thoughtful, relevant feedback.

Finally, we want to thank our editor, Virginia Lanigan, for her assistance on both the first and second editions of this book, and to acknowledge the contributions of the following reviewers: Sharon Cerami, Baldwin-Wallace College; Kathleen Howe, University of St. Thomas; and Andrew Johnson, Mankato State University.

Essentials of
Elementary Reading

1 Introduction, Overview, and How to Learn from This Book

> The knowledge is now available to make worthwhile improvements in reading throughout the United States. If the practices seen in the classrooms of the best teachers in the best schools could be introduced everywhere, improvements in reading would be dramatic. —Anderson, Hiebert, Scott and Wilkinson 1985

We are writing at an exciting time in the field of reading education. In our judgment and that of virtually all of our colleagues, the past 30 years have produced a rich and powerful wellspring of information and ideas about teaching children to read. Together, classroom teachers, university professors, and researchers in various settings have identified and investigated a host of approaches and activities for reading instruction. Using these approaches and activities, we can now help all children become competent readers, confident readers, and lifelong readers—youngsters, and later adults, who use reading as an avenue to learning, to personal fulfillment, and to enjoyment throughout their lives. In this book, we present the most practical and compelling of these ideas, the information we believe is most central to building and maintaining effective reading programs.

LOOKING AHEAD

Although this is a short chapter, it is an important one for getting the most from this book. In this chapter, we describe our basic orientation to teaching children to read, give a brief summary of each of the book's chapters, and make some suggestions for learning from the book. Knowing the general approach we take to reading instruction, knowing what topics the book covers and in what order it covers them, and considering the learning strategies that we recommend you use in studying this book will make your reading and studying efficient. Knowing as much as possible about the content and organization of material you are trying to learn is a great aid in learning material and remembering what you read. This fact, not incidentally, holds equally true for you and for your students. We are writing with the expectation that the introduction and overview we give you here will serve as a model for the introductions and overviews you give your students when you prepare them to read informational texts. We are also writing with the expectation that the study strategies we suggest in the last section of this chapter are ones that both you and your students will use.

KEY CONCEPTS

- Two major approaches to elementary reading instruction
- Crucial topics to consider in planning reading instruction
- General principles of effective study
- Techniques useful in studying this chapter and other informational texts

INTRODUCTION

For as long as we can remember, there have been debates about how to teach reading (Graves and Dykstra 1997). As Jeanne Chall (1967) has pointed out, during the 1950s and 1960s, the primary debate was over whether to teach beginning reading using a code approach (an approach that emphasizes the sounds of individual letters) or a whole word approach (an approach that presents students with whole words to learn as intact units). More recently—as illustrated by articles in educational journals such as the *American Educator* (for example, Adams and Bruck 1995; Beck and Juel 1995; McPike 1995) as well as articles in popular magazines such as *Time* (for example, Collins 1997)—the debate has shifted to the advocacy of either a fairly traditional approach, sometimes called the *basal approach,* or a newer and quite different approach, most commonly called *whole language.* Although we discuss each of these approaches in somewhat more detail in Chapter 2, here we briefly sketch them so that we can note our position with respect to this debate. The traditional or basal approach typically employs systematic phonics instruction, uses a graded series of readers specifically constructed for teaching reading, and teaches a sequenced set of skills. In contrast, the whole-language approach typically teaches much less phonics, employs trade books (books not specifically written for instructional purposes) rather than a graded series of readers, and does not teach skills in a preset sequence.

The approach suggested here is a balanced combination of elements from both traditional and whole-language approaches. Thus, for example, we have included a chapter on emergent literacy, a construct that recognizes, celebrates, and suggests ways to nurture children's natural and growing proficiency in reading, writing, speaking, and listening. Emergent literacy is a concept developed and endorsed by whole-language advocates. We have also included a chapter on teaching students strategies for recognizing words, and one of these strategies is using phonic analysis. Phonics, of course, is strongly endorsed by those favoring a traditional approach. We have adopted this moderate position which combines aspects of traditional and whole-language approaches for two reasons. First, we believe in it; like Dixie Lee Spiegel (1992), we believe that both approaches have a lot to offer. Second, your choices between a whole-language approach and a traditional approach are likely to be somewhat limited. Most schools either have graded series, which they ask or require teachers to use, or do not have graded series and encourage or require teachers to use whole-language approaches. Of course, there is always room for you to modify and complement your school's approach within your own classroom, and we believe that the balanced approach we present here gives you the knowledge, tools, and flexibility to do so.

CHAPTER-BY-CHAPTER OVERVIEW

Here, we first describe the contents of each chapter. Then we explain the common components and organization of each chapter.

Chapter 1: Introduction, Overview, and How to Learn from This Book

This, of course, is what you are reading now; it includes a brief statement about our instructional orientation, this overview of the book, and a section on study strategies.

Chapter 2: Learning to Read

This chapter is divided into three parts. The first part examines American students' proficiency in reading, changes in reading proficiency over time, and the adequacy of that proficiency in today's world. The second part describes the two main approaches to reading instruction—the traditional, or basal, reading approach and the whole-language approach. The third part discusses cognitive and constructivist orientations to teaching and learning and some of the major constructs that have emerged from these orientations.

Chapter 3: Developing a Classroom Reading Program

In this chapter, we discuss critical factors to consider as you plan the reading program for your classroom. The first two sections discuss classroom management and grouping students for instruction. The next section examines a small set of concepts and principles that have proven particularly useful in planning and delivering instruction. The two sections after that consider cultural and linguistic diversity and students with special needs, and answer several questions that teachers frequently ask about reading instruction. Finally, the last section stresses the importance of students being successful in the reading tasks we give them.

Chapter 4: Emergent Literacy and the Beginnings of Reading Instruction

Here we briefly examine children's early encounters with language and their growing ability to deal with printed language, their *emergent literacy*. Next we discuss some factors that influence emergent literacy and some ways to foster it. Here we consider ways of facilitating children's print awareness, interest in books, knowledge of letters, awareness of basic story elements, and recognition and discrimination of English sounds. We also consider the importance of immersing children in print, developing a basic sight vocabulary, and engaging children in rich and varied experiences with language.

Chapter 5: Strategies for Recognizing Words

Using word-recognition strategies—approaches readers use to figure out words they do not immediately recognize—is one of many reading skills that can lead students to become independent readers. The two word-recognition strategies we discuss in this chapter are phonic analysis—which includes using letter-sound correspondences, decoding by analogy, and blending sounds to form words—and structural analysis—which includes identifying roots, prefixes, and suffixes to arrive at the pronunciation of words that are not at first recognized as wholes. Although these word-recognition strategies require students to dissect words and deal with their parts, one goal of reading instruction is to have students recognize words as wholes and do so instantaneously. Thus, word-recognition strategies are a means to an end, tools that students will use until they reach the point at which they easily and automatically recognize most of the words in the material they read. Phonics and structural analysis have at times been treated as if they were ends in themselves—the ultimate goals of reading instruction. In this chapter, we repeatedly emphasize that the goal of reading is getting meaning from what is read and that word-recognition strategies are merely tools that can be used in reaching that goal.

Chapter 6: Developing Vocabulary

This chapter is divided into five parts. The first part examines how many words students know and how thoroughly they know most words. The second part considers the importance of wide reading for developing a rich and powerful vocabulary; of course, there are many reasons for engaging students in wide reading, but building vocabulary is certainly one of them. The third part deals with the various word learning tasks students face, selecting vocabulary to teach, and methods of teaching specific words. The fourth part describes strategies students can use to learn vocabulary on their own; these include examining context, working with word parts, and using the dictionary. The last part describes ways of fostering students' word consciousness, which we define as their interest in words and the pleasure they take in using words well and seeing others use them well.

Chapter 7: Fostering Comprehension of Specific Selections

In this chapter, we present a framework and a comprehensive plan for assisting students in reading, comprehending, and enjoying specific selections. First, we explain how the purpose, the reading selection, and the students who are doing the reading need to be considered as one plans reading activities. Next, we describe types of prereading, during-reading, and postreading activities that you and your students can use to ensure successful reading. Prereading activities motivate and prepare students to read a selection. During-reading activities are those that take place as students read and that assist them in building meaning. Postreading activities are those that occur after reading and that encourage students to analyze, synthesize, and apply what they have read. We conclude the chapter with a sample of a complete reading lesson made up of the prereading, during-reading, and postreading activities we consider appropriate for a particular group of students reading a particular selection for a particular purpose.

Chapter 8: Teaching Comprehension Strategies

The chapter begins by defining comprehension strategies, noting some of their principal characteristics, and describing eight key strategies. Next, it considers some central concepts underlying our approach to strategy instruction. Following that, it presents a specific approach to teaching comprehension strategies and describes some widely recommended sequences of strategies. Finally, because there are more strategies than you can teach in a single year, it examines the matter of your selecting which strategies to teach.

Chapter 9: Classroom Assessment

Here, we first consider the ongoing nature of assessment, the audiences for assessment, its purposes, and its relationship to instruction. Next, we discuss the major types of assessment and the types of records to keep. After that, we describe what aspects of students' reading performance to assess and how to do these assessments. Finally, we consider student self-assessment, teacher self-assessment, and some general guidelines for assessment.

Chapter 10: A Day in a Fourth-Grade Classroom

The chapters preceding this one present a variety of theories, principles, components of reading and learning to read, and instructional approaches. In this chapter, we present one possibility for reading instruction—a day in a fourth-grade classroom. In it we describe how the day's activities had their genesis, how they evolved, and how they are implemented. No two classroom reading programs can be or should be just alike. Many excellent programs will differ markedly. Here we present just one possible program for one day of the school year with one particular group of students.

The Components and Organization of Each Chapter

We have designed each chapter to facilitate your reading and make learning as efficient as possible. Each chapter has the same components and organization. Each begins with a brief personal statement or scenario in which we try to convey our interest in the topic of the chapter and suggest one or more of the major themes of the chapter. Next comes a section titled Looking Ahead, which presents an overview of the chapter and a very brief review of the previous chapter. After this comes a set of topics titled Key Concepts. These are the major topics in the chapter. Following this list of key concepts comes the body of the chapter, usually consisting of two to four main sections with some subsections. The last main section in the body is always titled Concluding Remarks and includes a summary and a few comments on the chapter. This is followed by a section titled Self-Check. The Self-Check includes specific questions on the topics listed in Key Concepts and more general questions that ask you to apply what you have learned to some instructional situation. The final section common to all chapters, References, lists articles that either support and explain information in the chapter or extend learning to related topics.

In addition to components included in all chapters, two features are included in selected chapters. Chapters 3 through 9 include information on dealing with cultural and linguistic diversity and students with special needs. Chapters 2, 4, 5, 7, 8, and 9 are followed by lists of children's books.

HOW TO LEARN FROM THIS BOOK

You have been reading and studying for a number of years and have, no doubt, discovered a number of approaches that are effective for you. Here we consider five general principles of studying and five specific study strategies that research and practice have shown to be generally effective. As we have already noted, in addition to your using these strategies in studying this book—and in studying generally—we believe strongly that these strategies are also applicable and appropriate for your students, and we encourage you to share the principles with your students and guide them in learning and using the study strategies. We also suggest that you share the principles and strategies with students' parents. A lot of studying is done at home, and parents are in a terrific position to help their children become effective and efficient learners.

General Principles of Studying

Taking Studying Seriously
A frequent problem that many students have with studying is that they do not take it seriously—they don't do much of it. The first rule of studying, then, is "Do it!" If you want to learn the material in this book or in other books, there is simply no substitute for putting in a serious amount of time studying. If there is a lot of information in the book, if the book examines complex issues or issues unfamiliar, then studying it adequately is going to take a lot of time. There is no alternative.

Finding the Time and a Place to Study
It makes good sense to try to estimate the time that studying is likely to take, and that is not easy to do. Each of you reads and learns at different rates and, to get an accurate estimate of the rate at which you will be able to read and learn from this book, you really need to study a chapter until you have mastered most of the material in it and see how long that takes. However, you can get a rough estimate by considering the length of the text and a rate of reading and studying that you can probably achieve. This book contains about 90,000 words, and many people can initially read a book of this complexity at about 100 words a minute. This means the whole of the book would take about 15 hours to read and the average chapter would take about 1½ hours. Add to this the time needed for some sort of surveying and note taking—two activities we will discuss—and the total time needed for studying an average chapter comes to about 2½ hours. Add to this some time for review, perhaps half an hour for reviewing an average chapter, and the time needed totals about three hours.

Assuming that you will be dealing with most chapters in about a week, this obviously means that you need to plan for about three hours a week. With the shorter chapters, we suspect that the surveying, reading, and initial studying can best be done in a single session. With the longer chapters, it may be best to survey the whole of the chapter and read and study half of it in one session, and then read and study the other half of it in another session. In either case, we suggest spending some time reviewing the chapter at the end of the week and, of course, you will need some extra time for reviewing before exams. Assuming you have a busy schedule, it would be a good idea to set aside specific days and times for studying and reviewing, for example, initially reading and studying on Monday or Monday and Wednesday mornings and reviewing on Thursday afternoons.

Having an appropriate place to study is almost as important as finding the time to study. The place where you study should be free from distractions and should give you room to lay out your materials and take notes or jot down ideas and questions. Regarding distractions, the main point we want to make is that our minds can only attend to one thing at a time. Attempts to study and do something else at the same time simply do not work. To learn the most in the least amount of time, your studying should be focused and uninterrupted. Regarding having a place to lay out your materials and take notes, we recommend a straight chair and a good sized desk. Again, our advice is to study seriously when you are studying and then relax and enjoy yourself when you are not studying.

Active Learning

As we explain somewhat further in Chapter 2, learning is not a process in which a teacher or textbook can somehow pour information into a student's mind. Learning can only be accomplished by the learner. Learning is an active process in which the learner considers, manipulates, and grapples with the ideas he is attempting to understand and remember. Learning is in fact a constructive process in which the learner plays an active role in building and shaping the meaning a teacher or text is attempting to convey.

All of this means that reading a text passively simply will not work. To understand a text, to come away with something solid that you understand and that you can apply in your teaching, you need to do much more than simply read it. You need to engage with the text—really get involved with the ideas presented. You also need to manipulate the ideas presented—for example, by putting them in your own words—and, if possible, you need to apply what you have learned. Fostering such involvement requires several steps. First, you must actively search for information in a text—have some questions you want answered or a problem for which you seek a solution. Second, you must engage with the text and reflect on it—pause periodically to answer the questions you initially posed, ask other questions, sum up what has been said thus far, agree or disagree with points made, or decide how you might use the information in an actual teaching situation. Third, for the majority of readers, such engagement and reflection require writing. You can certainly engage, grapple, and argue mentally, but oftentimes that's difficult. Thus, as a rule, you need to do something to force yourself to be active—take notes, jot down questions, or write out summaries. Finally, if at all possible, attempt to apply the information presented in the text—at this point, for example, stop and ask yourself what three topics on studying have been covered thus far; then briefly summarize what has been said about each of them.

Getting a Sense of the Whole

One part of being an active learner is putting bits and pieces of information together so that they fit into some general scheme of things and make up a meaningful whole. One step in putting the pieces together to form a meaningful whole is finding out what the whole of a text or chapter looks like. To facilitate your doing this, we znamed the chapters of the book, described the contents of each chapter, used a common organization for each chapter, and described the organization of each chapter. We were attempting to give you an overview of what was coming and in what order it was coming. If you skipped that section of this chapter or briefly skimmed it, we suggest strongly that you go back and read it carefully, and probably take some notes as you do so. This will be time well spent and will make your study of the rest of the text more efficient and more effective.

Relating New Information to Things You Already Know

Another part of being an active learner is relating new information to information you already know. In fact, some authorities have defined comprehension as relating the unknown to the known. Any time you can tie information in this text to things you already know or things you have at least heard about, it will be to your advantage to do so. Thus, for example, if you have had an educational psychology course, you are likely to have encountered the notion of active learning there. Ask yourself how the explanation of active learning given here is similar to and dissimilar to that presented there. You might also ask yourself what other concepts were associated with the concept of active learning in your psychology course. Building such relationships will give more meaning to the ideas presented here. Also, establishing such relationships will help you remember, recall, and deepen your understanding of the concepts over time.

Specific Study Strategies

Surveying

As one of the general principles of studying, we stressed the importance of getting an overview of the organization and a sense of the whole of a book or chapter before reading it. Surveying is the most common method of doing so. Surveying refers to going through a text rather quickly to get an overview of it. In surveying a book, you might read the flyleaf, preface, introduction, table of contents, and introductory and concluding sections of each chapter. You would also consider any supporting material available —index, bibliography, appendices, and so forth—and the length of the book. In doing this, you would be trying to get an idea of the content, how the book is organized, how much you already know about the topics, how difficult the book is going to be and how much studying it will take, and how you will study it. If the book is not required, you would also consider whether it is something you want to read.

In surveying a chapter or article, you would probably read the title, the introductory paragraphs (in this book, this would include the personal statement in italics, the Looking Ahead section, and the Key Concepts section), the main headings, and the chapter summary if there is one (in this book, this means the Concluding Remarks section). You would also consider supporting material, such as questions (here, the Self-Check section). As with books, you are trying to get an idea of the content and organization, how much you know about the topics, how difficult the chapter is likely to be and how much studying it will take, and—if the chapter is not required—whether you want to read it.

When surveying materials the length of chapters and articles, it is particularly important to be an active learner. Writing questions that you expect to be answered in the chapter, jotting down notes about the major topics and what you already know about them, or making a skeletal outline that you can later add to are active-learning strategies that will pay excellent dividends in understanding and remembering the material. Also, if chapters include introductory questions, try to answer them. If you cannot, write them down so that you can answer them as you read the chapter.

The time spent in surveying the book, surveying the chapter, and engaging in an active-learning strategy with the topics in the chapter will make your reading and studying of the chapter much more efficient. Moreover, such activities will leave you with information that you understand well and can remember when you need it.

Underlining or Highlighting

We include the topic of underlying or highlighting with some reservations. Underlining and highlighting are probably the most frequently used procedures for studying textbooks. They are also the easiest, the quickest, and the least cognitively engaging approaches one could take; and, consequently, they are often not very effective. However, we believe that there is one way in which they can be made more effective, and we certainly recommend that if you do use underlining and highlighting you use them as effectively as possible. The most effective way to use them is to underline and highlight only after you understand the material. This means (1) reading a complete section of the material—everything that is said about a topic or subtopic, usually several pages, (2) deciding what is important in the section, and (3) underlining or highlighting the important material. Note that this process forces you to work with the material and understand it *before* you underline or highlight. To be sure, this will take more time than underlining as you go, but in this way you both understand the material and have the relevant material identified for review. Underlining or highlighting before you really understand what you are reading is likely to leave you with little other than a messy book and a false sense that you have studied and learned the material.

Note Taking

We recommend note taking over underlining or highlighting because with note taking it is much harder to fool yourself into believing that you have studied and learned material when you have not. We also recommend note taking over underlining or highlighting because note taking is a more active process.

The first two steps in note taking are the same as those in underlining: First, read a complete section of the material—everything that is said about a topic or subtopic, usually several pages; and, second, decide what is important in the section. The third step of note taking, however, is different in two important ways. In note taking, you need to actively write something, not passively underline or highlight it. Also, and more importantly, in note taking you should strive to write down the information from the chapter in your own words rather than using the words of the author. This last point is crucial to truly effective note taking. Deliberately taking notes in your own words rather than in those of the author forces you to actively process the information in the text and to understand it. You simply cannot rephrase something in your own words without understanding it, and the sort of understanding it takes to rephrase ideas is the sort of understanding that will help fix those ideas in your memory.

Two additional aspects of note taking deserve mention. The first is the various forms that notes can take. Thus far, we have been talking about notes that are summaries or condensations of material in the book, and such notes are frequently appropriate. However, notes can also take other forms. For example, notes can be questions about what the author has said or will say—"Hmm. These authors don't think much of highlighting; I wonder what they'll say about note taking." Notes can link the ideas in the present text with ideas from other sources—"I remember that one of my high school social studies teachers used to rant and rave against underlining. I wonder if his arguments against it were the same as those here." Notes can be used to express your response to ideas in the text—"I agree that note taking is effective, but it also takes time. I know there will be some times when all I can do is underline."

The final aspect of note taking we consider is where to take notes—in the text itself or separately from the text. Both serve useful purposes and have their advantages. The advantages of taking notes in the book are that you can easily do it as you are reading and the notes are in a place you can find them. The disadvantages are that space is limited and you may end up with writing in the book you would rather not have there. One advantage of taking notes separately from the text is that you have plenty of room. Another advantage is that you can return to separate notes and further annotate or otherwise mark them up. One approach to note taking, for example, suggests that you put your basic notes on one side of the page and then come back and comment further on the other side of the page. Other things that you can do with separate notes are to highlight key terms or show relationships between ideas. Of course, a potential disadvantage of separate notes is that they may take more time than textual notes; however, this is not really a disadvantage because that extra time is going to pay extra dividends in learning and remembering the material.

Summarizing

We have already discussed the fact that a lot of notes take the form of summaries. We include summarizing as a separate topic so that we can further stress its value and give some specific guidelines for summarizing, guidelines that really press you to be an active learner.

The guidelines, which were developed and tested by Ann Brown and Jeanne Day (1983), are shown below:

1. Read a cohesive block of text, several pages that focus on a single topic.

2. Summarize the paragraphs in the section by (1) deleting trivial or redundant information, (2) using superordinate categories and terms when possible, and (3) identifying and recording a topic sentence for the paragraph.

3. Summarize the section as a whole by constructing an overall summary of these paragraph summaries.

By now, you are likely to realize why we highly recommend summarizing. We recommend it highly because it is exactly the sort of active, constructive study that we have repeatedly endorsed and that we believe is essential to learning.

Reviewing and Studying for Tests

This is the last studying technique we will discuss here. It is important to recognize that reviewing and studying for tests is not the most important part of studying. Instead, the most important part of studying is the day-to-day work that goes on throughout the period you are in a particular class or investigating a particular topic. No amount of reviewing can substitute for not studying well initially. This said, we move on to the topic of reviewing and present four guidelines.

First, reviewing should be done as soon as possible after material is learned and not just before tests. The new information you gain from a text or other source is very quickly forgotten and, because of this, the best time to prop up your fading memory is very soon after initially learning material. Thus, an excellent time to review lecture notes is just after the lecture, and a good time to review reading notes is shortly after taking them.

Second, reviewing should be done frequently and not just once. For example, when taking a quarter or semester course, we recommend that you take a short period of time each week to review all of the material you have covered up to that point in the course. Spending several 30-minute study sessions spaced a week or so apart will produce better and more permanent learning than spending a single long cramming session just before an exam.

Third, in addition to your initial studying and periodic reviews, you should include a block of study shortly before an exam. If you have been studying and reviewing all along, this final push certainly does not need to be a prolonged, all-night effort. But a good review shortly before an exam is essential—the motivation is certainly there, the test will come before you have forgotten the reviewed material, and you will go into the test confident of your performance.

Fourth, like any studying and learning, reviewing should be an active and constructive process. Answering questions orally or in writing, filling in blank diagrams, and completing outlines or other graphic summaries—all without looking back at the material unless you have to—are excellent activities. Also, reviewing is an excellent situation in which to cooperate with a partner or group of partners. Working together makes it easy to have one person in the group ask questions while others answer them or to have people check each others' answers. Working together also allows members of the group to share ideas and learn from each other. Finally, working together provides some motivation for studying and makes it easier to stick with it and put in a prolonged period of effort.

CONCLUDING REMARKS

In this chapter, we have done three things. First, we briefly described the traditional and whole-language approaches to reading instruction and explained that our approach represents a middle ground that incorporates the best of both approaches. Second, we outlined the chapters of the book and explained the common organization and contents of each chapter. Third, we listed some general principles of studying and some specific study strategies. Again, we stress that these strategies are intended for you to use in studying this and other texts and for you to teach your students to use in studying informational material.

SELF-CHECK

In this chapter and in those that follow, we have included a set of questions to check your understanding of the chapter. Here, the first five questions check your knowledge of the key concepts listed at the beginning of the chapter. The last three questions give you an opportunity to manipulate or apply what you have learned. Try to answer the questions without looking back at the chapter. However, if you do not know an answer, take the time to reread to get the answer. Rereading to fill in missing information immediately after first reading a selection is an efficient approach to learning material.

1. Describe the two major approaches to reading instruction.

2. Name or very briefly describe each of the ten chapters in the book.

3. State the five general principles of effective study presented.

4. Define active learning, and explain why active learning is extremely important.

5. Name the five specific study strategies presented.

6. If possible, get together with a colleague and discuss what you know about the two major approaches to reading instruction and the tensions between them.

7. Consider each of the five general principles of effective study and try to list someplace that you have heard each of them before. If you cannot think of anyplace where you have heard of one of them before, try to think of a place where you might hear about it in the future.

8. Consider each of the five specific study strategies and note an instance in which you have used each of them in the past or will use each of them in the future.

REFERENCES

Adams, M. J. and Bruck, M. (1995). Resolving the "Great Debate." *American Educator, 19* (2), 7, 10–20. Description of a beginning reading approach that would appropriately balance elements of whole language with decoding instruction.

Anderson, R. C., Hiebert, E. F., Scott, J. A. and Wilkinson, I. A. G. (1985). *Becoming a nation of readers.* Washington, DC: National Institute of Education. A concise summary of what we know about reading instruction.

Beck, I. L. and Juel, C. (1995). The role of decoding in learning to read. *American Educator, 19* (2), 8, 21–25, 39–42. Clear and concise suggestions for designing effective decoding instruction.

Brown, A. H. and Day, J. D. (1983). Macrorules for summarizing text: The development of expertise. *Journal of Verbal Learning and Verbal Behavior, 22,* 1–14. This well-known research study presents some very practical rules for summarizing text.

Chall, J. (1967). *Learning to read: The great debate.* New York: McGraw-Hill. This classic text describes the debate between code and meaning emphases to beginning reading instruction and presents what Chall saw as the evidence favoring the code approach. Although the text is now dated, it is an important part of the history of reading instruction.

Collins, J. (1997, October 27). How Johnny should read. *Time,* pp. 78–81. A brief but well-reasoned look at the two major approaches to teaching beginning reading and at what constitutes a reasonable blend of the two.

Gall, M. D., Gall, J. P., Jacobsen, D. R. and Bullock, T. L. (1990). *Tools for learning: A guide to teaching study skills.* Alexandria, VA: Association for Supervision and Curriculum Development. This straightforward text written specifically for teachers presents fairly brief discussions of a wide range of study skills.

Graves, M. F. and Dykstra, R. (1997). Contextualizing the first-grade studies: What is the best way to teach children to read? *Reading Research Quarterly, 32,* 342–344. A brief introduction to the long-standing debate over methods of teaching beginning reading.

McPike, E. (1995). Learning to read: Schooling's first mission. *American Educator, 19* (2), 3–6. A brief and balanced look at the components of an effective beginning reading program.

Pauk, W. (1997). *How to study in college* (6th ed.). Boston: Houghton Mifflin. A popular and very readable book written for college students.

Spiegel, D. L. (1992). Blending whole language and systematic direct instruction. *The Reading Teacher, 46,* 38–44. A cogent presentation on the value of including elements from both whole-language and traditional approaches.

2 Learning to Read

We assume that some of you reading this book have had a good deal of experience teaching reading while others have had none. As a consequence, what we have to say here will be quite familiar to some of you and largely unfamiliar to others. In either case, we urge you to give serious consideration to the ideas presented. Our understandings and beliefs about the matters discussed here heavily influence our instructional recommendations throughout the book. If you are already generally familiar with some of these topics, you still need to know what we think about them. If you are not familiar with the topics, then you need the general knowledge presented here to get the most out of the book.

While some of the information we discuss can be sobering—for example, some of the data on American students' achievement in reading—a good deal of it can be exciting—for example, information about how children learn. We hope you consider both the sobering parts and the more exciting ones as you plan and refine your approach to fostering students' reading ability.

LOOKING AHEAD

This chapter is divided into three parts. In the first part, we look at American students' proficiency in reading, the way that proficiency has changed over time, the reading proficiency of disadvantaged students, and the adequacy of that proficiency in today's world. In recent years, the United States has periodically assessed students' reading proficiency with a nationwide program named the National Assessment of Educational Progress. Results from this and other sources provide both encouraging and sobering information on students' proficiency.

In the second part of the chapter, we look at current practices for teaching reading in elementary schools. Although practices are diverse and in the process of changing, it is still possible to characterize two main approaches to reading instruction: the basal-reader approach and the whole-language approach.

Finally, in the third part of the chapter, we examine two general orientations and several important theories that have influenced our understanding of the reading process and, consequently, our approach to reading instruction. The past 30 years have seen a huge outpouring of theory and research on reading, and we now know a good deal that is useful in planning effective instruction.

KEY CONCEPTS

- American students' reading proficiency

- The proficiency of disadvantaged and advantaged students

- The reading skills needed in today's world

- Instruction in basal reading programs

- Instruction in whole-language programs

- Schema theory and the importance of schemata

- The interactive model of reading

- Automaticity and its importance in reading

- Metacognition and types of metacognitive knowledge

- The social constructivist orientation

- Types of context to consider in promoting literacy

STUDENT ACHIEVEMENT

As we have already noted, recent reports reveal both positive and negative aspects of students' reading achievement. Two large-scale assessment projects—the National Assessment of Educational Progress (NAEP) and the International Association for the Evaluation of Educational Achievement (IEA)—provide the most reliable data we are familiar with. The National Assessment of Educational Progress was established by the federal government 30 years ago to provide a periodic report card on American students' achievements in reading and other academic areas. In other words, it was established to do exactly the job we are trying to do here—communicate about how American students are doing in school. NAEP typically tests about every four years, and reports data for 9-, 14-, and 17-year-olds. Results of the nine administrations of the NAEP reading tests for which we have comparative data (Campbell, Voelka and Donahue 1997) show that American students in the 1990s read just about like American students did in the 1970s. Comparisons with earlier times, though difficult to make because comparable data are in short supply, show very similar results (Anderson, Hiebert, Scott and Wilkinson 1985).

The International Association for the Evaluation of Educational Achievement was established in the late 1950s to conduct international studies. It is by far the most experienced body conducting such comparisons and presents the most comprehensive and representative studies available. The most recent IEA study of reading achievement was conducted during the 1990–91 school year in 34 countries (Elley 1992). Comparisons of American students to those in other highly industrialized nations generally considered to have high educational standards—countries such as Canada, Finland, and Singapore—show that for all practical purposes American students read as well as students in comparable industrialized countries.

In summary, the best data we can locate indicate that American students reading proficiency has not declined in recent years and is about like that of students in other industrialized nations. However, there is still cause for concern. Recent NAEP data (Campbell, Donahue, Reese and Phillips 1996; Mullis, Campbell and Farstrup 1993) suggest the following pattern of performance among U.S. students: By fourth grade, the vast majority of students can read easy material and answer simple questions on it. However, once texts become slightly more difficult, involving the sorts of things middle-grade students are expected to deal with, a large percentage of middle-grade students cannot read and understand them and neither can a sizable percentage of high school seniors. And once both texts and questions become demanding, the sorts of material one would need to read in understanding political and social issues or enjoying sophisticated literature, very few students, even those about to graduate from high school, can deal with them. Additionally, the data indicate that certain groups of U.S. students are not as well prepared for school as others and will need your help in becoming proficient readers. Most notably, students of poverty, students whose preschool and out-of-school experiences have not prepared them for middle-class schools, are likely to need particular assistance. The reading proficiency of students attending schools in economically disadvantaged communities lags very significantly behind that of students attending schools in economically advantaged communities.

Additional understanding of students' achievements in reading comes from considering what it means to be literate in today's world. At one time, literacy was defined as the ability to sign your name. At another time, it was defined as the ability to read aloud a simple text with which you were already familiar—typically something from the Bible. Today, while there is no single definition of literacy, there is universal agreement that the demands of literacy are far greater than they were at any time in our past and will continue to grow and take many forms. David Perkins (1992), for example, notes that contemporary education must go beyond simply presenting students with information and must ensure that students retain important information, understand topics thoroughly, and actively use the knowledge they gain. And Robert Calfee (Calfee and Patrick 1995) argues that success in today's society demands what he calls *critical literacy*—the use of reading and the other language arts for thinking, problem solving, and communicating.

Technology

Thus, literacy often requires that we be able to do something not just know something. Moreover, literacy today requires that we be able to do something with a variety of different texts—not only short stories, novels, poetry, and history texts but also tax forms, computer manuals, complex directions for operating even more complex machines, and technical documents related to business, economics, agriculture, the military, and a huge variety of other enterprises. Literacy today also requires that we be competent and comfortable accessing electronic texts—from online card catalogs, to airline schedules, to up-to-date scientific reports.

To be sure, students do not read all of these texts in elementary school, but the reading experiences students have in their elementary years have a powerful influence on their future reading abilities. All in all, we need to do more to improve all students' reading performance, and we need to work especially hard to improve dramatically the performance of many disadvantaged children. We particularly need to improve children's higher-level skills, what is sometimes called *critical thinking*. We need to move as many students as possible to a literacy level that enables them to read challenging material, to analyze it closely, to learn from it, to reason from it, and to problem solve; that is, we need to prepare children to be competent readers in today's increasingly complex and demanding world.

CURRENT TEACHING PRACTICES

Several reports have characterized the reading instruction elementary school students typically receive and the instructional material they use (for example, Anderson et al. 1985, Hoffman et al. 1994). Until fairly recently, most children have been taught with traditional basal reading programs. Traditional basal reading programs consist of large packages of graded readers, worksheets, teachers' manuals, tests, and supplementary material specifically constructed to be used in teaching children to read. The earliest books often employ severely controlled vocabularies, generally contain very brief narratives, and rely on extensive use of pictures for much of their meaning. The books used in the remainder of the primary grades continue to employ controlled vocabularies, contain largely fiction, and often contain rather impoverished stories. At about the fourth grade, selections become longer, vocabulary control is eased, the fiction included becomes increasingly children's literature, and more expository selections are included.

At the elementary level, much instruction has been given to students grouped by reading ability and has consisted of what is called the directed reading lesson. Very often, students are placed in one of three ability groups, and the teacher works with one group while the other two do some sort of seatwork, often workbook exercises. A directed reading lesson includes preparing students for reading a selection, silent reading of the selection, and follow-up questions and discussion. Typically, these activities are followed by skills work of some sort—work on decoding, vocabulary, comprehension, and a number of other areas. Although all basals give some attention to each of these topics, classroom observations indicate that students receive very little direct instruction in comprehension and that much of the teacher's time is taken up with giving assignments, checking assignments, and questioning. Additionally, it appears that students using basal readers spend much of their time, far too much in the opinion of most authorities, completing worksheets.

In recent years, basal readers have changed considerably (Hoffman et al. 1994), and much of that change is for the better. Current basal readers include good children's literature, employ more varied and interesting vocabulary, and contain informational articles as well as narratives. Still, analyses of both comprehension instruction (Durkin 1990) and vocabulary instruction (Ryder and Graves 1994) indicate that the instruction presented in even the most recent material is inadequate and not in keeping with current knowledge about effective instruction.

As noted, until recently most children were taught with basal readers. However, a significant number of students are now being taught with whole-language approaches. It is difficult to characterize whole-language programs because, as one of the major promoters of whole language, Kenneth Goodman (1986), has pointed out, an important whole-language tenet is that whole-language instruction does and should differ from one teacher to another. Still, one can list a number of general principles of whole language instruction. Goodman includes the following: Reading programs should be built on students' existing knowledge and should employ intrinsic motivation. Reading skills should be built as part of language experiences that are functional, meaningful, and relevant for students. The teacher's role is that of monitoring and supporting the development of reading rather than directly instructing students in reading. The most important question to ask a reader is whether what she is reading makes sense. Instruction must employ whole texts that are meaningful and relevant to students. Finally, basal readers, hierarchical sequences of skills and subskills, workbooks, worksheets, and teaching practices that fractionate the use of language are not acceptable.

Additionally, in whole-language classrooms, students typically are not grouped by ability. They spend a lot of time reading self-selected material independently, and they often work together on projects of mutual interest. When instruction is given, it is typically in response to a particular need of one or more students, it is relatively brief, and it is integrated with the reading that students are doing as part of their regular classroom activities.

THEORIES THAT MOTIVATE THE APPROACH TAKEN IN THIS BOOK

In this section, we consider two psychological orientations that underlie much current work in reading and motivate the approach to reading instruction presented here. The two orientations are cognitive psychology and social-constructivist thinking.

Cognitive Psychology

The principal orientation behind many current conceptualizations of reading is cognitive psychology (Gardner 1985). By focusing on how the mind processes information, cognitive psychology attempts to provide a window on the brain. The cognitive orientation first became prominent in the late 1960s and has been the dominant force in educational psychology for much of the past 25 years. Two characteristics of cognitive psychology are particularly relevant. First, it views individuals as active searchers for meaning rather than as passive respondents to external stimuli; much of the meaning an individual derives from a situation is thought to be constructed by the individual. Second, it places great importance on the development of knowledge as a crucial part of an individual's intellectual development and views knowledge as central to intellectual activity. What a student already knows has a great deal to do with what she can learn and how much time and effort that learning will take. In addition to endorsing these two positions, cognitive psychologists have developed a number of theoretical constructs important to understanding and fostering students' learning. Here we describe four that are particularly relevant to sound teaching: schema theory, the interactive model, automaticity, and metacognition.

Schema Theory
One of the central theories of cognitive psychology and one of the most important concepts influencing current thinking about reading is that of schemata (the plural of *schema*). Schemata are units of knowledge that individuals internalize. As David Rumelhart (1980) has pointed out, they constitute our knowledge about "objects, situations, events, sequences of events, actions, and sequences of actions" (34). We have schemata for objects, such as cars; for situations, such as being in a restaurant; for events, such as weddings; and for sequences of events, such as driving to and from work. Schemata constitute our knowledge about the world. We make sense out of what we read by attempting to fit the information we glean

from a text to an existing schema. If, for example, we read about a waiter serving a meal, we immediately evoke our restaurant schema, and evoking that schema provides us with a wealth of information beyond that in the text. We know that customers can order a variety of foods from a menu, that the waiter will bring their food, that they will need to pay for it when they are finished, and much much more.

Among the types of schemata that influence our understanding as we read are general knowledge of the world and its conventions; specific knowledge about various subjects; and linguistic knowledge, which includes some understanding of different patterns of textual organization. Importantly, having appropriate schemata for texts we read is crucial to understanding. As Marilyn Adams and Bertrand Bruce (1982) put it, "Without prior knowledge, a complex object such as a text is not just difficult to interpret; strictly speaking, it is meaningless" (23).

The Interactive Model of Reading

The interactive model, another concept advanced by Rumelhart (1977), presents a number of concepts closely related to the concept of schema theory. Interactive models can be best understood when contrasted to text-based and reader-based models. Text-based models assume that the text is of utmost importance and that the reader processes text by first recognizing lower-level units and then repeatedly synthesizing lower-level units into more and more complex units. In this view, the reader might first perceive letters, then synthesize several letters to form words, then synthesize several words to form a phrase, and so on. The point is that in this view the processing operates in a single direction, from the text to the reader.

Reader-based models are the antithesis of text-based models. Reader-based models assume that the reader is of utmost importance and that the fluent reader processes text by first hypothesizing about the content of text and then selectively sampling the text to confirm or disconfirm the hypothesis. In this view, the reading process begins with the highest-level unit possible (meaning in the mind of the reader) and deals with lower-level units (for example, words) to a limited extent. Again, the processing operates in a single direction, in this view, from the reader to the text.

Interactive models differ from these one-directional models by assuming that readers arrive at meaning by simultaneously using information from several knowledge sources. These knowledge sources include letter-level knowledge, word-level knowledge, syntactic knowledge, and various types of world knowledge or schemata. Information moves simultaneously in two directions; the reader's background knowledge and the information that she gleans from the text interact to produce meaning.

Recognizing that reading is an interactive process serves as a caution against overemphasizing the role of readers' schemata in text comprehension. As we noted, readers' schemata are vital to their understanding texts; however, that does not mean texts are unimportant (Stanovich 1994). For example, you would not understand much from a description of a baseball game unless you knew something about baseball. However, a *Sports Illustrated* article about the Oakland A's will convey a very different meaning than a *Boy's Life* story about a Little League team. Although no text is ever fully explicit, neither are texts vacuous. Texts constrain meaning; for example, no competent reader who knew anything about sports would interpret the Little League story as being about basketball. Good readers learn to rely appropriately on the text and on prior knowledge, and to adjust their relative reliance on the two so that it is appropriate for a particular text and a particular situation.

Automaticity

David LaBerge and Jay Samuels first explained the importance of automaticity to proficient reading in 1974, and since that time the importance of this straightforward concept has been universally recognized. An automatic activity is one that can be performed instantaneously and without conscious attention. Reading demands that a number of processes—for example, recognizing letters, recognizing words, assigning meaning to words, linking words to form propositions, and linking propositions to form larger units of meaning—be performed at the same time. If these processes are not automated, they demand attention. The mind's attentional capacity is limited. In reading, some processes—dealing with the meanings of sentences and longer units—demand attention. Other processes must be automated so that they do not demand attention. Otherwise, the brain's limited attentional capacity will be overburdened, and the reader will not be able to read with understanding.

In particular, two closely related processes must be automatic. One of these is recognizing words. Readers must automatically recognize the vast majority of words they encounter as they read. They cannot afford a mental process such as, "Oh. Let's see. Yes, this word is *intervention*." The other process that must be automatic is assigning meaning to words. Readers must develop rapid access to word meanings. Thus, in addition to recognizing a word automatically, they must automatically (instantly and without conscious attention) assign meanings to the majority of words they encounter as they read. They cannot afford to go through a mental process such as, "*Intervention*. Now, what does that mean? Oh, yes. It means to interfere with something."

Metacognition

As applied to reading, metacognition refers to a person's knowledge about his or her understanding of a text and about what to do when comprehension breaks down. As Ruth Garner (1987) has noted, accomplished readers have metacognitive knowledge about themselves, the reading tasks they face, and the strategies they can employ in completing these tasks. For example, on beginning this section, a reader might realize that she has no prior knowledge about metacognition (self knowledge), notice that the section is brief (task knowledge), and decide that the strategy of reading the section through several times would be fruitful (strategy knowledge).

In this example, the reader exhibited metacognitive knowledge prior to beginning reading. However, readers can also make use of metacognitive knowledge as they are reading or after they have completed a text. In fact, active awareness of one's comprehension while reading and the ability to use effective fix-up strategies when comprehension breaks down are essential to becoming an effective reader, and lack of such metacognitive skills is viewed as a particularly debilitating characteristic of poor readers.

Arthur Whimby (1975) has given a particularly apt characterization of a metacognitive reader.

> A good reader proceeds smoothly and quickly as long as his understanding of the material is complete. But as soon as he senses that he has missed an idea, that the track has been lost, he brings smooth progress to a grinding halt. Advancing more slowly, he seeks clarification in the subsequent material, examining it for the light it can throw on the earlier trouble spot. If still dissatisfied with his grasp, he returns to the point where the difficulty began and rereads the section more carefully. He probes and analyzes phrases and sentences for their exact meaning; he tries to visualize abstruse descriptions; and through a series of approximations, deductions, and corrections, he translates scientific and technical terms into concrete examples. (91)

Teaching students to be metacognitive is one of the most important and challenging tasks you face, and it is a task we address in detail in Chapter 8, Teaching Comprehension Strategies.

The Social-Constructivist Orientation

The social-constructivist orientation has become increasingly influential in education over the past decade (see Fosnot 1996). Although this orientation reflects some of the same thinking found in cognitive psychology, there are important differences between the two. Here, we discuss three aspects of constructivist thinking and its relevance to teaching. First, we discuss the general concept of constructivism; next, we deal specifically with social constructivism; and, finally, we consider the importance the social-constructivist orientation gives to the contexts in which students learn.

Constructivism

We introduced the notion of constructivism in discussing cognitive psychology when we pointed out that much of the meaning an individual derives from a situation is thought to be constructed by the individual himself or herself. For those who take a strong constructivist position, our knowledge of the world—whether it is knowledge gained from a text or knowledge from any other source—is not the result of phenomena in the real world. It is the result of our interpretation of those phenomena. The meaning we attain is in fact constructed. Inherent tendencies in the ways we think, categorize, and process information shape the meanings we construct.

Social Constructivism

Social constructivism begins with acceptance of the basic constructivist position, but then goes beyond this to take the position that it is the social world within which we live—our interactions with our friends, acquaintances, and the larger community—that shapes our understanding of reality. As Kenneth Gergen (1985) has explained, we understand the world in terms of social considerations, considerations that are themselves the result of interchanges among people. Therefore, the process of understanding is not a direct outcome of viewing the real world; rather, it is influenced greatly by the social world in which we live. Social constructivism is a relativistic notion; because our social backgrounds vary, whether we are interpreting a text or some other phenomena, we do not all see the same thing.

Social-constructivist thinking has influenced educational practice in two principal ways. First, social-constructivist thinking is one of the factors motivating the interest and endorsement of small-group work, particularly cooperative learning. If much of what a child learns or understands comes from her social interactions with others, then schools need to provide students with many opportunities for productive social interactions. We certainly agree with this position, and we point out opportunities for cooperative work throughout the book.

Second, social-constructivist thinking is one force undergirding the reader-response orientation to reading literature. According to reader-response theory (see Galda and Guice 1997), interpreting literature is and should be a very personal thing. We should not attempt to force students to adopt our interpretations of a literary text. Instead, we should recognize that students differ a good deal from each other and are likely to interpret literary texts quite differently, and we should celebrate and nurture these differing responses.

In considering the applications of reader-response theory, it is important to distinguish between literary texts (novels, short stories, poetry, and the like) and expository texts (textbooks, manuals, directions, and the like). While many literary texts are open to a variety of interpretations, many expository texts are not. To cite some extreme examples, instructions on how to take a certain medicine or what to do if there is a fire are meant to be interpreted in a certain way and alternate interpretations to such instructions are both incorrect and potentially dangerous. Consider also a less extreme example—this text. We have a good deal of information we are trying to convey and we are trying to convey that information as clearly as we can. Of course, not all of you reading this book will interpret everything just as we intend it to be interpreted, but we certainly hope most readers will interpret most of what we say as we intended it to be interpreted. Finally, we should point out that literature varies in the extent to which it admits a variety of responses and that even with literature there are some limits to defensible responses. For example, an abstract poem such as Lewis Carroll's *Jabberwocky* is open to more varied responses than a straightforward children's novel such as Beverly Cleary's *Ramona Quimby, Age 8*. Additionally, we would certainly not want students to interpret Patricia MacLachlan's *Sarah, Plain and Tall*, a book set on the American Prairie, as being about a trip to a deserted island.

The Significance of Context

One additional concern prompted at least in part by social-constructivist thinking has been a realization of the importance of the contexts of students' reading. There are at least three types of context to consider.

The first is the textual context. Reading educators have come to believe that the majority of the texts children read should be authentic and complete. Authentic texts are texts written by children's authors for the primary purpose of engaging or informing children. Authentic texts are contrasted to contrived texts, which are texts written or modified by educators—usually editors employed by publishers of basal readers—for the purpose of teaching some sort of reading skills. For example, the selections in many primary-grade basal readers are contrived. They are written with a severely controlled vocabulary that displays only certain letter-sound correspondences. Although many educators believe there is a place for such texts in the very early stages of reading instruction, almost all believe in moving to more authentic selections as soon as possible. As noted, reading educators also believe that most texts should be complete. Complete texts are simply texts that are not excerpts from longer works. However, what is most important about a text is that it constitutes a whole, understandable, and enjoyable unit. If an excerpt of a longer text is itself whole, understandable, and enjoyable, then it is an acceptable text.

Another type of context we consider is the immediate context in which instruction takes place. Of concern here is the danger of using artificial materials in artificial settings. Thus, for example, such practices as teaching students words using flash cards, teaching them to identify main ideas by working with paragraphs specifically written to teach main ideas, or having students complete worksheets that require them to circle prefixes and suffixes deserve scrutiny. A very strong position on the importance of providing authentic contexts is that material should never be pulled out of its natural context and isolated for instructional purposes. Our position is more moderate. We believe that it is sometimes efficient and effective to pull material out of context for instructional purposes. However, if this is done, it is vital that students work with the newly learned material or skill in an authentic context as soon as possible after the initial instruction. Thus, for example, you might initially present some sight words—words that are in students' oral vocabularies but that they cannot read—to first-grade students by writing them on the board. But later the same day, you should have students read some interesting and enjoyable stories that contain those sight words.

The third type of context we consider is the broad context in which children read. Recently, educators have used the term *literate environment* to describe the sort of classroom and school atmosphere in which children are most likely to learn to read. In promoting literacy, we need to consider the physical environment as well as an intellectual and social environment in which children spend their time. This means having a room with plenty of enticing books prominently displayed, a room with a place—perhaps a rug-covered floor or perhaps a quiet corner—where students can read comfortably, and a room in which children are frequently given the time to read and are frequently read to. It also means creating an environment that values the knowledge, satisfaction, and enjoyment one can get from reading. Sometimes, you can demonstrate your endorsement of such values by directly stating them; other times, you can demonstrate such values by reading yourself, by sharing what you gain from reading with students, and by reading to students.

CONCLUDING REMARKS

In this chapter, we have presented a brief overview of American students' proficiency in reading, briefly considered the two most common broad approaches to reading instruction, and outlined two psychological orientations and a handful of theoretical constructs that influence reading instruction. We revisit many of these ideas in upcoming chapters, and you will learn more about them as we do. However, the discussion here has been a very brief review, and you may well want to know more about some of these topics. You will find additional information listed in the references at the end of this chapter.

SELF-CHECK

As in Chapter 1, we have included a set of questions to check your understanding. The first 11 questions will help you check your knowledge of the key concepts listed at the beginning of this chapter. The last three give you an opportunity to apply what you have learned. As before, we recommend trying to answer the questions without looking back at the chapter. However, if you do not know an answer, take the time to reread to get the answer.

1. How does American students' reading performance today compare to what it was 20 years ago? What source provides you with this information?

2. How does the reading performance of economically-disadvantaged students compare with that of economically-advantaged students?

3. Briefly describe the kinds of reading skills all students need to develop.

4. Characterize the type of instruction students typically receive in classes that use basal readers.

5. How is the instruction that students receive when they are taught with a whole-language approach likely to differ from the instruction that they receive with a basal approach?

6. Define *schemata* and describe a schema you have. Also, name something for which some of your classmates might have a schema but you do not.

7. Name the two sources of information that interact in the interactive model of reading.

8. Define *automaticity* and note why it is important. Give an example of something you do automatically and something you do not.

9. Define *metacognition;* then describe a reading situation in which you have demonstrated metacognitive behavior.

10. Explain two basic tenets of the social constructivist orientation.

11. Note three types of context that are important to consider in promoting literacy.

12. Suppose that a neighbor learned that you were a teacher and called you on the phone to complain that American children can't read. What would you tell him or her?

13. If you were to visit a first-grade class during reading time in a school that endorsed the whole-language approach to reading, what would you expect to see? What might the teacher be doing? What might the

students be doing? How might the room be arranged, and what sorts of materials might it contain?

14. Briefly describe a particular group of third-grade students and their backgrounds. Think of a short story or expository article that might require schema this group of children is unlikely to have. Finally, explain what these schema are and why the children might not have them.

REFERENCES

Adams, M. and Bruce, B. (1982). Background knowledge and reading comprehension. In Langer, J. A. and Smith-Burke, T. M. (eds.), *Reader meets author: Bridging the Gap.* Newark, DE: International Reading Association, pp. 2–25. A very readable discussion of the importance of background knowledge.

Anderson, R. C., Hiebert, E. F., Scott, J. A. and Wilkinson, I. A. G. (1985). *Becoming a nation of readers.* Washington, DC: National Institute of Education. This concise summary of what we know about reading instruction is probably the most widely circulated and influential text on reading published in the last decade.

Calfee, R. C. and Patrick, C. L. (1995). *Teach our children well: Bringing K-12 education into the 21st century.* Stanford, CA: Stanford Alumni Association. One teacher-scholar's view of active, constructive elementary classrooms.

Campbell, J. R., Donahue, P. L., Reese, C. M. and Phillips, G. W. (1996). *NAEP 1994 reading report card for the nation and the states.* Washington, DC: Department of Education. Detailed report on the 1994 NAEP reading findings.

Campbell, J. R., Voelka, K. E. and Donahue, P. L. (1997). *Report in brief: NAEP 1996 trends in academic progress.* Washington, DC: Department of Education. Reports trends in NAEP results between 1970 and 1996.

Durkin, D. (1990). *Comprehension instruction in current basal reading series.* Technical Report No. 521. Champaign, IL: Center for the Study of Reading. Describes the comprehension instruction Durkin found in the series.

Elley, W. (1992). *How in the world do students read?* The IEA study of reading literacy. The Hague: International Association for Evaluation of Educational Achievement. A detailed report on this international study of reading.

Fosnot, C. T. (ed.) (1996). *Constructivism: Theory, perspectives, and practice.* New York: Teachers College Press. A challenging and informative introduction to constructivism in education.

Galda, L. and Guice, S. (1997). Response-based reading instruction in the elementary grades. In S. A. Stall and D. A. Hayes (eds.), *Instructional models in reading.* Mahwah, NJ: Erlbaum, pp. 311–349. A concise overview of reader response theory as it applies to elementary-age students.

Gardner, H. (1985). *The mind's new science: A history of the cognitive revolution.* New York: Basic Books. A concise history of cognitive psychology and related areas.

Garner, R. (1987). *Metacognition and reading comprehension.* Norwood, NJ: Ablex. A fairly technical summary of research on metacognition.

Gergen, K. J. (1985). The social constructionist movement in modern psychology. *American Psychologist, 40,* 266–275. An introduction to the concept of constructionism.

Goodman, K. (1986). *What's whole in whole language?* Richmond Hill, Ontario, Canada: Scholastic. One of the best-known statements of the whole-language position by one of the principal whole-language advocates.

Hoffman, J. V., McCarthey, S. J., Abbott, J., Christian, C., Corman, L., Curry, C., Dressman, M., Elliott, B., Matherne, D. and Stahle, D. (1994). So what's new in the new basals? A focus on first grade. *Journal of Reading Behavior, 26,* 47–73. Very complete description of the differences between the pre-1993 and post-1993 first-grade basal readers.

LaBerge D. and Samuels, S. J. (1974). Toward a theory of automatic information processing in reading. *Cognitive Psychology, 6,* 293–323. The original work on automaticity and reading.

Mullis, I. V. S., Campbell, J. and Farstrup, A. E. (1993). *NAEP 1992 reading report card for the nation and the states.* Washington, DC: Department of Education. A detailed report of the 1992 NAEP findings in reading.

Mullis, I. V. S., Owen, E. H. and Phillips, G. W. (1990). *America's challenge: Accelerating academic achievement.* Princeton, NJ: Educational Testing Service. A convenient summary of 20 years of NAEP findings in reading and other subject areas.

Perkins, D. (1992). *Smart schools: From training memories to educating minds.* New York: The Free Press. An extremely readable and excellent book on ways to foster deep understanding in students.

Rumelhart, D. E. (1977). Toward an interactive model of reading. In Dornic, S. (ed.), *Attention and performance* (Vol. 6). Hillsdale, NJ: Erlbaum, pp. 573–603. The original presentation of the interactive view of reading.

Rumelhart, D. E. (1980). Schemata: The building blocks of cognition. In Spiro, R. J., Bruce, B. C. and Brewer, W. F. (eds.), *Theoretical issues in reading comprehension.* Hillsdale, NJ: Erlbaum, pp. 33–58. The original statement of the concept of schemata.

Ryder, R. J. and Graves, M. F. (1994). Vocabulary instruction presented prior to reading in two basal readers. *Elementary School Journal, 95,* 139–153. A description of vocabulary instruction presented in current basals.

Stanovich, K. E. (1994). Constructivism in reading education. *The Journal of Special Education, 28,* 259–274. Examines various elements of constructivism and cautions against some interpretations of the theory.

Whimby, A. (1975). *Intelligence can be taught.* New York: Dutton. An interesting perspective on intelligence and the source for the quote on metacognitive behavior presented in this chapter.

CHILDREN'S BOOKS CITED

Carroll, L. (1992). *Jabberwocky.* New York: Disney Press.

Cleary, B. (1981). *Ramona Quimby, Age 8.* New York: Morrow.

MacLachlan, P. (1985). *Sarah, plain and tall.* New York: Harper & Row.

3 Developing a Classroom Reading Program

No matter what reading materials you have, no matter what your training in teaching reading, and no matter what sort of supervision and support you receive in your school, the nitty-gritty day-to-day and week-to-week task of operating a classroom reading program is up to you. Once the door is closed—or even if there is no door—once students are in their seats—or even if they sit on the floor for much of their reading—just what does and does not happen to create able and avid readers depends on your skill and ingenuity.

A challenging task? Yes. An achievable goal? Absolutely. Creating an environment in which students learn, work together effectively, and feel good about themselves and their learning requires a host of skills, as well as knowledge, commitment, and confidence. We believe that the contents of this chapter will help you build the knowledge you need to develop an effective reading program in your classroom. We believe it will encourage you to consider the skills necessary to organize and maintain such a program. We hope it inspires you to be committed to establishing a program that is well run, effective, and caring. Your confidence will come in knowing you can design and implement such a program. As you go out into the classroom and find yourself succeeding in creating a well-managed classroom—one in which students are learning to read, to love reading, and to respect themselves and each other—your confidence will grow along with your students' reading proficiency.

LOOKING AHEAD

In the first two chapters, we considered matters that are in some ways preliminary—the organization of the book, ways of studying it, American students' proficiency in reading, current approaches to instruction, and theories that motivate the approach we present. In this chapter, we turn to more concrete matters—to matters that will affect the daily activities in your classroom. The chapter is divided into six sections. In the first section, we discuss classroom management. Both recent research and common sense highlight the importance of ensuring that students spend adequate amounts of time on important learning tasks and suggest ways of getting the most out of classroom time. In the second section, we examine grouping. Although ability grouping has been a prominent feature of reading instruction for many years, today many educators are concerned with some of the negative effects of ability grouping and are investigating other ways of organizing students for instruction.

In the third section, we describe instructional considerations, concepts and principles that have proven useful in planning and delivering instruction. In the fourth section, we take up the matter of diversity in the classroom and suggest guidelines for dealing with diversity. In the fifth section, we consider several specific questions that teachers and those preparing to be teachers often ask about instruction.

Finally, we emphasize the importance of students being successful in the reading tasks we give them, as well as the importance of students realizing that success is something they have control over. This is a brief section, but it is a theme to which we will return frequently because we believe that being successful and feeling in control of their success is essential to students becoming accomplished readers.

KEY CONCEPTS

- Essential matters to attend to before school begins and during the first few weeks of class
- Methods of keeping students engaged during day-to-day activities
- Advantages of grouping students for reading instruction and disadvantages of using ability as the sole basis for grouping
- Characteristics of effective student groups
- Specific grouping arrangements
- Distinguishing between instruction and practice
- Implications of the constructive nature of learning
- Scaffolding and the gradual release of responsibility model
- Guidelines for meeting the needs of a diverse group of students
- When silent reading is appropriate and when oral reading is appropriate
- Ways of responding when students mispronounce words
- Passive failure in reading and helping students avoid it

TEACHER EFFECTIVENESS

Until recently, years of research on teaching had produced few consistent and generalizable results about just what constitutes effective teaching. Over the past two decades, however, research has yielded some very consistent results about the characteristics of effective instruction, and these findings have led to a number of principles that are vital to providing effective reading instruction (see, for example, Brophy 1986, Walberg 1990). It is particularly worth noting that, although these principles are important in providing appropriate instruction for all students, they are vital for students who experience some difficulties in learning to read.

The most basic principle is that creating and maintaining a smoothly running classroom is an absolute prerequisite to providing effective instruction. Good classroom managers provide sufficient time for instruction and maximize the effectiveness of the time they provide.

Providing Sufficient Time on Task

Without question, the most basic principle emerging from the teaching effectiveness research is that the time students spend on academically relevant tasks is of utmost importance. This is obvious. The more time students spend on a topic, the more likely they are to master it. The more time students spend reading and learning reading skills and strategies, the better readers they will become.

Maximizing the Effectiveness of the Available Time

Of course, optimizing the use of time requires more than providing sufficient time on task; it also demands using that time as effectively as possible. From a management perspective, the key to effective use of time is preventing problems before they occur. Research has shown that both getting off to a good start and keeping students purposefully engaged in daily lessons throughout the year are vital.

Getting Off to a Good Start

Three factors have been shown to be particularly important to getting off to a good start: academic planning, clear behavioral guidelines, and the use of managerial routines. Thorough academic planning needs to take place before the school year begins. Once school begins, the days are just too busy. Such matters as what books you are going to use, whether you are going to group students, how you are going to group students, how much time you are going to spend on reading instruction, and what instructional techniques you are going to use need to be decided beforehand. Of course, once school begins and you are working with a particular group of youngsters, plans will need to be modified, but modifying an existing plan is a much more feasible task than creating a plan from scratch.

In addition to having an academic plan, it is vital to have clear behavioral guidelines for students. Students need and deserve to know just what is expected of them. Equally important, they need and deserve to know what is *not* expected of them. During the early weeks of a school year, a significant amount of time needs to be spent establishing those expectations. This does not mean that all classes need to have the same guidelines or that varying levels of student choice and responsibility are not acceptable. Teachers differ greatly on how structured or open classrooms should be, and there is no compelling evidence that certain levels of structure or openness are optimal. Some teachers run traditional classrooms with fixed desks, a good deal of large-group work with the teacher as the center of attention, and definite rules about what students should be doing most of the day. Other teachers prefer informal arrangements of desks that change as activities change, a lot of small-group work in which students serve as teachers and sounding boards for each other, and an atmosphere in which students make many decisions about what they will do each day. Both of these structures have their place; what is crucial is that students understand the structure that is being used and what is expected of them.

It is also very useful to have some definite managerial routines in place. Managerial routines are prescribed sequences of activities that students engage in. Having such routines avoids wasted time and makes what is expected of them very clear to students. For example, students might routinely begin the reading period by reading quietly from a book of their choice and writing down an interesting thought or an interesting word that they find in the reading. In the same vein, students might be routinely expected to place completed work in a basket on your desk well before the end of the reading period.

Maintaining High Levels of Time on Task

Once students have gotten off to a good start, they need to continue to work productively. Five types of teacher behaviors have proven to be particularly effective in fostering productivity: "withitness," overlapping, maintaining lesson continuity and momentum, prompting all students to attend, and providing variety and purpose to seatwork. Withitness refers to being on top of things. Effective classroom managers are constantly aware of what is happening in the classroom and are thus able to detect inappropriate behavior early and do something about it before it escalates. Overlapping refers to the ability to do more than one thing at a time when necessary. This, of course, is no simple task. Eventually, however, parts of running a classroom become virtually automatic, allowing a teacher to attend to several aspects of a class at the same time. For example, a good classroom manager is able to continue to monitor the class as a whole while working with an individual student.

Effective classroom managers maintain lesson continuity and momentum by being fully prepared for each lesson and by not allowing disruptions to interrupt lessons any more than necessary. For example, a good manager is more likely to deal with an inattentive student by establishing eye contact with the student or asking the student a question directly related to the content of the lesson than by interrupting the lesson to reprimand the student. Of course, this does not mean that good teachers plunge blindly ahead ignoring what is happening in class. If, for example, children are halfway through a story and you realize from their comments that many of them have missed a crucial point at the beginning of the story, it is usually appropriate to back up and review the beginning.

Effective classroom managers help keep all students attentive by looking around the room before asking a question, calling on students in a way that does not broadcast who is and is not going to be called on next, and getting around to each student as frequently as possible. Such practices as calling on students systematically by going up and down the rows, only calling on students who raise their hands, or centering attention on certain parts of the room make it likely that there will be long periods of time during which many students are not attending.

Finally, although it has been shown that students often do too much seatwork and that seatwork is often an unproductive enterprise, in most classrooms students continue to do a substantial amount of seatwork. Good classroom managers ensure that seatwork is varied and purposeful and that students are clearly informed of the purpose of any seatwork they do.

Admittedly, being an effective classroom manager is a real challenge. Moreover, no one can be an optimal manager every minute of every day. However, the goal of being an effective manager is an extremely important one and one that is well worth striving for.

GROUPING STUDENTS FOR INSTRUCTION

One of the most important decisions you make in your classroom is that of how to group students. Students can be grouped in a variety ways for a variety of purposes. In this section, we discuss some of the reasons for grouping, some of the problems caused by homogeneous ability grouping, various types of groups, and some guidelines for grouping.

A typical class of 25 to 30 students brings with it 25 to 30 different sets of interests, attention spans, personalities, and reading abilities; and it is very difficult to attend to each of these when working with the class as a whole. When teaching the entire class as a single group, teachers tend to teach to an imaginary mean; that is, they gear their instruction to what they perceive to be the middle range of interest, attention span, personality, ability, and so on. Such instruction does not meet the needs of those who are not in this range. Furthermore, in large-group situations, it is tempting for the teacher to do most of the talking, asking only an occasional question and, even then, allowing only one or two students to respond. Thus, most students play a passive role.

Dividing students into smaller groups is often helpful for a number of reasons. First, it is generally easier to keep smaller groups of students on task than it is to keep larger groups on task. Smaller groups tend to facilitate direct instructional engagement for more children and for a longer period of time. Second, smaller groups allow you to provide instruction designed to meet the needs of specific students, thus individualizing your reading program. Finally, smaller groups allow more students to be actively involved in instructional activities. In a group of five, for example, it is possible for each student to respond to a question before you either run out of time or test the patience of the other students.

Given these advantages, it is not surprising that students have often been grouped for reading instruction. Unfortunately, however, grouping has typically been based exclusively on ability. During much of this century, American students have been grouped homogeneously, with the typical classroom having one high, one middle, and one low ability group (Anderson et al. 1985). Recently, teachers and researchers have found that ability grouping results in a number of disadvantages, particularly for students in low ability groups. As compared to students in other groups, students in low ability groups are often given less time to read, spend more time on worksheets and less time being actively instructed, and are asked fewer higher order questions. Additionally, lower ability group students often suffer affective consequences of grouping, including lowered self-esteem, lowered motivation to succeed, and negative attitudes toward reading (Allington 1995). Finally, there is much concern about the permanence of group membership; students who are placed in a low ability group in kindergarten and first grade are all too likely to stay in the low ability group throughout the elementary school years (Juel 1990).

These findings have led teachers to develop a variety of grouping options, many of which deliberately include heterogeneous groups of students. Using a variety of groups gives children opportunities to learn how to interact with and learn from others who are in some ways different from them. Using a variety of groups also allows you to select appropriate groups for the various goals you have for students.

Types of Groups

Here, we describe some specific grouping arrangements. Keep in mind that your objective is not to select the best group or even the best pair of groups. Rather, your goal is to learn to work with a range of grouping options so that you can provide appropriate alternatives for your students and for the knowledge, skills, and strategies they are learning.

Literature Groups

Literature groups, sometimes called literature circles, literature study groups, or book clubs, are primarily designed for use with trade books. Of course, stories found in basal readers or literature anthologies can also be used. As the name implies, literature groups are arranged around pieces of literature. Thus, students who are reading the same book or story are grouped together. Such grouping can be particularly motivating because students usually have some choice in which book they are reading.

In literature groups, students generally spend a good deal of time discussing what they are reading. The discussion can be prompted by questions provided by the teacher and monitored by a member of the group who has been selected for this role for the day. Student-generated questions and entries in reader response journals can also be used as a springboard for discussion. Another group member might record the ideas generated in the discussion, or the discussion might be tape recorded for the teacher to listen to at a later time (Keegan and Shrake 1991). Through discussion, students come to better understand and to think critically about what they read. One thing to keep in mind when selecting groups in which students will work independently is that students' needs cannot be ignored. Unless each member of the group is indeed able to *read* the selection, the experience will do little to enhance members' reading abilities. Some teachers use literature groups as the core of their reading programs (McMahon and Raphael 1997, Roser and Martinez 1995).

Interest Groups

In this grouping arrangement, students are allowed to select an area to pursue through reading. Perhaps you will have the class brainstorm ideas that they would be interested in pursuing in their reading, list the ideas on the board, and then have students vote for the five they find most interesting. After narrowing the list to five, you can have students rank the topics they wish to pursue in order from first to fifth, explaining that you will try to see that they get one of their top three choices or that those who do not get their top choice this time will get it next time. Groups are arranged accordingly. Within each group, all students may read one text or they may read several different texts and share the information they obtain.

Groups Based on Student Needs

Here, students are grouped because they share a common instructional need. Thus, students who would benefit from further development of their sight vocabulary might meet in one group, while another group of students might focus on the long *e* vowel sound. Similarly, a set of students who can read silently and stay on task for 10 minutes might meet together, while another set of students who need smaller sections of text taken at one time might meet as a group. Such practices, of course, represent a particular sort of ability grouping. However, it is very different from traditional ability grouping because these groups are based on specific needs rather than on general abilities, exist for only a short period, and are not the only type of grouping that children experience. Groups such as these allow teachers to engage in guided reading instruction, which is an important part of a strong reading program, especially in the early grades (Fountas and Pinnell 1996).

Formal Cooperative Groups

Cooperative grouping is based on the notion that students are capable of working together, that students can learn from each other, and that instilling a sense of cooperation among students rather than a sense of competition is one important goal of schooling. Formal cooperative groups, the sort suggested by David Johnson and his colleagues (1994), for example, are carefully structured and well organized. Such groups usually give students specific roles, such as team leader, recorder, praiser, and checker.

Formal cooperative groups require a good deal of student preparation. Students must learn how to assume various roles, how to work cooperatively toward a common goal, and how to monitor and evaluate their learning and the performance of their group. However, time spent teaching students how to work cooperatively pays off in the long run when students can work independently, leaving you free to work with students who need your assistance. Moreover, working in cooperative groups prepares students for the cooperative efforts needed throughout life.

Student Selected Groups

Here, students are allowed to select others to work with using whatever criteria they choose. The rationale behind this type of grouping is that choice is a strong motivator. When students are involved in the formation of the groups, they are more likely to be active participants in the group. Of course, students will often need some guidance in the selection process, particularly when they are just beginning to self-select groups. For example, you might give them a list of half a dozen classmates from whom to choose. One thing to be particularly attentive to is that shy and less popular students are included and welcomed in groups. Also, because groups will include many friends, you will need to ensure that students are actively engaged in academic tasks, and not simply actively engaged in chatting with their friends.

Pairs

Students with similar abilities can work in pairs on such activities as oral reading and responding to discussion questions after reading. Often, one student may know a word the other doesn't. So, too, the different interpretations two students bring to discussion questions are likely to enrich both students' understanding of the selection. Alternately, students may be grouped in pairs for peer tutoring. Peer tutoring involves pairing a student who has mastered a particular strategy or skill with a student who is still developing that strategy or skill. The student who has mastered the strategy acts as a tutor for the other student. Such pairing is often very effective, resulting in initial learning on the part of the tutee and reinforced learning and a sense of accomplishment on the part of the tutor. If possible, all students should have opportunities to serve as both tutors and tutees.

One-to-One Instruction

Here, we are referring to instruction in which you work individually with students. One benefit of having students work in small groups rather than as a whole class is that it provides time for you to work individually with students on areas that are causing them difficulty or to simply touch base with students on a one-to-one basis. Spending five to ten well-planned minutes with a student can provide you with a great deal of information about his reading skills, be highly instructive for him, and show him that you care.

Whole-Class Instruction

Although we have focused most of this discussion on relatively small groups, the entire class can be thought of as a group as well. Whole-class instruction is useful when you wish to inform everyone of the same thing. Spending five or ten minutes with the entire class before having students work in smaller groups allows you to touch base with all students, answer their questions, and hear their concerns. Because lengthy whole-class instruction can invite off-task behavior, whole-class instruction should generally be kept brief and focused.

Guidelines for Making Grouping Decisions

When deciding how to group students, there are many matters to consider. These include your general instructional objectives as well as your more specific objectives for individual children, the material your students will be reading, your students' individual strengths, which children in the classroom work well together, and the number and type of groups you can successfully manage.

Despite the complexity of deciding how to group students for instruction, there are three basic questions that should guide you. First, what are your purposes for instruction? What is it that you hope to accomplish with each of your students at this particular time? Note that what you want to accomplish will differ from day to day and from student to student.

Second, what are your students' strengths? By looking not only at areas in which your students are still developing but also at areas in which they have competence, you will gain insight into ways to group students so that they can benefit from each other's strengths. For example, if students are reading an informational selection, you may want to be sure that each group includes at least one student who is able to identify the main points in the selection.

Finally, how will you monitor each of the groups? Even when groups are working independently, you need to know what is going on in them and be there to lend a helping hand if necessary. In the final analysis, you must feel comfortable with managing your groups, and the number and kinds of groups you can effectively monitor is limited.

In addition to answering these questions, it is worthwhile to consider some general characteristics of effective groups. Here are four of them:

- Effective groups are purposeful. Group students in order to accomplish some task—to identify the main characters in a story, identify the main points in an essay, or write a play based on a news story they recently read. Moreover, ensure that all groups, including the ones not in direct contact with you, are engaged in meaningful learning activities.

- Effective groups consist of a carefully chosen mix of individuals who know what they are doing. Thoughtfully assign students to groups and instruct them as necessary. Students should get specific instruction in what they are doing, how they are to do it, and why they should do it. Do not assume that students will automatically be able to work together well.

- Effective groups monitor their learning and their performance as a group. Groups tend to run most smoothly when their members are responsible for the reading tasks assigned and the mechanics of group operation. They will need instruction in doing both types of evaluation.

- Effective groups are flexible. The process of forming and reforming groups is continual because you are repeatedly informed and updated by incoming information about students' needs and abilities. Moreover, students' needs and abilities are relative to specific reading tasks; thus, grouping needs change with tasks and with time.

As is the case with becoming an effective classroom manager, becoming adept at grouping students is a challenge. We suggest that you meet that challenge by first becoming comfortable with two or three types of grouping and then gradually adding other grouping alternatives over time.

INSTRUCTIONAL CONSIDERATIONS

In addition to considering matters of classroom management and ways of grouping students for instruction, there are a number of general instructional considerations, concepts, and principles that can be helpful when planning instruction. Here, we list seven such considerations that are particularly important.

Distinguishing Instruction from Practice

Instruction needs to be clearly distinguished from practice. Practice involves asking students to do something they can already do. Instruction involves showing or telling students how to do something. Both instruction and practice have their places; however, it needs to be clearly understood that asking students to do something does not constitute teaching them to do it. In exploring this concept, Gerald Duffy and Laura Roehler (1982) have coined the terms *proactive teaching* and *reactive teaching*. Proactive teachers fully prepare students to perform a task before asking them to do it. Reactive teachers, on the other hand, assign students a task and then provide instruction only if students experience difficulty with the task. Like Duffy and Roehler, we favor proactive teaching in the majority of cases. Proactive teaching leads students to success. Reactive teaching puts them in the position to fail. Thus, for example, before asking students to explain the conflict in a particular short story, check to see if they understand the concept of conflict as used in literature. If they do not, teach the concept before they deal with the story. Note that with a difficult concept, such as conflict, instruction could take some time.

Direct Explanation of Reading Strategies

One important part of reading instruction is direct explanation of reading strategies (Winograd and Hare 1988). In teaching strategies such as how to sound out words, how to glean a word's meaning from context, and how to identify the important information in a selection, teachers can greatly aid students by fully explaining the strategy and its uses. Such explanations should include five components: what the strategy is, why the strategy is worth learning, how to use the strategy, when and where the strategy should be used, and how to evaluate whether the strategy is effective. Of course, you usually cannot explain all of this at one time; but, if students are to use strategies effectively, these are things that they need to know and be able to do.

Cognitive Modeling

Modeling is another very important part of instruction. When teachers model, they actually *do* something rather than just tell students how to do it. A specific type of modeling, cognitive modeling, is particularly useful in teaching students difficult concepts and strategies. Cognitive modeling consists of teachers using explicit instructional talk to describe their thought processes in performing the tasks they are asking students to perform. For example, a teacher might model the mental process of determining the meaning of an unknown word in context as shown here.

Suppose I'm reading along and I come to this sentence, "It was raining heavily and water was standing in the street, so before he left for work Mr. Nelson put on his raincoat, buckled on his

_____ (galoshes) over his shoes, and picked up his umbrella."
Let me see—*guh-lahsh-es.* I don't think I know that word. Let's see.
It's raining, and he picks up his raincoat and umbrella and buckles
something over his shoes. *Galoshes* must be some sort of waterproof
boots that go over your shoes. I can't be certain of that, but it makes
sense in the sentence, and I don't think I want to look it up right now.

Such modeling is a window on the mind and certainly one of the most
powerful tools for showing children how to think.

Recognizing the Constructive Nature of Learning

As explained in Chapter 2, much of the meaning an individual derives from
a situation is constructed by the individual. Different students will construct different meanings from reading the same text. In some cases, these
different meanings will be quite acceptable; many texts have more than one
possible interpretation, and some texts allow a number of valid interpretations. In other cases, however, students' constructed understanding will be
incorrect or inadequate. Teachers need to be constantly aware of this possibility. They need to check students' understanding of what they read, provide feedback, and further explain and elaborate on matters that are
misunderstood or partially understood. Sometimes, these misunderstandings will be minor and easily cleared up. At other times, however, the misunderstandings will be major ones that will require significant amounts of
time and energy to remedy. It is very important that they be remedied, for
if students continue to hold misconceptions, they will only cement those
misconceptions in their minds.

Metacognition and Strategic Behavior

Teachers are not always available to check students' understanding and to
reteach if necessary. Over time, students need to increasingly undertake these
tasks themselves. To do this, they must develop metacognition. Metacognition refers to readers' awareness of whether they are comprehending a selection as they are reading it and to their ability to remedy comprehension
problems when they occur. To remedy comprehension problems, students
need to learn specific strategies, sequences of voluntary actions that they employ when what they are reading is not making sense. Many poorer readers
are profoundly in need of help, both in recognizing when things are not making sense and in using specific fix-up routines to restore comprehension.

Scaffolding

A scaffold is a temporary support teachers use in helping a student or
group of students accomplish a task they could not do alone. Scaffolding
enables teachers to stretch students' thinking and performance as they

move students toward becoming accomplished and independent readers. A concrete example from the arena of children's games may be useful. The game we are alluding to is t-ball, and the scaffold is the tee that holds up the ball so that the preschooler can hit it. The tee allows preschoolers to hit a ball well before they are able to hit a thrown ball; the tee is temporary, and using the tee will prepare preschoolers to later hit balls that are thrown. Scaffolds for reading abound—reading part of a story to students, telling them where to look for the answers to questions, letting them know that an essay they are about to read deals with three main topics. Scaffolding plays a central role in the instruction we suggest throughout the book.

The Gradual Release of Responsibility Model

The gradual release of responsibility model suggests an instructional plan for carefully dismantling the scaffolding used to support students' initial efforts. A slightly modified version of the model first presented by David Pearson and Margaret Gallagher (1983) is shown in Figure 3–1. The model shows a sequence in which the teacher at first does all the work, students do more and more of the work under the teacher's guidance as time pro-

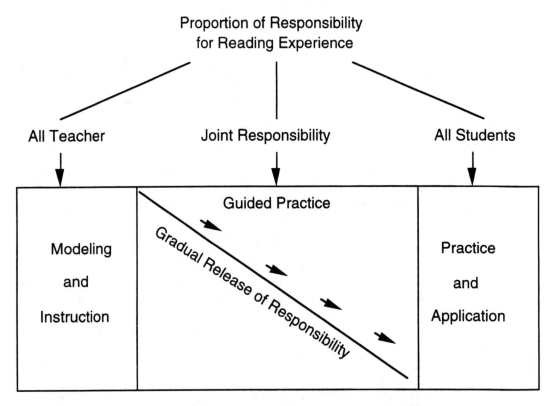

Figure 3–1.   The Gradual Release of Responsibility Model

gresses (in other words, the teacher scaffolds their efforts), and eventually students do the work independently. The word *gradual* is crucial here. The teacher first shows students how to do a task, and then gradually—over time—has them assume the responsibility of completing the task. Like scaffolding, the gradual release of responsibility model plays a central role in much of the instruction we suggest.

DIVERSITY IN THE CLASSROOM

Although the term *diversity* has recently come to the forefront in education, diversity is nothing new in American schools. Each year, each student brings with himself a set of individual interests, strengths, and needs that is unique. In this section, we will address three specific dimensions of diversity: culture, language, and educational needs.

As the number of ethnic minority students in the United States continues to increase, elementary school classrooms grow more heterogeneous. As of 1990, ethnic minorities comprised nearly one-third of the school-age population and this figure continues to grow (Educational Research Service 1995). During your career, you are likely to teach children of various ethnicities including European Americans, African Americans, Hispanic Americans, Native Americans, and Asian Americans. Additionally, some of these students are likely to be recent immigrants for whom English is a second language. Thus, your classroom will be both culturally and linguistically diverse.

Special-needs students will add a third dimension of diversity to your classroom (U.S. Department of Education 1997). Federal law guarantees all children the right to an education in the most appropriate instructional setting, and for many students experiencing specific learning difficulties, the regular classroom is identified as the most appropriate setting in which to learn.

Because diversity is an integral part of the elementary school experience, approaches to effectively instructing diverse learners are integrated throughout the book. At this point, however, we provide some general guidelines for meeting individual needs in your classroom. It is important to realize that these guidelines merely extend the ideas discussed previously in this chapter and are applicable to all students. The most important guideline to follow when attempting to meet the needs of a diverse student body is to be a good teacher, a teacher who is knowledgeable, well organized, and caring. Good teaching does not require many special changes to meet the needs of individual students because good teaching is already student centered.

Guidelines for Meeting the Needs of a Diverse Student Body

Monitor Instruction Carefully
When teaching special-needs students and second-language learners, it is particularly important to monitor what, how, and when you teach. Often,

this will mean breaking larger tasks into smaller subtasks to ensure learning before moving on.

Reinforce Appropriate Behavior

Behavior management will be a challenge for some special-needs students. Especially at the beginning of the school year, they will spend a good deal of time learning the codes of the classroom. Because they will learn many of these codes by trial and error, it is important to positively reinforce appropriate behavior as soon as it occurs. Actively seek opportunities to reward appropriate behavior rather than waiting for opportunities to punish inappropriate behavior (Bos and Vaughn 1998).

Make Use of Cooperative Learning

Allowing students to work together will benefit all students, especially those with special needs. Cooperative learning is particularly helpful for second-language learners because it provides students with much needed opportunities to practice speaking English. In addition, cooperative work styles may be more congruent with the cultural practices of some groups than are competitive work styles.

Pair ESL Students with Native English Speakers

As we just noted, cooperative learning can provide second-language learners with many opportunities for speaking English. Pairing second-language students with American-born partners with whom they can interact over time will give them still further opportunities to communicate in English as well as frequent chances to learn more about American culture.

Assess Prior Knowledge

Remember that students may possess qualitatively different kinds of knowledge depending on their cultural and educational backgrounds. By actively involving students in discussing their prior knowledge relevant to what they are about to read, you will allow more opportunity for talk, legitimize the background experiences of all cultural groups in your class, and learn what additional information students need to succeed with the task you have planned.

Expect and Promote Higher-Order Thinking

With students who differ from you or from what you consider to be the norm, it is critical that you avoid the trap of thinking that they are incapable of higher-order thinking. Regardless of their culture, English language proficiency, or educational background, students are most likely to meet high academic standards when their teachers believe that they can (Flores, Cousin and Diaz 1991; Ladson-Billings 1994). In addition, engaging ESL students in activities that require critical thinking provides fertile ground for authentic language development (Pérez 1996).

Work with Others in Your Building, District, and Community

You cannot be an expert at everything, but you should be good at using the resources that are available. Work with special educators in your district in getting ideas for helping special-needs students, and work with community organizations and parents to glean information about the various cultures your students come from. Also, be aware of school policy regarding referrals for special services and translation services for parents who do not speak English.

Use Multiple Modes of Instruction

Technology

The wider the variety in your class, the more beneficial it is to give students many ways to learn. Instruct students by talking, writing, showing, and modeling; and ensure that students are active participants in their learning by giving them many opportunities for talking, writing, showing, and modeling. For nonnative speakers of English, visuals such as graphs, charts, and pictures as well as gestures that accompany speech are critical to the communication process. Aso for nonnative speakers who may read English slowly, or for any group in which students read at quite different rates, computer-presented instruction that lets individuals proceed at their own rates can be extremely useful.

Provide Many Opportunities for Genuine Success

Praise is important for students' belief in their ability to succeed and their willingness to work toward success. However, false praise is easily discernable. Therefore, it is important to provide students with opportunities for genuine success.

SOME COMMONLY ASKED QUESTIONS

Here, we consider three commonly asked questions about reading instruction. Of course, each of these questions is probably best answered with the phrase, "It depends," because the answers depend on factors such as the particular students involved and the classroom environment. Still, the discussion will give you some ideas to consider when these questions come up in your classroom.

Is It Better for Students to Read Orally or Silently?

Beginning readers tend to read orally, while accomplished readers tend to read silently. When children first begin to read, reading aloud reinforces the new concept that print represents words that, up to this point, are familiar only in their spoken forms. Further, beginning readers often comprehend what they are reading only after they hear themselves say the printed words, as opposed to comprehending directly from print, as do older readers. With increased proficiency comes a natural transition to silent reading because it is more efficient than oral reading. For older students who are not reading far below grade level, silent reading is generally more conducive to comprehension than oral reading. So, before asking students to discuss or answer questions about what they have read, silent reading is in order. There are, however, cases when oral reading is appropriate for all readers. Choral reading, readers' theater, and plays are natural outlets for oral reading. Also, if your purpose in having students read is to check their ability to recognize words and their fluency, then obviously oral reading is the only option. Finally, if the reading is recreational, students should be allowed to read however they feel most comfortable.

What Should I Do When Students Mispronounce a Word?

Some students pronounce words differently than you do simply because they are using speech that is natural to them. Often, these students speak a nonstandard form of English or speak English as their second language. Unless these mispronunciations are associated with a breakdown in comprehension, they need not be corrected. For some students, however, mispronouncing a word reflects an absence of comprehension. If the word is critical to the text, you should correct these mispronunciations so that comprehension is not inhibited. This can be done by providing immediate correction or letting students read to the end of the sentence, asking whether what they read makes sense, and providing correction at that point. In any case, you should make a note of the words that cause difficulty so they can be addressed later. Sometimes, you will want to encourage students to use decoding strategies and context cues to figure out words for themselves—if, of course, they are able to use such techniques. Also, consider student preference. Some students become anxious if they cannot get a word and need to be given the word so they do not lose confidence. Other students prefer to figure out words for themselves.

In addition to the matter of your pronouncing words for students, there is the question of students' pronouncing words for each other. As a general rule, students should not provide words for their peers unless they are asked to do so, either by you or by the student who is reading.

How Can I Meet the Needs of All Students in the Limited Amount of Time I Have?

Having a well-managed classroom in keeping with the principles suggested in the first section of this chapter is the starting point here. Beyond that, we have several suggestions. First, get to know each of your students and his or her strengths, weaknesses, likes, and dislikes as fully as possible. In addition, find ways to create time to meet individual needs. For example, if the classroom routine is structured so that students begin an independent activity upon arrival in the morning, brief student conferences or mini-lessons can be held at this time. Similarly, if most students are productively involved in small-group work, you can focus on one or two students who need some special help. Finally, maximize the help a classroom aide, parent volunteer, or older student can provide. Many schools provide teachers with at least some classroom assistance each week. It is worth spending some time training an aide well so that the time spent with students is productive.

CONCLUDING REMARKS

Thus far in this chapter, we have discussed classroom management, grouping students for instruction, some instructional considerations, diversity in the classroom, and some questions teachers often ask. Here, we discuss the critical importance of students experiencing success. Nothing, we believe, is more crucial than ensuring that students are successful in their reading experiences. There is abundant evidence that most good readers start out as good readers, succeed in the reading tasks they are asked to do in school, and, as a consequence, become both able and avid readers. There is also abundant evidence that most poor readers start out as poor readers, experience difficulty and failure in many of the reading tasks they are asked to do in school, and, as a consequence, do not become either able or avid readers.

In addition, there is evidence that one frequent result of repeated failure in reading is for students to attribute their failure to forces beyond their control, for example, to their lack of ability or to bad luck. Given such attributions, students may fall into a pattern of passive failure in reading (Johnston and Winograd 1985). Students who exhibit passive failure in reading believe that they will not succeed and so they don't try. Teachers need to make every effort to convince each and every student that he is capable of reading and can succeed at the reading tasks school presents. The main way to do this is to give students doable reading tasks and to provide them with whatever scaffolding they need to successfully complete these tasks. Additionally, teachers can cultivate two positive attitudes in their classrooms. One of these is termed *expectancy*. Teachers need to communicate to each student, with their actions as well as with words, their belief that each and every student can learn. Effective teachers create a "you can do it" atmosphere. The other is termed *efficacy*. Teachers need to communicate to every student their belief that they can effectively help each and every student to learn. Effective teachers radiate an "I can help you do it" attitude.

SELF-CHECK

The first 11 questions check your knowledge of the key concepts listed at the beginning of the chapter, while the last three give you an opportunity to apply what you have learned.

1. Note two essential matters that you need to attend to before the school year begins and during the first few weeks of class to ensure that your class gets off to a good start.

2. Describe five methods of keeping students engaged during day-to-day activities.

3. Describe some of the advantages of grouping students for reading instruction, and some of the disadvantages of using ability as the sole basis for grouping.

4. Describe four characteristics of effective groups.

5. Describe four or five types of groups you might have in your classroom, and explain in what way each of them could be useful.

6. How does instruction differ from practice?

7. Explain why it is important for teachers to recognize the constructive nature of learning.

8. Define *scaffolding*, and describe the gradual release of responsibility model.

9. Suggest some situations in which silent reading is appropriate and some situations in which oral reading is appropriate.

10. Note some of the factors you would consider and some of the ways you might respond when students mispronounce words.

11. Explain how students acquire an attitude of passive failure about reading and suggest ways in which we can help students avoid it.

12. List half a dozen management procedures that you now employ or plan to employ in order to keep your classroom a smoothly running environment conducive to students' learning. Then, prioritize them and consider why you have prioritized them as you did.

13. Identify two grouping procedures that you plan to implement first or use most frequently in your classes, and explain why you believe these two will be particularly useful.

14. Think about your experiences as a college student and identify one class in which you were particularly successful and one in which you were not so successful. How did you feel about the subject matter

being studied after each class? What might both you and the teacher have done to improve your performance in the class in which you were less successful?

REFERENCES

Allington, R. L. (1995). Literacy lessons in the elementary schools: Yesterday, today, and tomorrow. In Allington, R. L., & Walmsley, S. A. (eds.), *No quick fix: Rethinking literacy programs in America's elementary schools.* New York: Teachers College Press. Suggests new ways to provide literacy instruction to better meet the needs of all learners.

Anderson, R. C., Hiebert, E. H., Scott, J. A. and Wilkinson, I. A. G. (1985). *Becoming a nation of readers: The report of the Commission on Reading.* Washington, DC: The National Institute of Education. A concise summary of much that we know about reading and reading instruction.

Bos, C. S. and Vaughn, S. (1998). *Strategies for teaching students with learning and behavior problems* (4th ed.). Boston: Allyn & Bacon. Discusses approaches for teaching, across the curriculum, that are appropriate for students who experience difficulty learning.

Brophy, J. (1986). Teacher influences on student achievement. *American Psychologist, 41,* 1069–1077. A cogent review of the research on teaching.

Duffy, G. G. and Roehler, L. R. (1982). Commentary: The illusion of instruction. *Reading Research Quarterly, 17,* 438–445. Looks at the way in which practice is sometimes mistaken for instruction.

Educational Research Service. (1995). *Demographic factors in American education.* Arlington, VA: Author. A resource of demographic data related to American schools.

Flores, B., Cousin, P. T. and Diaz, E. (1991). Transforming deficit myths about learning, language, and culture. *Language Arts, 68,* 369–379. Addresses the notion of educational disadvantage in relation to cultural and linguistic minorities in the U.S.

Fountas, I. C. and Pinnell, G. S. (1996). *Guided reading: Good first teaching for all children.* Portsmouth, NH: Heinemann. A very useful text on how to provide guided reading instruction for students in the early grades.

Johnson, D. W., Johnson, R. T. and Holubec, E. J. (1994). *The new circles of learning: Cooperation in the classroom and school.* Alexandria, VA: Association for Supervision and Curriculum Development. An extremely readable and informative description of cooperative learning.

Johnston, P. H. and Winograd, P. N. (1985). Passive failure in reading. *Journal of Reading Behavior, 17,* 279–301. An insightful view of the way in which less-successful readers often resign themselves to being unsuccessful.

Juel, C. (1990). Effects of reading group assignment on reading development in first and second grade. *Journal of Reading Behavior,* 22, 223–254. Points out the large and enduring effects of grouping.

Keegan, S. and Shrake, K. (1991). Literature study groups: An alternative to ability grouping. *Reading Teacher,* 44, 542–547. A concise description of one way to implement this grouping practice.

Ladson-Billings, G. (1994). *The dreamkeepers: Successful teachers of African-American children.* San Francisco: Jossey-Bass. Reveals the results of an in-depth study of the characteristics of teachers who successfully teach African-American children.

McMahon, S. I. and Raphael, T. E. (eds.) (1997). *The book club connection: Literacy learning and classroom talk.* Newark, DE: International Reading Association. Discusses the planning, implementation, and results of book clubs as a core component of a classroom reading program.

Pearson, P. D. and Gallagher, M. C. (1983). The instruction of reading comprehension. *Contemporary Educational Psychology,* 8, 317–344. A discussion of contemporary approaches to comprehension instruction.

Pérez, B. (1996). Instructional conversations as opportunities for English language acquisition for culturally and linguistically diverse students. *Language Arts,* 73, 173–181. Illustrates the importance of academic talk in the development of English language proficiency for a group of children.

Reutzel, D. R. and Cooter, R. B. (1991). Organizing for effective instruction: The reading workshop. *The Reading Teacher,* 44, 548–554. Describes one way to implement this approach to reading instruction.

Roser, N. L. and Martinez, M. G. (1995). *Book talk and beyond: Children and teachers respond to literature.* Newark, DE: International Reading Association. A collection of insights gained from and ways to facilitate genuine responses to literature.

U.S. Department of Education. (1997). *The condition of education: 1997.* Washington, DC: U.S. Department of Education. Describes characteristics of educational programs in this country.

Walberg, H. J. (1990). Productive teaching and instruction: Assessing the knowledge base. *Phi Delta Kappan,* February, 470–478. A concise review of 25 years of research on teaching.

Winograd, P. N. and Hare, V. C. (1988). Direct instruction of reading comprehension strategies: The nature of teacher explanation. In Weinstein, C. E, Goetz, E. T. and Alexander, P. A. (eds.), *Learning and study strategies: Assessment, instruction, and evaluation.* New York: Academic Press, 121-139. Presents a very useful model for strategy instruction.

Young, T. A. (1990). Alternatives to ability grouping in reading. *Reading Horizons,* 30, 169–183. Discusses a number of viable alternatives to traditional ability grouping.

4 Emergent Literacy and the Beginnings of Reading Instruction

If you were asked to recall your first year of school, you might remember days of listening to stories; playing Duck Duck Goose; singing the alphabet song and Old MacDonald; playing games with shapes such as triangles, circles, and squares; learning your colors, your numbers, and your ABCs; going on field trips and walks; and anxiously awaiting your turn at Show-and-Tell. Hopefully, your memories of your early schooling are fond and warm. Perhaps they even make you think of a happy time when school was easy—after all, all you did was play. Or did you? Actually, much of the playing you did in your early school years was related to your literacy development. Singing songs, going to the zoo, and playing with shapes helped build a foundation for reading and writing

In fact, the foundation for beginning reading instruction was laid, for all of you, long before entrance into school. You heard other people talking to you well before you began to talk yourself. Then, at about age 1, you said your first word, and soon you were using sentences of increasing complexity—two-word sentences, three-word sentences, and sentences that sounded much like those of adults. You probably scribbled with crayons on walls and paper and enjoyed being read to long before you could actually read or write yourself. Yet, all of these experiences helped you in learning to read. In this chapter, we consider how these seemingly disparate activities are all tied to literacy development.

LOOKING AHEAD

In Chapter 3, we discussed some general principles of effective reading instruction. This chapter focuses on young children's early encounters with language, the experiences that bring them a growing awareness of language and a growing ability to create meaning from printed language—an ability referred to as *emergent literacy*—and the beginnings of reading instruction that follow. We begin this discussion by examining four modes of language: listening, speaking, reading, and writing. We then provide an overview of emergent literacy and explain how children's early experiences with language affect their readiness for reading instruction.

Following these two sections is a section on some specific factors that influence emergent literacy, factors related to children's physical, cognitive, and affective development. After considering these dimensions of literacy development in young children, we discuss several ways to directly foster literacy skills. These include creating a rich environment in which children can learn, as well as providing specific reading, writing, listening, and speaking activities.

In the next section, we describe various types of books that foster the development of beginning reading. We then discuss the importance of an initial sight vocabulary and explain how to use the whole-word method to build sight vocabulary. Finally, we suggest two pervasive guidelines for working with emergent readers, and we provide a list of predictable books that can be part of a classroom library for young children.

KEY CONCEPTS

- The four modes of language and their interrelationship
- Emergent literacy and its relationship to children's environments
- Characteristics of a language-rich preschool environment
- Factors influencing emergent literacy
- Creating a classroom environment to foster literacy
- Reading activities that foster emergent literacy
- Writing activities that foster emergent literacy
- Invented spelling and the development of spelling proficiency
- Listening activities that foster emergent literacy
- Speaking activities that foster emergent literacy
- Types of books that foster emergent literacy and facilitate beginning reading instruction
- The whole-word method of developing sight vocabulary

MODES OF LANGUAGE

There are many ways to communicate. Humans can communicate with gestures, facial expressions, sounds, pictures, and words. We do most of our communicating through words and, in our culture, these words are either spoken or written. Because speech and writing involve the expression of ideas, to others or to ourselves, these two modes of language are known as *expressive* language. Listening and reading, on the other hand, involve receiving the ideas that have been put forth by others or by ourselves and are, thus, *receptive* modes of language. The development of language is a holistic process, a process in which various expressive and receptive aspects of language are interwoven. Emergent literacy is part of children's overall language development.

EMERGENT LITERACY AND CHILDREN'S READINESS FOR READING

As stated previously, the four language modes are inextricably woven together. The development of language skills is an ongoing process beginning at infancy. Before speaking their first words, for example, toddlers will often respond to the words *bottle, no,* and *stop.* Later, having learned a word, they may try it out in a variety of contexts, each time eliciting or failing to elicit the desired response. Based on these and a myriad of other experiences, children's understanding and control of various aspects of language grows as they are repeatedly exposed to the four modes of language and successively approximate adult performance—thus the term *emergent literacy.*

Emergent literacy is an important concept, brought to the forefront with the whole-language movement because it highlights the relationship among all four sorts of language. Since listening, speaking, reading, and writing are related, progress in one mode positively affects the others. It is important to note that literacy development is closely related to children's environments—that literacy emerges naturally when children are in an environment that is filled with opportunities to listen to language, practice speaking language, read language, and write language. Thus, you will want to create such an environment—a *language-rich environment*—in your classroom. We discuss the development of a language-rich environment in more detail later in this chapter.

When children are read to, they first become aware of the existence of books. Soon thereafter, they learn about the features of books—that they have pages and that these pages have pictures and print. With time, they also glean the fact that the pages must be turned—that each page holds only a fraction of the entire story—and that the pages are turned from right to left. If the reader (a parent, grandparent, teacher, or older sibling) happens to point to the words on the pages during the reading, the child will soon learn that it is the print rather than the pictures that actually indicate what the reader says. At the same time that they are learning about the mechanics of reading, children are learning about the meaning of reading. They begin to develop a sense of what a story is—the fact that it has a beginning, a middle, and an end, and the fact that often there is a meaningful sequence of events in the story. With repeated exposure to books over several years, children learn that lines of print consist of individual words and that the white space between the print separates these words. Multiple exposures to words over time facilitates the ability to identify them. If, during these early years, adults or older siblings are teaching children to recognize letters in print, they will soon learn that the words are composed of individual letters.

As you can see, reading development can begin early in a child's life. In fact, some children are able to read quite well before they begin school. Other children entering school may read only a few words or no words, but possess a wealth of knowledge about the reading process as a result of having been read to and watching family members reading and writing. Still other children come to school without having been exposed to the kinds of literacy experiences we have discussed. Given the range of experiences with print that children will bring to your classroom, beginning reading instruction exists on a continuum. What some students do before entering school or in kindergarten, others will do in first grade or later.

FACTORS THAT INFLUENCE EMERGENT LITERACY

This section focuses on specific factors that influence emergent literacy. Here, we discuss a set of physical characteristics that includes general physical fitness, visual acuity, and auditory acuity; a set of perceptual characteristics that includes visual discrimination and auditory discrimination; and a set of language characteristics that includes phonemic awareness, print awareness, word awareness, syntactic awareness, and awareness of the structure of stories. Finally, we consider the critical influences of experience, interest, and school language.

Physical Characteristics

Obviously, children who are in good health tend to be more successful with reading than children who are not. Being in good health means that they are well nourished and, if physically handicapped, are under a physician's care and have the appropriate equipment needed to facilitate movement and comfort.

Each year, most elementary school children receive tests of visual and auditory acuity. *Acuity* simply refers to sharpness of perception, so tests of visual and auditory acuity are tests of how well one sees and hears. These are particularly important during the first few years of school because it is at this time that previously unrecognized problems may first become apparent. It is often when children are required to focus on something as small as the print on a page that they first begin to squint or rub their eyes excessively, indicating that they may need glasses. Similarly, when children enter school and are seated at varying proximities to the teacher, it may become apparent for the first time that they cannot see or hear things from a distance. Thus, it is particularly important to watch for signs of vision or hearing problems during the early school years.

Perceptual Characteristics

After determining that children possess the visual and auditory acuity for reading, it is important to determine that they possess the visual and auditory discrimination necessary for reading. Not only must children be able to see the word *cat*, they must also be able to tell that it looks different from the words *sit* and *cab*. Obviously, it is easier to distinguish *cat* from *sit* than it is to tell *cat* from *cab*. Children go through developmental stages of visual discrimination, first being able to make gross discriminations, then being able to make fine discriminations. Auditory discrimination functions similarly. It is easier to distinguish between the sounds at the beginnings of the words *gate* and *zip* than it is to distinguish between the sounds at the beginnings of the words *sip* and *zip*. Similarly, the whole words *cat* and *cab* sound very much alike, whereas the words *cat* and *sit* do not.

A related step on this continuum is the development of *phonemic awareness*, the ability to hear the specific sounds that make up English words. In the word *phoneme*, for example, you hear a total of five sounds, which are represented by the *ph*, the *o*, the *n*, the *e*, and the *m*, respectively. As you know, one part of learning to read involves learning to associate letters with the sounds they represent. The nature of letter-sound correspondences and approaches to teaching them are discussed in the next chapter. Children's phonemic awareness—their ability to hear the individual sounds in words —is an extremely important prerequisite to their developing knowledge of the relationship between specific letters and specific sounds.

Language Characteristics

In Chapter 2, we discussed the influence of schema theory on our approach to learning and, concomitantly, our approach to teaching. In this section, we discuss the development of schemata related to the reading process. *Print awareness* refers to knowledge of the fact that the graphic symbols on pages in books correspond to spoken language—the notion that, in a way, print is talk written down. When children first develop this awareness, they tend not to distinguish among individual words in a line of print. With time, they develop word awareness—the notion that lines of print are composed of individual words and that these words are separated by white space on the page. Some students may take longer to develop print awareness than other students because some cultures rely heavily on an oral tradition of literacy. In some cultures, being able to read what has been written is much less important than being able to tell stories and histories that have been heard. In still other cultures, there is no written form of the language or the written form is a recent development. In these cases, the very concept of reading may be new to students and to their families.

Syntactic awareness refers to tacit knowledge of the grammar of the language—knowledge about word order and the effects it has on meaning. In English, syntactic awareness includes the tacit knowledge that adjectives come before nouns. For example, we would say, "the red balloon" rather than "the balloon red." Understanding syntax is important to reading because reading is a meaning-getting process and meaning is influenced by the structure of the language.

While the term *grammar* refers to the structure of sentences, the term *story grammar* refers to the structure of stories. Awareness of story grammar is important to the development of early literate activity. At least in Western cultures, most stories that young children encounter have a predictable structure. They include a setting, a main character with a goal, a plot with complications and outcomes, and a final resolution. Even fairy tales and other narratives that depict events that are not realistic generally follow this standard structure. Children learn about these story elements not by having a lecture on them but by listening to stories over and over again. The knowledge that they glean from repeated readings helps them as they later attempt to make meaning of print for themselves by both reading the print of others and by writing their own stories.

Experience

Children's experiences are important to their success in beginning reading because, again, reading is a meaning-getting process. As mentioned in Chapter 1, comprehension involves the process of connecting the new with the old. Children need information firmly planted in their heads to serve as anchors for the new information they encounter in reading or listening. Thus, it is important for them to have as many experiences as possible so that they can comprehend as many different types of text as possible. Experience and imagination—which grows out of experience— are the meat of communication; they are what children talk *about*, write *about*, read *about*, and listen *about*.

It should be noted that no two children bring the same experiences to a classroom. A key to success in developing early literacy is learning about the variety of experiences that your students possess and providing them with books that are commensurate with those experiences and yet still provide them with new experiences. This is a particularly important consideration for ethnic minorities and for students from other countries because the majority of American children's literature reflects European-American culture. In order to excite children about reading and in order to ensure that reading is a process of deriving meaning, the material that students read must carry meaning for them. It must connect to their experiences. Therefore, it is critical that your classroom library reflect the diversity of your classroom. In addition, it is important to share books representing a variety of cultures with all of your students so that all students can broaden their experiences.

Interest

Children must be interested in books if they are to develop their full potential in reading. Interest and motivation are strongly related to success in anything we do. We tend not to engage in activities that we do not enjoy, are not interested in, or see no purpose in. Children are much the same way. If we want them to engage in literate activity, we must pique their curiosity, provide materials that they find interesting, and motivate them.

School Language

When children first enter school, one of the biggest adjustments they have to make is that from the language used at home to that used at school. Common phrases such as, "Look at the picture on the front of the book," "Let's look at the next page," "We need to stop talking before we look at the book," and "Write your name at the top of your paper," seem straightforward to adults, but actually assume a great deal of prerequisite knowledge. In order to understand these sentences, students must distinguish between *front* and *back;* know the meaning of the word *next;* distinguish among *before, during,* and *after;* and distinguish the *top* of the page from some other part of the page. Words such as *in, out, top, bottom, up,* and *down* are frequently used during instruction to teach about other things. However, many children need first to learn the meanings of these words.

In addition to learning meanings of words, children also need time to get used to the way language *functions* in school. Gordon Wells (1986), Shirley Brice Heath (1982), and others have found great differences between home and school language, particularly when the students' culture is different from that of the teacher as, for example, when children come from different economic and ethnic backgrounds than their teachers. Obviously, the challenge is even greater for students who have recently moved from other countries and are trying to learn American customs generally as well as the customs of the classroom. Even when such differences do not exist, the home represents one culture and the classroom another. Children typically spend much of their first year in school learning about this new culture.

FOSTERING EMERGENT LITERACY: THE BEGINNINGS OF READING INSTRUCTION

Here, we consider ways of making the environment conducive to developing literacy and describe reading activities for children who are just beginning to read.

The Environment

The most effective way to foster the emergence of literate activity is to make your classroom a language-rich environment—one in which students are immersed in print. A language-rich environment is one that is permeated with things to read, write, listen to, and talk about, as well as a host of opportunities to read, write, listen, and talk. Therefore, your classroom walls should be covered with posters, signs, labels, and student work. You should have a special part of the room designated for reading— a classroom library. It should contain books that your students find interesting (which means you need to observe your students' responses to various types of books and really get to know what they like), comfortable chairs, pillows, stuffed animals, a rug, and anything else that will make it an enticing and secure spot for young children.

Technology

In addition to a classroom library, there should be a special area of the room designated for writing. This area should contain paper of various sizes, textures, and colors, as well as a variety of pencils, pens, markers, and crayons. Having a computer in the writing area provides children with a whole new way of exploring literacy. Graphics programs allow students to create visual stories, and word processing programs help them to express their ideas through letters and words.

In addition to providing the materials needed to read and write, children should be provided with the time needed to engage in these activities. Time should be set aside each day for students to read and to write. Of course, as we discuss later, this reading and writing can take many forms.

Beyond providing the materials and the time necessary for reading and writing, you need to continually show children that these activities are valuable and enjoyable. The best way to do this is to model the activities you want children to value and engage in. Therefore, when students are reading, you should be reading. When students are writing, you should be writing as well. You need to share with your students information about what you are reading and writing as well as information about your reactions to what you are reading and writing. While it may be tempting to use reading and writing time to correct papers or straighten the room, we urge you to read and write along with students instead. If you don't, you will be sending mixed messages. On the one hand, you are telling students that reading and writing are important and fun. On the other, you are *showing* them that they are not important or enjoyable enough for you to do them. Of course, you will sometimes need to interrupt your reading to help students who need assistance.

Throughout all of your activities with children on the threshold of literacy, there should be a focus on reading for enjoyment and reading for meaning. Remember, the fact that print conveys meaning is the central concept you're trying to develop, and this is not a concept that all students already know. Of course, there should also be multiple opportunities for children to talk and to listen because skills in these areas will enhance skills in the area of reading. As you read the following sections, you will see that literacy activities, like the four modes of language, are highly interrelated and that your opportunities to create worthwhile, interesting, and motivating activities are endless.

Reading

The Morning Meeting

At the beginning of each school day, it is a good idea to spend anywhere from 10 to 20 minutes meeting with students. The amount of time you spend will depend on how long they are able to focus without becoming restless and may be relatively short at the beginning of the year and increase as the year progresses. During this meeting, many activities can take place. This is an opportunity to prepare students for the day as well as allow them to explore valuable concepts such as time, weather, the days of the week, and the months of the year. The meeting usually begins with an attendance count. As students become more adept with print, attendance might be taken by showing name cards and having students respond to their names in print.

The morning meeting is a good time to write the day and date on the board with students, reminding them of what day came just before and what day will come after (thus, simultaneously teaching and reinforcing the days of the week and the concepts of *before* and *after*). It is also a good time to talk with students about the weather, teaching words like *sunny*, *rainy*, *cold*, and *warm*. In addition, it is an excellent time to catch up on the latest news. Students always enjoy sharing the events of their lives, and the morning meeting is perfect for such sharing, perhaps with students rotating turns (depending on how much time you wish to spend on this) so that several students share each day. Certainly, you will have information that you wish to share as well, and one way to do this is to write messages to your class.

The Morning Message and the Daily Schedule

We recommend writing a short message to your class each day so that when they arrive, they know that they will be "reading" a note from you. This message serves two major purposes. First, it reinforces the notion that print conveys meaning. Second, it provides children with practice in tracking print as you read aloud, especially if you point to each word as you read it. In fact, it is often worthwhile reading the message several times. At this time, you might also ask students whether they recognize any of the letters or words and have them come up and circle those they recognize. Along with the morning message, a daily schedule is particularly helpful. Going over the schedule at the beginning of the day gives students a sense of what the day holds and, more importantly, illustrates another use of print. As the day progresses, you can refer back to the schedule from time to time.

Read-a-Room

As stated previously, your room should be language rich. One of the easiest and most effective ways to fill your room with print is to label objects in the room, a task that children may be able to help you with. Labels can be attached to objects such as your desk, your chair, the bulletin board, the clock, the coat rack, the windows, and so on. Labels illustrate the point that words represent things that exist in the world, some of which are concrete objects. Of course, abstract concepts can be labeled as well. You could label a bulletin board filled with pictures of your smiling students with the word *happy*. During the morning meeting, or at some other time during the day, you can offer your students the opportunity to "read the room." That is, students can look around the room and read any labels they wish to. At first, they will not really be reading the labels; they will take their cue from the objects labeled. However, they will be learning that the words they are looking at stand for something, a very important message. With time, they will begin to associate specific labels with the objects they name.

Free Reading

Each day, students should be given several chances to engage in free reading. These are times when they are able to read books of their choice in any way they choose. Many will share a book with a friend by telling a favorite story that they have committed to memory using the pictures as cues for turning the pages, especially if you model this activity for them. Others will silently look at books. Still others will want to be read to or listen to a book that has been tape recorded. However they choose to do it, children should get some experience with books during these times. These sessions need not be long, since the attention spans of young children tend to be relatively short, but the opportunities for such engagement with books should be frequent throughout the school day.

Environmental Print

In addition to books, there are several other things that children can "read." These include such items as posters, greeting cards, cereal boxes, bumper stickers, names of toys, letters, charts, magazines, coloring books, and milk cartons. By using things that exist in the child's environment for them to read, you will reach most all of your students. While not all children in your classroom will be from homes where there are rich stores of books, most will be surrounded by other forms of print that can reinforce the notion that print carries meaning and thus enhance their literacy development.

Writing

Doing some writing themselves will do a great deal to help students develop their reading skills, and a variety of types of writing should be encouraged.

Journals

When children write, they begin to internalize the notion that ideas can be represented symbolically. We know several kindergarten and first-grade teachers who have students keep journals, beginning on the first day of school. The journal need not be elaborate—several sheets of paper folded over to make a little book is quite sufficient. In the journal, students are encouraged to express themselves in whatever way they choose. They can be given ideas to write about or they can be allowed to write without prompts. One way is to draw pictures, another is to make squiggles, another is to make letters, and still another is to combine several forms of expression. Thus, children can "write" even if they do not yet know the letters of the alphabet. They can then read back what they have written, a task that they will find easiest if they are given the opportunity to read it back right away. As with most emergent literacy activities, journal writing should be modeled for children and, in your modeling, your attempt should be to show children that there are many ways to express themselves in writing. Another way that young children can write is to dictate a sentence that you or a classroom aide writes down. As children experiment with writing, they should be encouraged to get their ideas down in print even if they do not know some letters or spellings. The term *invented spelling* refers to spelling patterns that children experiment with during their early literacy development. Regie Routman (1994) and others have observed the following pattern of spelling development:

- Pictures
- Scribbling
- Random letters and numbers
- Prephonetic/invented spelling
- Phonetic spelling
- Conventional spelling

As Richard Gentry (1987) explains, most students progress through each of these stages and, at some point in their literacy development, "spelling" in each of these ways is an appropriate and useful part of their growth.

Language-Experience Activities

Language-experience activities are group or paired writing activities based on students' own experiences. With the whole class, a small group, or one child, an adult or older student writes down the words spoken by a student or group of students. As the students tell the story, the able writer writes it down, using the students' language. Thus, when the story is read back, it is familiar, and students can readily read along. In addition to using familiar language, prior knowledge is guaranteed in such stories because the stories are based on the students' experiences. Since this approach is entirely student centered, it is particularly useful for meeting the needs of students who vary in ethnic background, English-language competence, and educational needs. As an additional bonus, students see each word written as it is spoken, which reinforces the correspondence between spoken and written words.

Making Books

Children can be encouraged to take their language-experience stories or perhaps write their own stories and make them into small books with illustrations. In fact, making and illustrating books is a wonderful way to actively involve children in writing and reading. Book making can be as elaborate or as simple as you wish. Books can be laminated and bound with a plastic spiral or hand-sewn binding or simply stapled together. We recommend saving the more elaborate bindings for class books that can be saved and read over and over again.

Mailboxes

A classroom mailbox system in which students can post one letter a day and have pen pals to correspond with reinforces print awareness and gives students motivation for writing and for reading their own writing (since early on they will probably be the only ones who can read their messages).

Listening and Speaking

Of course, listening and speaking are normal parts of the kindergarten and first-grade school day. Here, we briefly mention some specific activities that enhance skills in these areas and, as you know by now, enhance skills in reading and writing as well.

Reading Aloud

We cannot overemphasize the importance of reading aloud to all children, but reading aloud is especially important for emergent readers. It is also doubly important for students who have not had the benefits of being read to at home. When you read to your class, you give students a chance to hear fluent reading and to develop the critical skill of listening comprehension.

You also give them the pleasure of hearing a good story and sharing your enjoyment and enthusiasm for the story. As Judith Slaughter (1993) explains, when reading aloud your goal is to share the experience of the book with students and to support their growing literacy. In order to create an effective shared book experience, it is helpful to bear four hints in mind.

- Select a story that interests you as well as your students.

- Practice the story so that you use the most effective intonation and show the pictures effectively. Also, pick good stopping points for elaborating on the information presented in the story and making sure that students understand the action.

- Pay attention to students as you read the story so that you can respond if they appear to grow restless or confused. Encourage active participation by stopping at appropriate points to ask questions and responding to any students may have. You might, for example, ask whether students have any idea what will happen next or whether they have ever experienced something similar to what the main character is experiencing.

- Whenever possible, invite students to join in! If a word or phrase is repeated, or if you are reading a story students have heard before, encourage them to read along with you. Also, some stories lend themselves to gestures and simple movement.

Choral Reading
Choral reading simply refers to having children read passages aloud in unison. The passage may be as short as a phrase or as long as a poem or story, but it should definitely be something that is fun to read. Choral reading gives children an opportunity to experience the cadence of oral language, the structure of various forms of text, and the correspondence between print and talk.

Tape Recordings
Taping stories yourself or having a classroom aide or older student tape stories can provide you with an inexpensive and very useful resource. Of course, commercially prepared tapes are also available for many popular trade books. With tapes available, a number of children can listen to the stories any time during the day, and you are freed to give attention to other students.

Sing-Alongs
Singing with students encourages listening and speaking development because lyrics are, of course, words. Whenever possible, lyrics should be posted on the wall or put on an overhead projector during singing so that children can follow along.

BOOKS TO FOSTER EMERGENT LITERACY

The next time you visit a local public library, take a look at the preschool and primary-age children's section. If the library is well organized and books are categorized by type, you may be surprised at how many different types of books you find. Many of these books are suitable for sharing aloud with children. In this section, we describe several different types of books and explain why they are useful for young children. Also, because becoming familiar with books is crucial for emergent readers, we have included several bibliographies of appropriate children's books in the References section of this chapter and provided a list of predictable books at the end of the chapter.

Big Books

Big books are just what their name suggests—enlarged copies of books. Big books might be as tall as some children! Big books are generally larger copies of books that exist in a regular size as well. However, big books are suitable for sharing with large groups of children because the print is big enough to allow children to see it clearly and follow along. At the beginning, following along will mean realizing that what you are saying is what is printed on the page. Later, it will mean realizing that each individual word you say is represented by an individual word on the printed page (assuming that you point out the words), and that individual words are separated by white space. Still later, it will mean literally following the words as you are reading.

Little Books

Little books are books that are smaller than regular books. Because they are just the right size for little hands, many children enjoy reading them to themselves or in pairs.

Repetitious Stories, Predictable Books, and Pattern Books

These books are those that have a phrase or word that is repeated several times throughout the story, thus making it predictable. A pattern is established so that, after the first few pages, children can "read" along because they know that the pattern will be followed throughout the book.

Picture Books

This large category of books simply refers to books with illustrations on all or most of the pages. These illustrations entertain children and help them follow the story.

Wordless Storybooks

Some picture books tell a story without using words. The story that is told is very much dependent on the reader. Thus, these books give children the opportunity to tell stories themselves, something that most children really enjoy.

Touch and Feel Books

These are books designed to be handled as they are read. They are books that focus on textures that can be felt with the hand and help children to learn the meanings of words and distinguish textures. For example, concepts such as *rough, smooth, soft*, and *bumpy* might be shown with pieces of sandpaper, foil, cotton, and a sample of braille.

Concept Books

These books are designed to teach the meanings of words such as *top* and *bottom, large* and *small, inside* and *outside, up* and *down*, and similar words for spatial and directional concepts. Additionally, some concept books focus specifically on social studies concepts, science concepts, or concepts related to other school subjects. These books are useful because they help students learn school language—words that are typically used in instruction and are necessary for children to understand in order to profit from instruction.

Alphabet Books

These books focus on the correspondence between letters of the alphabet and the sounds they represent. Each page is usually devoted to one letter and a picture of something that illustrates that letter's sound. Of course, as discussed in the next chapter, many letters in the English language represent more than one sound, so alphabet books are usually used as a prelude to teaching letter-sound correspondences rather than as a vehicle for teaching them.

Number Books

The numeric counterpart to alphabet books, these books focus on teaching numbers. Usually, each page is devoted to one number and an illustration shows the number of items indicated by the number on the page.

Shape Books

These books deal with shapes such as circles, squares, triangles, and rectangles. They may also deal with other geometric concepts, such as straight lines and curves. They are important to the development of reading because letters are made up of shapes. Though not true for all children, shape discrimination helps many children prepare for letter discrimination.

Nursery Rhymes

These books contain what will be for many children old favorites. Because they rhyme, they are easy to remember and easy for children to follow when they hear them read aloud.

Caption Books
These are books that consist primarily of labels for items that are drawn or pictured on the page. They do not tell a story. They represent a collection of items and labels. Because there is little print in these books and children may be familiar with the items pictured, they can be used to help children develop print awareness.

Fairy Tales, Fables, Myths, and Folktales
These traditional stories, which often involve imaginative settings and plots, are enjoyed by children and are often committed to memory. They may contain some repetitive and predictable phrases and often follow a predictable format. Because the format may be similar across stories, they are useful illustrations of the structure of stories—story grammar—and facilitate the creation of student stories based on similar patterns.

Poetry Books
Poetry has the appeal of being short and easy to enjoy in relatively brief time periods. Poetry can be used when you have a few free minutes, perhaps just before lunch, in addition to being a regular part of the literature experience.

Series Books
Books in which one or more characters are followed in a number of books are wonderful because they encourage reading other books by the same author and give children a chance to become friends with familiar characters and follow their development through several stories.

Multicultural Books
The books considered here are those that represent various cultures. Such books may represent culturally diverse writing styles, stories and characters from various cultures, illustrations depicting a variety of cultures, and authors of various cultural origins. High quality, multicultural books should be an integral part of all classroom libraries thus allowing children to see themselves in what they are reading and to experience the lives of others through literature.

Books Written by the Teacher, the Class, or a Child
Books written about the events, places, and people with which children are directly familiar are the most meaningful for young children. Children particularly appreciate books about themselves. They also appreciate photographs or illustrations to accompany these books. Often, these books can be joint projects with some children dictating the story, other students bringing in photographs or making drawings to accompany the books, and you doing the actual writing. Also, at least some of the time, the finished product should be a book that students can be especially proud of, something they can read repeatedly, share with each other, and display for class visitors.

DEVELOPING AN INITIAL SIGHT VOCABULARY

Our recommendations for developing beginning reading have included attention to all four modes of language—listening, speaking, reading, and writing. Not only can we talk about four modes of language, we can also talk about four modes of vocabulary—that is, listening, speaking, reading, and writing vocabulary. The focus of this discussion is reading vocabulary—specifically, on teaching an initial set of words that students can identify on sight. As we will explain in a bit more detail in Chapter 6, which deals specifically with vocabulary development, most children begin school knowing the meanings of several thousand words. They understand these words when they hear them and they use many of them in their own speech. During the initial stages of reading instruction, it is important to teach children to read these words for which they already have meanings so that they can concentrate on one task—learning the graphic representation of the word—rather than on two tasks—learning the graphic representation of the word and the meaning of the word.

It is also extremely important that children move beyond the point at which they are simply accurate in recognizing these words on sight to the point at which they automatically recognize them on sight. Students need to recognize these words instantaneously—without thought, without hesitation, and without any interruption of the process of reading a selection in order to understand it.

Many students come to school with some words already in their sight vocabularies, already recognized automatically. Children are likely to have words such as *McDonald's* and *Pepsi*, as well as their own names, the names of their favorite toys, and the names of other familiar and valued objects already in their sight vocabularies. They respond automatically to these words because they have seen them countless times in their homes, on television, on family outings, or while riding in a bus or car. The fact that students already know some sight words is, of course, a tremendous boon to their learning others, and you will want to celebrate and nurture their accomplishment and their interest in words by complimenting them and prominently displaying words they know in your room.

After beginning by focusing on the words students already know, the next set of words you will want students to learn on sight are those associated with their safety, words such as *stop, danger,* and *Exit.* Of course, many students will know these words, too, and those who do know them can be encouraged to use their knowledge to help you teach the words to others.

After learning these words, the next most important words to learn are those that students will meet most often in their reading The word *the,* for example, the most frequently used word in English, occurs about once in every 10 words a student reads. If a student has not mastered *the* as a sight word, if she balks for even a second every time *the* appears in a reading selection, reading will not be very enjoyable or yield much meaning. Don

Holdaway's (1990) list of basic sight words or the first several hundred words in Edward Fry's list of frequent words (Fry, Polk and Fountoukidis 1993) are two convenient sources of sight words.

When you examine sight word lists, you will find that they contain three types of words. Some of the words are content words that have a concrete referent—words like *ball, balloon,* and *hand*. These words stand for things that children can see, touch, smell, taste, or hear. They have concrete referents you can point to or show in a picture and they are likely to be the easiest words for children to learn. Other words on the list are content words that lack concrete referents—words like *think, wish,* and *maybe*. These words represent abstractions and they are likely to be more difficult for children to learn and for you to teach. Still, children have had experiences with the concepts represented by these words and, when these words appear in meaningful contexts, such as stories, rhymes, and written directions, students can tap those experiences. The third type of words are function words, the grammatical markers and glue of the language—words like *a, of,* and *the*. These words usually give children the greatest difficulty. Therefore, it is vital that children repeatedly practice these words in meaningful contexts. Even with such practice, you should be aware that these words may cause some students problems and be ready to reteach them when it seems necessary.

As explained in the next chapter, children will learn several strategies for learning words as they progress in school. However, the quickest, easiest, and most appropriate way to teach students a basic set of sight words so that they can begin reading meaningful materials is to teach them as whole words. As the name suggests, the whole-word method treats words as intact units without giving attention to individual letters or their sounds. The method is simple and straightforward: Show children the word to be taught and say it aloud so that they can recognize the association between the written word, which they do not recognize, and the spoken word, which they already know. To be sure that children recognize the association, it is a good idea to have them say the word as they are looking at it. Then, once children have learned this initial association, they need to practice it a myriad of times, using different learning modes.

Initially, you can introduce students to sight words by putting them on the board, calling students' attention to the labels you have placed around the room, or asking them to look at a specific word in something they are reading. However sight words are initially introduced, by far the best practice for mastering them is for students to read them repeatedly in meaningful materials. Thus, just as soon as possible, you want students to read the sight words you are teaching in big books, little books, nursery books, poetry books, language-experience books, or any other sorts of books that they find meaningful and enjoyable. Repetition—many encounters with the words in written contexts that children find enticing, engaging, and nonthreatening—is the key to their becoming automatic at recognizing an increasingly larger store of words.

Patricia Cunningham (1995) suggests several useful strategies for teaching sight words. One of them has to do with words that are easily confused by young learners such as *of, for,* and *from; on* and *no;* and *was* and *saw.* For words such as these, Cunningham suggests teaching one "confusable" word at a time (e.g., saw). Once students have mastered this word, teach the second confusable word (e.g., was). Once students have mastered both words, and can distinguish them, teach the third word, if there is one.

Another useful device suggested by Cunningham (1995) is the Word Wall, a part of a classroom wall (or the inside of a manilla folder for an individual word wall) dedicated to high frequency, usually irregularly spelled, words that should be learned by sight. The letters of the alphabet are placed on the wall in three or four rows, with plenty of space between letters. (The letters A–F might make up the first row.) As sight words are introduced to students, each one is written on a piece of construction paper, cut out (following the shape of the word), and placed on the Word Wall near its beginning letter. The Word Wall grows throughout the year and serves as a constant reference to students as they read and write. In addition, it can be used for reading activities such as Read-a-Room.

That is really all there is to it. The challenge you face is straightforward. You need to introduce students to a lot of words that occur very frequently in material they will enjoy reading and then you need to entice them to read and reread those words in a variety of meaningful contexts.

CONCLUDING REMARKS

In this chapter, we have described emergent literacy and beginning reading instruction. We have presented some ideas for fostering emergent literacy in kindergarten and first-grade students and, hopefully, provided you with enough of an understanding of emergent literacy to develop many more ideas on your own. As we close the chapter, we want to reemphasize the fact that emergent literacy must be nurtured by a literate environment. Students will make rapid and appropriate progress in becoming fully literate only if we provide them with opportunities, encouragement, reading materials, and physical settings that support and foster their growing proficiency in reading, writing, speaking, and listening. There are numerous ways to create such an environment and we have outlined many of them here. In closing, we suggest just two guidelines:

- Model the behavior and attitudes you are trying to develop in your students. Read a lot and share your joy and fulfillment in reading with your students.

- Focus on reading as a meaning-getting process. Do everything possible to show students that we read—and write—to learn things, to share information with each other, and to have fun.

SELF-CHECK

As in the preceding chapters and those that follow, the questions here check your knowledge of the key concepts listed at the beginning of the chapter and give you several opportunities to apply what you have learned.

1. What are the four modes of language and how are they related?

2. Define *emergent literacy* and explain its significance during the first year of school.

3. Describe several characteristics of a language-rich preschool environment.

4. Name and discuss some of the factors that influence emergent literacy.

5. Characterize the type of classroom environment that is likely to encourage literacy development.

6. Describe two reading activities that foster emergent literacy and explain how they do so.

7. Describe two writing activities that foster emergent literacy and tell how they do so.

8. Define *invented spelling* and list the stages of spelling development.

9. Describe two listening activities that foster emergent literacy and explain how they do so.

10. Describe two speaking activities that foster emergent literacy and tell how they do so.

11. Name and discuss several types of books useful with emergent readers.

12. Define sight vocabulary and describe some ways to develop children's sight vocabularies.

13. Visit several kindergarten or first-grade classrooms and take notes on what the teachers have done to create a language-rich environment that nurtures children's developing literacy. Then, sketch a plan showing how you might arrange and stock a kindergarten or first-grade room. Once you have completed the sketch, write a brief description of your arrangement and the items you have included and explain why you designed the room as you did.

14. Assume that you are teaching in an ethnically diverse kindergarten or first-grade class, and describe the cultural and linguistic backgrounds that children in the class might represent. Use the bibliographies included here and other resources you have to select at least one book appropriate for each of the groups of students that make up the class. Then read each book, taking enough notes to remember them over time.

Keep in mind that some of your students may have limited English skills and that you may need to provide them with some books written in their primary languages.

15. Select half a dozen or so of the types of books that foster emergent literacy and read at least one book of each type. After you read each book, think about how and when you could use it and write a brief note in which you consider the importance and place of this type of book in promoting young children's emerging literacy.

REFERENCES

Bridge, C. (1986). Predictable books for beginning readers and writers. In Sampson, M. (ed.), *The pursuit of literacy: Early reading and writing.* Dubuque, IA: Kendall-Hunt. A bibliography of predictable books suitable for the early elementary grades.

Butler, A. and Turbill, J. (1984). *Towards a reading-writing classroom.* Portsmouth, NH: Heinemann. Discusses the connection between reading development and writing development and suggests ways to integrate the two in the classroom.

Cullinan, B. E. (ed.). (1987). *Children's literature in the reading program.* Newark, DE: International Reading Association. Introduces several genres of literature and provides suggestions for integrating them into the development of early literacy and higher-order thinking skills.

Cullinan, B. E. (ed.). (1992). *Invitation to read: More children's literature in the reading program.* Newark, DE: International Reading Association. An extension of the earlier book by Cullinan described above.

Cunningham, P. M. (1995). *Phonics they use* (2nd ed.). New York: Harper Collins. A valuable resource for teaching phonics so that children can apply what they learn to their reading and writing.

Fields, M. V., Spangler, K. L. and Lee, D. M. (1991). *Let's begin reading right: Developmentally appropriate beginning literacy* (2nd ed.). New York: Macmillan. Presents information on literacy development in infants, toddlers, and preschoolers.

Fry, E. B., Polk, J. K. and Fountoukidis, D. (1993). *The reading teacher's book of lists.* Englewood Cliffs, NJ: Prentice-Hall. A good source of a basic sight wordlist and many other lists that are very useful in teaching reading.

Gentry, J. R. (1987). *Spel . . . is a four letter word.* New York: Scholastic. An inviting discussion of invented spelling, early writing, and some of the ways parents can be involved.

Heath, S. B. (1982). Questioning at home and at school: A comparative study. In Spindler, G. (ed.), *Doing the ethnography of schooling: Educational anthropology in action.* New York: Holt, Rinehart and Winston. Reports the results of a study of African-American students' communication patterns at home and school and discusses the implications for classroom teaching.

Holdaway, D. (1990). *Independence in reading* (3rd ed.).Sidney: Ashton Scholastic. A whole-language perspective on reading instruction and the source for Holdaway's list of basic sight words.

Huck, C., Hepler, S. D. and Hickman, J. (1987). *Children's literature in the elementary curriculum.* New York: Holt, Rinehart and Winston. A thorough analysis of genres and styles of writing as well as implications for classroom use.

Norton, D. A. (1995). *Through the eyes of a child: An introduction to children's literature* (4th ed.).Columbus, Ohio: Merrill. Provides a history of children's literature, suggestions for selecting literature, and profiles of several illustrators as well as discussions of traditional literature, modern fantasy, poetry, contemporary realistic fiction, historical fiction, multiethnic literature, and nonfiction.

Pilar, A. M. (1992). Resources to identify children's books. In Cullinan, B. E. (ed.), *Invitation to read: More children's literature in the reading program.* Newark, DE: International Reading Association, pp. 150–165. An absolute gold mine of bibliographies of children's books.

Routman, R. (1994). *Invitations: Changing as teachers and learners K–12* (2nd ed.). Portsmouth, NH: Heinemann. Presents a framework for becoming a whole-language teacher, including the theoretical underpinnings and practical ideas.

Slaughter, J. P. (1993). *Beyond storybooks: Young children and the shared book experience.* Newark, DE: International Reading Association. Describes the shared book approach to reading aloud and includes a rich set of practical teaching ideas to include as part of the shared book experience.

Trelease, J. (1995). *The read-aloud handbook.* New York: Penguin. Presents books to read aloud, hints for reading aloud, and ideas for exciting children about reading.

Wells, G. (1986). *The meaning makers: Children learning language and using language to learn.* Portsmouth, NH: Heinemann. Discusses the ways in which children's speaking, listening, reading, and writing skills are interrelated.

PREDICTABLE BOOKS

Because we believe that predictable books are particularly valuable and because many of you may not be familiar with these books, we have listed some of our favorite predictable books here. Although we have listed only one book by each of the authors represented, in most cases these authors have produced more than one predictable book (sometimes involving the same characters); so, if you find a book you particularly like, we encourage you to look for others by that author.

Barrett, J. (1987). *Animals should definitely not act like people.* New York: Aladdin.

Flack, M. (1986). *Ask mister bear.* New York: Macmillan.

Martin, B. and Archambault, J. (1988). *The braggin' dragon.* Allen, TX: DLM.

Martin, B. (1983). *Brown bear, brown bear, what do you see?* New York: Holt, Rinehart and Winston.

Livingston, M. C. (1988). *Dilly dilly piccalilli.* New York: McElderry.

Kent, J. (1987). *The fat cat.* New York: Scholastic.

Carle, E. (1997). *From head to toe.* New York: Harper Collins.

Prater, J. (1985). *The gift.* New York: Viking.

Antle, N. (1993). *The good bad cat.* Grand Haven, MI: School Zone.

Aliki. (1974). *Go tell Aunt Phody.* New York: Macmillan.

Fox, M. (1987). *Hattie and the fox.* New York: Bradbury.

Peppe, R. (1985). *The house that Jack built.* New York: Delacorte.

Stevens, J. (1985). *The house that Jack built.* New York: Holiday House.

Westcott, N. (1980). *I know an old lady who swallowed a fly.* Boston: Little Brown.

Allen, R. V. (1985). *I love ladybugs.* Allen, TX: DLM.

Shaw, C. (1947). *It looked like spilt milk.* New York: Harper.

Asch, F. (1981). *Just like daddy.* Englewood Cliffs, NJ: Prentice-Hall.

Cowley, J. (1987). *Mrs. Wishy-Washy.* Bothell, WA: The Wright Group.

Munsch, R. (1982). *Mud puddle.* Buffalo, New York: Firefly.

Young, E. (1984). *The other bone.* New York: Harper.

Wadsworth, O. (1985). *Over in the meadow.* New York: Viking.

Sendak, P. (1962). *Pierre.* New York: Harper & Row.

Lobel, A. (1984). *The rose in my garden.* New York: Greenwillow.

Hutchins, P. (1988). *Rosie's walk.* New York: Macmillan.

Galdone, P. (1984). *The teeny, tiny woman.* New York: Clarion.

Mayer, M. (1973). *What do you do with a kangaroo?* New York: Scholastic.

5 Strategies for Recognizing Words

Upon arriving home from school, a 6-year-old is greeted by his babysitter, who shows him this note.

> Josh, please feed Homer. I will get home late.
>
> Love,
>
> Mom

Josh looks at the note. There are some words that he knows automatically. For example, he can read his own name easily. The next word that pops out at him is the name of his dog, *Homer*, since Homer's name is printed on his dog food dish and the dog has been part of the family since Josh was born. Josh recognizes the words, *I*, *Love*, and *Mom* without hesitating. When he glances back at the first sentence, he realizes that he also recognizes the word *please*, since his first-grade teacher has the words *Please* and *Thank You* printed on the board. The other words, however, are more of a challenge for Josh. Because he does not recognize them automatically, he must work at decoding them.

As Josh studies the word *feed*, he is thinking about what word could possibly fit there—What would his mother want him to do with Homer? What word would make sense? Josh knows what sounds the letters *f*, *ee*, and *d* represent, and he can blend these sounds together. Blending the sounds together, Josh comes up with a word that he knows, the word *feed*— a word that is in his oral vocabulary—and a word that makes sense in the sentence.

Josh figures out the word *home* because it is a part of a larger word that he already knows—*Homer*. As he did with *feed*, Josh figures out *late* by blending its sounds and then predicting its meaning—what word would make sense in the sentence? Usually, Josh's mother feeds the dog. Why can't she do it today? At the same time, he remembers that he's encountered many other words with the same spelling pattern—consonant-vowel-consonant-e—and most of them carry a long vowel sound, so he guesses that this word will carry a long *a* sound rather than a short *a* sound. As he says the word *late* to himself, Josh recognizes the sound of it. He has heard it before and realizes that it makes sense in the sentence, so he does not bother trying a short *a* sound for the word. All of this effort took Josh only a minute or so.

As is evident in this brief scenario, the purpose of word-recognition strategies is to empower readers by giving them tools to unlock meaning from text. Good readers use a combination of word-recognition strategies and they use the strategies so rapidly that they are not even aware that they are using them. As a beginning reader, Josh expends more time and energy on word-recognition strategies than he will when he is older. With each passing month, he will recognize more and more words automatically. Automatic word-recognition allows readers to turn more attention to the meaning of words, sentences, and passages. This construction of meaning on the part of the reader is the ultimate goal of all word-recognition strategies.

LOOKING AHEAD

In the previous chapter, we talked about the beginnings of reading instruction. These include ways to facilitate print awareness, interest in books, knowledge of letters, awareness of basic story elements, the provision of many and varied experiences, and ways to develop phonemic awareness. We emphasized immersing children in print and developing a basic sight vocabulary by teaching words as intact units in meaningful contexts. We also stressed the importance of meaningful contexts to the emergence of literacy in children, highlighting the role of prediction, confirmation, and self correction as central to the reading process. In this chapter, we continue the discussion by focusing on the role word-recognition strategies play in the continuing literacy development of young students.

Sight words are invaluable to children because time not spent figuring out individual parts of words and putting them together is time that can be spent on comprehending text. However, children will not immediately recognize all of the thousands of words they eventually need to learn as whole units nor will context alone always be sufficient. Therefore, it is important to provide them with a repertoire of strategies for figuring out unrecognizable words. In this chapter, we discuss two types of cues that can be used in conjunction with context to decode unrecognized words: graphophonic cues and structural cues. Used within the context of meaningful reading, these cues provide ways of figuring out words when context alone is not sufficient.

The remainder of this chapter is divided into three major sections. In the first section, we discuss the meaning of word recognition and its relationship to the reading process. In the second section, we focus on phonic analysis, a word-recognition strategy based on letters and the sounds they represent. The third section focuses on structural analysis—a related word-recognition strategy based on larger groups of letters and the sounds they represent in words. We conclude the chapter with a suggested progression for instruction and a discussion of five important guidelines for teaching word-recognition strategies.

KEY CONCEPTS

- The purpose of teaching word-recognition strategies

- Types of letter-sound correspondences

- Methods for providing initial instruction in and practice with basic letter-sound correspondences

- The importance of careful observation in phonics instruction

- Blending and ways to teach children how to blend

- The process of decoding by analogy

- The general information children need about any reading strategies they will use

- Structural analysis and the significance of compound words, root words, suffixes, and prefixes

- A method of teaching children to decode suffixed and prefixed words

- Five guidelines for teaching word-recognition strategies

A FRAMEWORK FOR WORD RECOGNITION

In our discussion of emergent literacy and building a sight vocabulary, we stated that students should constantly be making sense of what they read, an idea revisited in this chapter's opening scenario in which Josh used several letter-sound clues to figure out the unknown words in his mother's note while *simultaneously* asking himself, "What would make sense here?"

In addition to using letter-sound correspondences, figuring out unknown words is a complex process that often includes the following steps:

- Asking, "What would make sense here?" when coming across an unknown word and making a prediction about what the word is

- Confirming or disconfirming this prediction by asking, "Does this make sense here?"

- Self-correcting and trying other predictions when the answer to the above question is, "No"

During the early stages of learning this process, strategic readers use context combined with their knowledge of the first letter of a word and the sound associated with this letter. Don Holdaway (1990) refers to this use of context plus the initial letter as a "central method of word attack." As they become more fluent in reading, students begin to use additional information about words, such as associations between groups of letters and sounds, common spelling patterns, and common structural components of words. In addition, they consider letters appearing in the medial and final positions of words. The more sophisticated their knowledge of the way words are put together, the more sophisticated students' predictions become.

Simply stated, *word recognition* is the ability to pronounce a word when it is seen in print. For most children, certain words will be pronounced automatically and without hesitation when they are seen in print. As indicated in Chapter 4, these words comprise children's sight vocabularies. Other words children encounter will not at first be pronounced automatically. However, by using the context of the sentence along with other clues, children can usually decode these words. The purpose of teaching word-recognition strategies is to lead children to an awareness of the clues available to them and the knowledge of how and when to use these clues to construct meaning from text.

Instruction in word-recognition strategies has one primary goal—comprehension. Indeed, comprehension is the goal of all reading instruction. Word-recognition strategies provide a means to this end and, quite obviously, do not represent an end in themselves. The ultimate goal is not for students to use phonic analysis or structural analysis to decode every word they read. The goal is for them to use these strategies *until* words become automatically identifiable for them.

Automatic word identification, also known as automaticity, is important because the less mental energy used to determine the pronunciation of a word, the more energy the reader has for comprehension. The more students practice decoding words, the less necessary such decoding becomes because students automatically recognize more and more words. Thus, students must be given many opportunities to read and reread stories so that words can be learned to the point of automaticity. Word-recognition strategies should be taught within the context of the reading students do during the school day so that students can see that using these strategies has purpose—they are tools to unlock meaning.

PHONIC ANALYSIS

Many of the "unknown words" encountered by young readers are unknown only in the sense that their graphic representation is unfamiliar; students recognize such words with ease when they hear them. Using letter-sound clues can help students arrive at a pronunciation that leads to meaning if the word is in fact in the student's listening vocabulary. For words that are unrecognizable in their spoken forms as well, you will need to provide instruction in word meanings. Teaching word meanings is a very different matter from teaching students strategies for recognizing printed versions of words in their oral vocabularies. Methods of teaching word meanings are discussed in Chapter 6.

Successful readers use the context of sentences in conjunction with their knowledge of letters and the sounds they represent to identify words when seen in print. By helping students discover the patterns and consistencies in the language (that the letter *b*, for instance, makes the sound they hear in *Bob, bicycle, bear,* and *boat*) as well as the inconsistencies (that the same letter *b*, for example, makes no sound in the word *lamb*) and by showing them that individual sounds and groups of sounds plus context can lead to word identification, you are facilitating their construction of meaning from what they read and helping them to become independent readers.

Some Inappropriate Approaches to Phonics Instruction

In the past, phonics instruction often consisted of drill and practice activities using flashcards, wall charts, and workbook pages. Letter-sound correspondences were sometimes emphasized to the exclusion of meaning. For example, in a lesson focusing on the short *i* sound, children might have read lists of unrelated words containing short *i*'s, thus focusing on the short *i* sound without giving appropriate attention to meaning. Children might also have read through lists of nonsense words such as *bif, sil, kiv,* and *min.* While reading such a list allows children to demonstrate the ability to apply the short *i* sound in decoding, nonsense words obviously do not yield meaning. Further, in some cases there was so much emphasis on learning letter-sound correspondences themselves that whether children could apply them to obtain meaning was de-emphasized. Rather than being viewed as a means to an end—the end being comprehension—phonic analysis was often viewed as an end in itself.

Another misuse of phonics instruction occurred when students who were accomplished readers were made to participate in phonics drills—for example, drills in which they copied long lists of words containing the short *e* sound—often causing them to dislike reading or to make a sharp distinction between the reading they did for enjoyment and reading instruction as it occurred in school. Finally, phonics was misused when it was taught as the sole word-recognition strategy. Good readers apply several strategies, and phonics is one of them.

Clearly, reading instruction should reflect what is known about the reading process—that it is a constructive process of obtaining meaning. Thus, reading instruction should take place in contexts that allow children to be actively engaged in the construction of meaning (International Reading Association 1997). Within the past few years, there have been several discussions of the role of phonics in such an approach to reading instruction. In this chapter, we concentrate on ways of teaching phonics in meaningful contexts.

Overview of Basic Letter-Sound Correspondences

Once children develop phonemic awareness and learn the letters of the alphabet—two matters discussed in Chapter 4—they are ready to carry their knowledge one step further by learning the associations between these sounds and letters. In this section, we discuss the basic sounds represented by consonants and vowels in American English. Although we present all of them here, these correspondences should be taught over the course of the first three or four years of school. Later in the chapter, we differentiate content appropriate for beginning phonics instruction from content appropriate for intermediate and advanced phonics instruction. Because individual children will be ready to learn different letter-sound associations at different times, our recommendations are appropriate for any level of instruction.

In discussing the sounds that letters represent, it is useful to think of *generalizations*—sounds that letters *usually* represent. There are always exceptions because the English spelling system is not totally regular; that is, the same letters sometimes represent different sounds and the same sounds are sometimes represented by different letters. Irregularities in the English language is one reason our focus on sight words in Chapter 4 did not include a discussion of phonics. The words that occur most frequently in the English language, those that constitute basic sight words, are also the most irregularly spelled words in the language (Cunningham 1995).

Many other words do conform to regular spelling patterns. Figure 5–1 lists the major letter-sound correspondences that students should be exposed to during the first three or four years of schooling. For ease of reference, we have divided these into three developmental levels. As we have indicated several times throughout this book, we do not hold steadfast to stages of development, as we believe that the sequence in which children learn letter-sound correspondences varies. Further, we refer to beginning, intermediate, and advanced levels rather than to specific grade levels because the grade levels that correspond to each of these three levels will differ among your students.

Phonics instruction usually begins with the consonants. Of the 21 consonants in the English alphabet, all but five—*s, c, g, q,* and *x*—generally represent only one sound. These letters are located at the beginning level of Figure 5–1.

Intermediate instruction in letter-sound correspondences focuses on groups of consonants that represent special sounds: blends and digraphs. As the name implies, a blend refers to the combined sounds of two or three consonants. *Pl* in *play* and *spr* in *spring* are examples of blends. A consonant digraph, on the other hand, is a combination of consonants that makes a

Early Level

Consonants Related to One Sound

b – bid	d – sad	f – fit	h – hill	j – jade	k – bike
l – lap	m – more	n – neat	p – cope	r – run	t – tip
v – vest	w – wall	y – yell	z – zoo		

Consonants Related to Multiple Sounds

s – bus, busy	c – cat, cent	g – gum, gender	q – quick, unique
			x – xylophone ax exalt

Intermediate Level

Consonant Blends

bl	fl	pl	sl	st	br	cr	dr	fr	gr	tr	str
sm	sn	sw	pr	cl	gl	tw	sp	spr		

Consonant Digraphs

ph - phone	ch - beach	gh - cough	th - thin	sh -bush	ng - hang

Advanced Level

Long and Short Vowels

a – make, mat	e – read, bed	i – kite, kit	o – boat, cot	u – use, cup

Vowel Digraphs

oo – food, loose, wood, cook	ew – stew dew	au, aw – auto awesome	oi, oy – soil foil boy decoy	ou, ow – south allow

Figure 5–1.   Basic Letter-Sound Correspondences

unique sound unlike the sound made by any of the individual letters within the digraph. Examples include *ph* as in *phone* and *sh* as in *share* and *fish*.

Advanced instruction in letter-sound correspondences deals with vowels. Each of the vowels—*a, e, i, o,* and *u*—is associated with a long sound and a short sound. For example, the *i* in *kit* has a short sound and the *i* in *kite* has a long sound. In addition, *y* can function as a vowel when found in the middle, as in *myth*, or the end of a word, as in *sky*. As is the case with consonants, there are pairs of vowels that make distinct sounds. *Vowel digraphs* such as *oo* in *stool* or *stood* and *aw* in *straw* are examples. As is evident in the example of *oo* as in *stood* or *stool*, digraphs can make more than one sound. Further, the sounds that letters make are influenced by the differences in dialect and accents across individuals, which are in turn influenced by region of the country in which you are teaching, students' cultural backgrounds, and students' experience in other languages.

It should be noted that the important point here is not that some letters are called consonants and some are called vowels or that some letter combinations are called digraphs. We are using these terms to facilitate our discussion of letter-sound correspondences; however, children do not need to learn these terms. The goal for children is to be able to associate letters with their corresponding sounds. We make this distinction because sometimes teachers get so involved with terminology that students are better able to describe phonics than they are to apply it.

Teaching Letter-Sound Correspondences

In learning to use any reading strategy, including phonic analysis, children need to know what the strategy is, why and when they use it, and how to evaluate whether it has worked for them. Of course, they do not need to learn all of this in one sitting, but they do need to learn it over time. Thus, over time, you need to explain to students that what you are teaching them is the process of using a letter or several letters in a word as clues when figuring out an unknown word. It is important to tell students that they can use letter clues when they come across a word they do not at first recognize. It is equally important to explain to students that they will know these letter clues have worked for them if they come up with a word that makes sense in the sentence they are reading.

Although some students will have some concept of letter-sound correspondences before they come to school, the concept should be formally introduced to be sure that all students understand it. This can be done as a scheduled activity for the entire class or in a small group in which students are taking turns reading an interesting story aloud and one of the students stumbles over a word and cannot come up with it. In either situation, briefly explain the idea of letter-sound correspondences and model the use of them—including the critical component of checking to be sure the word you came up with made sense in the sentence. Finally, you could conclude this mini-lesson by telling students that using letter clues is one step in becoming an independent reader.

At this point, you may be wondering whether the acquisition of letter-sound knowledge should come incidentally for children as they engage in literacy activities throughout the school day or via direct instruction. The answer is that it should come in both ways (Wharton-McDonald et al. 1997). Some students will learn some letter-sound correspondences incidentally and informally through reading activities at home and at school. Some students will not. It is appropriate to directly teach the important correspondences that students have not learned rather than simply expecting students to recognize them. Such instruction can and should be brief. It should focus students' attention on the letter and sound to be learned while remaining connected to a meaningful context. Here, for example, is one instructional sequence.

Instructional Sequence for Teaching Letter-Sound Correspondences

- Tell students that you are going to be discussing the sound usually made by the letter *b*.

- Focus students' attention on the letter *b*, writing a lower case *b* and perhaps an upper case *B* on the board.

- Give examples of other words that contain the letter *b*. Have students look around the room for examples of words that contain *b* from those that you have printed labels for—*book, ball, basket, table,* for example. Write these on the board.

- Pronounce each word you have written on the board, emphasizing the sound /b/ as you underline the letter *b*.

- Have students say the words with you, and perhaps ask them to produce some words that contain the sound /b/.

This approach can be used either as part of a preplanned lesson or when an occasion for teaching the sound associated with the letter *b* presents itself. If the instruction is given as part of a preplanned lesson, be sure that students move quickly to reading interesting and engaging stories that include a number of words containing the letter *b*. An occasion that would prompt incidental instruction in the sound represented by the letter *b* would be one like this: Suppose Bill Martin's *Brown Bear, Brown Bear, What Do You See?* is a story you have read with your students several times. After sharing the story on yet another occasion, you might close the book so that the title is showing and remark, "You know, I really like this book, *Brown Bear, Brown Bear, What Do You See?* and I've noticed something interesting about the first two words in the title." You might then say and point to the words, "Brown Bear" and ask whether anyone notices something that these words have in common. You can then present the instruction just described.

Quite often the impetus for focusing on a particular word and the sounds that comprise it will come from your students themselves, as they proudly recognize a letter-sound correspondence they know as they are reading. Other meaningful contexts within which you can draw students' attention to letter-sound correspondences are described here.

Using Literature
Take advantage of read-aloud and shared reading experiences by pointing out frequently occurring letter-sound correspondences. For example, the story *Mrs. Wishy Washy* by Joy Cowley, available in large print format, provides a good opportunity to introduce and review the sound made by the

letter *w*. Big books, such as those described in Chapter 4, are especially useful because children can see the print clearly, which of course facilitates their making a clear connection between the letter and the sound. Phyllis Trachtenburg (1990) has prepared a list of books highlighting specific letters and their corresponding sounds, and a slightly modified version of that list is shown at the end of this chapter.

There are several ways to incorporate phonics instruction or review into activities involving stories. Children will often ask questions that provide the perfect moment for pointing out a letter-sound correspondence. In order to preserve the enjoyment of the stories, Trachtenburg suggests a whole-part-whole sequence for integrating phonics instruction with children's literature. A slightly modified form of her sequence is shown here.

- *Whole:* Read, comprehend, and enjoy the selection as a whole.

- *Part:* Provide instruction in a high utility letter-sound correspondence by drawing from or extending the preceding literature selection.

- *Whole:* Apply the new phonic skill when reading and enjoying other literature selections.

Note that, although the initial steps of phonics instruction can often be completed in a single day, reviewing and reinforcing children's knowledge of the correspondences taught should extend well beyond the initial instruction.

Guided Reading
In addition to participating in shared reading and read-aloud experiences, students at this stage of their literacy development should experience a guided reading activity each day. The guided reading experience involves a small group of children, with similar instructional needs, working with the teacher to read text that challenges them to learn and apply new reading strategies (Fountas & Pinnell 1996). During these interactions with text, you will have wonderful opportunities to introduce, practice, or reinforce both beginning level word recognition strategies, discussed here, and more advanced strategies discussed later in this chapter.

Using Students' Writing
Among the most meaningful texts students read are those they create themselves. Writing lends itself to both initial instruction in letter-sound correspondences and review of letter-sound correspondences that have been previously introduced. As they are writing, students often wonder how to spell a word. One way to facilitate their movement through the stages of spelling development discussed in Chapter 4 is to remind them to use correct spellings for the letter-sound correspondences they know. So, for example, if a few students are writing about their dogs and the class has discussed the sound that *d* makes, students should be encouraged to make

a *d* at the beginning of the word, regardless of whether they can spell the entire word. Similarly, when students who have discussed the sound made by *oo* are writing about their favorite books and they wonder how to spell the word *book,* they should be encouraged to think of letters that make the sound that they hear in the middle of the word and reminded that they studied those letters in yesterday's morning message. The teacher might say, "These are the same letters that you hear in the words *look, cook,* and *took."* All in all, students' free explorations and independent searches for ways to express themselves and make meaning for another reader will provide one of the most fertile instructional grounds you will ever find.

Phonics Charts

You may recall wall charts in the classrooms of your childhood with letters and corresponding pictures showing the sounds that the letters represent. Although such charts should not be used for isolated drills, they can be useful to remind students of the sounds made by various letters. In order to provide a meaningful context for your students, make phonics charts with your students instead of purchasing prepackaged charts. In making phonics charts, students become actively involved with words and letter-sound correspondences of interest to them.

There are a number of ways to make such charts. One is to spend two or three days focusing on a specific letter, having students cut out or draw pictures of things that begin or end with that letter. Another way to make a phonics chart with students is to have them think of as many words as they can that begin with a certain sound (a single consonant such as *f* in *food* or a consonant digraph such as *th* as in *think,* for example) and list these words on a chart, underlining the *f* or the *th* in each. Keep in mind that words appearing on the chart that are not part of the students' sight vocabulary will need a picture to be meaningful to them. Of course, the most meaningful pictures are often those that children draw themselves.

Personal Phonics Books

Routman (1994) has suggested encouraging students to keep personal records of letter-sound correspondences as they learn them. These can be part of the journals that students keep, an activity described in Chapter 4. If the letter-sound correspondence for *sh* has been recently discussed, for example, students can be encouraged to record as many words as they can with the *sh* sound. They can record words by drawing or cutting out pictures and pasting them into the book. For example, the teacher or the student can write the letters *sh* at the top of the page devoted to that sound, and the student can then dictate words beginning with *sh* or write words beginning with *sh* and invent the rest of the spelling. Not only does this allow students to practice letter-sound correspondences, it provides a written record of each student's achievement and progress in phonics that can be used for making instructional decisions. Growth in knowledge about letter-sound associations corresponds with the stages of spelling development discussed in Chapter 4. As students learn more and more letter-sound correspondences, their use of invented spellings will diminish.

Read-a-Room
As noted in Chapter 4, labeling objects in the classroom introduces and re-inforces the notion that objects in the world have names and that these names can be represented with graphic symbols. Giving children the opportunity to "read the room" introduces them to the notion that these graphic symbols correspond to spoken language and that they, the children, are readers. As you begin teaching letter-sound correspondences, you can key the signs so that certain aspects of words are highlighted. For example, all objects beginning with the letter *b* might be labeled with a red sign while all other objects are labeled with a black sign. Children's natural curiosity will spur them to ask why some of the signs in the classroom are printed in red while others are printed in black. At that point, you can ask the children to see whether they can discover what it is about the words printed in red that is similar. Naturally, they all begin with the letter *b* and the sound that *b* makes.

Write-a-Room
The interconnectedness of reading and writing can be made explicit when students are involved in writing the labels that appear around the room. As they label objects in the room, children get the opportunity to use their knowledge of phonics for spelling.

Poetry
Poems, especially those with rhyme or alliteration, provide practice with letter-sound correspondences and exposure to a new literary form. Check your local library for anthologies of children's poetry, including those by Shel Silverstein and Jack Prelutsky.

Tongue Twisters
Repetition of sounds is the very reason that children find tongue twisters so much fun (and the reason that they twist the tongue). Children enjoy saying them and making them up. *Marvelous Mary marched through the meadow merrily* provides practice with the initial *m*, and *Bickering brothers Bobby and Billy bother the barber* provides practice with *b*, for example.

Daily Schedule
As suggested in the previous chapter, you will probably have a daily schedule displayed in your classroom. By manipulating the schedule, you can teach many letter-sound correspondences. For example, in the following

schedule, the teacher is highlighting the sound the letter *m* makes whether it appears at the beginning, the end, or the middle of a word:

Today's Schedule

8:45–9:15	Morning Message
9:15–9:45	Art
9:45–11	Reading
11–11:15	Free Time
11:15–12	Lunch
12–12:30	Story Time
12:30–1:15	Math
1:15–2:00	Gym
2:00–2:30	Writing
2:30–2:45	Clean Up/Dismissal

Of course, you can also highlight the letter or letters you want to emphasize with colored markers. As a variation in this activity, you can leave blank spaces in words for children to fill in. When doing this, make sure to leave the blank for a letter that clearly makes its sound in the word, since some letters are sometimes silent in words.

The Morning Message

The morning message provides another opportunity to highlight various letter-sound correspondences. Single consonants, long and short vowel sounds, and digraphs can all be dealt with using the morning message. Consider the following example:

January 14, 1998

Good Morning Friends,

I hope you had a **good** weekend. I **took** a walk on Saturday to **look** at the new snow in the park. I **shook** in the cold but had fun **looking** at children playing in the snow. I left the park so I could get home to **cook** dinner. Later that night, I read a **book** by the fire. What did you do on Saturday?

Your friend,

Ms. Conklin

By highlighting certain aspects of this message, Ms. Conklin can point out some common letter-sound correspondences that students can use in other contexts. Such lessons can take place frequently. For example, similar messages can be written about topics in the content areas. As always, the meaning of the message remains the first priority, but using that same message to reinforce letter-sound correspondences is an efficient use of time and places letter-sound correspondences in a real communicative context.

The Importance of Careful Observation

At this point, you have no doubt realized that there are many ways of teaching and practicing letter-sound associations. Exposing your students to word-recognition strategies from many different angles is important to meeting the needs of learners who vary in learning styles, phases of readiness, and English-language proficiency. Many school districts have adopted basal reading programs in which these correspondences are taught in a specific order to the entire class. Other districts, using literature-based and whole-language approaches, allow greater teacher choice in determining when and how to teach correspondences. Whether you teach using a basal approach or a whole-language approach, careful observation and record keeping of student progress is vital. You should consistently monitor students' ability to use the correspondences taught in reading and writing situations.

One reason why observation and record keeping are important is that students are highly individual in their learning. There are differences in the number of letter-sound correspondences students learn in a given time period as well as differences in exactly which letter-sound correspondences they learn. While James may have mastered all of the single consonants by the middle of first grade, Maria will have mastered only half of the single consonants but all of the consonant digraphs. If you have a record of these differences, you can use them to enhance instruction for all your students. For example, you might have the two students just mentioned work together on a few writing projects, since each has an area of strength where the other is still developing.

Through careful observation you will also notice who is having difficulty with letter-sound associations because of oral language influences. It is not uncommon for children who speak nonstandard dialects of English to find letter-sound correspondences based on standard English particularly challenging, since their pronunciations will sometimes differ from those of standard English speakers. The challenge is even greater for non-native English speakers, who may not perceive some of the sounds English speaking children do. For example, having never heard the sound that *r* represents in English because the sound does not exist in their languages, some Asian children have difficulty saying or even recognizing this sound. However, these differences generally create problems only if they interfere with comprehension, and if letter-sound correspondences are taught in meaningful contexts such interference is unlikely. It is particularly important, therefore, to be certain that the contexts in which you work with letter-sound correspondence are meaningful to all students.

Another reason that careful observation and record keeping is important is because it prevents you from wasting valuable instructional time teaching something that a student already knows. While providing ample opportunities to practice strategies is important, if you were going to teach a mini-lesson on *ph* to a small group of students who were in need of such a lesson, you probably would not include a student who had already mastered consonant digraphs. Although most basals series will provide you with a preset sequence of instruction, you must be aware of what individual students are capable of doing so that you can monitor progress on an individual level. Following a certain scope and sequence of instruction does not guarantee the same scope and sequence of learning.

For students whose comprehension is inhibited because of difficulty in learning letter-sound correspondences, we recommend a multisensory approach. Having students focus on the visual representation of the letter while at the same time listening to the sound it makes and then making the sound while writing or tracing the letter can be effective. In addition, multiple exposures in a variety of forms, such as word games and magnetic letters, is often a helpful adjunct to more direct instruction. At the same time, it is important to remember that providing more detailed and direct instruction in letter-sound correspondences should always occur along with and in addition to—but never in place of—reading experiences involving meaningful, continuous text.

THE INTERMEDIATE AND ADVANCED LEVELS OF INSTRUCTION

Once students have learned most of the consonant sounds, they are ready to learn other strategies that can be used in conjunction with their growing repertoire of letter-sound correspondences. These include decoding by analogy, blending, syllabication, and the use of spelling patterns.

Decoding by Analogy

One of the simplest ways to decode an unrecognizable word is to think of a recognizable word that is like it. For example, a child encountering the word *snake* for the first time in its written form might hesitate for a moment, and then recognize the *-ake* part as being part of the word *cake*. A quick substitution of *sn* for *c* yields the correct word. This is called *decoding by analogy* (Cunningham 1995) and is the most straightforward way of decoding words. At first, students may benefit from putting a finger over the letter not in the familiar part of the word and making a mental substitution of a letter that would make the whole word familiar. Over time, they will be able to do this without physically covering letters. One way to facilitate the development of this strategy is to play games in which children substitute beginning sounds in words to create new words. You might ask, for example, "How many new words can we make by substituting the first letter in the word *bake*?" Examples include *cake, rake, make, fake*.

Blending

After identifying individual sounds in words, children must be able to put the sounds together to form words. This step is called *blending*. Too often, we think that blending is simple and fail to provide students with the direct instruction they need to be successful with it. This happens because, as accomplished readers, we already know what the final product—the word—should sound like. For someone who already recognizes a word, dissecting it and putting it back together is a simple task. It is also a totally unnecessary task because the person already knows the word. For beginning readers, blending can be a challenge.

The following steps can be used to teach students how to blend. Note that in this case, the explanation of the general purposes and nature of blending is included in the instruction itself.

- Write a sentence on the board with a word that is likely to be unknown to the students. The sentence should deal with a topic familiar to students. It might refer to a story they have recently heard or an event they have taken part in. Here, we will use the sentence *We had ice cream at lunch.* The new word for students is *cream.*

- Have the students look at the whole sentence and raise their hands if there is a word they do not know. Tell them to think quietly and not to blurt out words so that everyone gets a chance to think. Once it has been established that most of the students do not recognize the word *cream,* tell them that you will show them a way to figure it out. Be sure to tell students what they will be learning, why they are learning it, when they can apply it, and how they will know that it has been successful for them.

- Cover the beginning and the end of the word so that only the letters *ea* are showing. This can be done with your hands or with pieces of tagboard taped over the letters. Ask students for the sound that the letters *ea* usually make. Provide them with the sound if they are unsure.

- Uncover the beginning of the word and ask for the sound made by the letters *cr*. Then, have students put the two sounds together to make the sound /cree/. Say the sound with the students. You may wish to run your hand underneath the letters as students do this to reinforce the notion that they are no longer making isolated sounds.

- Finally, uncover the end of the word and have students add this sound to what they have so far. Again, you may wish to run your hand underneath the letters to illustrate the progression and joining of sounds. After doing this, reread the sentence with the students inserting the new word, and ask students whether the word makes sense in the sentence.

As we noted at the beginning of this section, blending appears deceptively simple to accomplished readers and it seems particularly simple to you when you are showing students how to blend the sounds of a word you know perfectly well. But blending will be a challenge to some children, and some children will require more instruction and more follow-up instruction and mini-lessons than others. We recommend that you keep careful track of your students' blending skills and give those that need additional help the additional help they need.

Syllabication and Spelling Patterns

Syllabication is the process of dividing words up into their component parts. Beginning readers sometimes need to break unknown words into their component parts so that they can deal with each of the parts in turn. For example, *sandal* can be divided according to a rule that indicates that when two consonants (that are not digraphs) are between two vowels, the word generally divides into syllables between the consonants. Thus, *san-dal* can be divided as *san-dal*. Once the word is divided in this way, the student can sound out *san*—yielding /săn/—and *dal*—yielding /dəl/. All of this makes good sense. The problem is that syllabication rules are themselves complex, there are many exceptions to the rules, and teaching syllabication rules is complex. For this reason, we do not deal with syllabication in this brief book. Instead, we recommend Dolores Durkin's *Strategies for Identifying Words* (1981) or Chapters 8 and 9 of her *Teaching Them to Read* (1993) for an in-depth treatment of the topic.

Spelling patterns are sequences of consonants and vowels commonly associated with certain sounds—the *an* in *ran, can, Dan, fan,* and *tan,* for example. If children recognize a particular spelling pattern, they will have a clue to the sound represented by letters that represent different sounds in different spelling patterns. For example, the word *came* follows the consonant-vowel-consonant plus *e* pattern (CVCe), a pattern that often signals a long vowel sound. As is the case with the concept of syllabication, the concept of spelling patterns makes good sense. As is also the case with syllabication, spelling-pattern rules are complex, there are many exceptions to them, and teaching them is complex. Again, we recommend Dolores Durkin's *Strategies for Identifying Words* (1981) or Chapters 8 and 9 of her *Teaching Them to Read* (1993) for an in-depth treatment of the topic.

Final Words on Phonics

You will notice that the instructional activities discussed do not involve the use of flashcards or worksheets. The reason for this is that children retain information best when they learn it in meaningful contexts. Because reading for meaning is the only meaningful context in which reading can take place, it makes sense that instruction in word-recognition strategies should take place in this environment. This is why phonics instruction is generally not begun until a student has a sight vocabulary of 50 words or more—without one, there would be no meaningful context within which phonics instruction could take place.

At this point, you may be wondering whether isolated practice is ever appropriate, especially since you may remember taking part in isolated practice when you were a child. Although we do not advocate practicing phonics in isolation, there are ways to give children practice opportunities that do not involve extended pieces of text. Word games and songs can be used to help students practice various phonics concepts. For example, children thoroughly enjoy trying to figure out riddles such as this, "I am an animal. I begin with the letter *d.* I say 'Quack, quack!.' What am I?"

One particularly effective word game is called Making Words (Cunningham 1995). In Making Words, all students are given the same set of letters with which they are instructed to make increasingly difficult words. Given the letters *t, p, r, i,* and *n,* for example, you might give students the following directions: 1. Select two of your letters and make the word *it.* 2. Now replace the *t* with another one of your letters to make the word *in.* 3. Now add a letter to make the word *pin.* 4. Now add a letter to make the word *pint.* 5. Now, let's see who can use all of their letters to come up with the mystery word. As your students work on each directive, you can walk around the room, checking their work or have them check with a neighbor. You should also show the correct answer before moving on to the next directive. You can include as many directives as you like (you will find that children will want to keep playing) but the final directive should be to figure out the mystery word, which uses all of the students' letters. We recommend this activity because it focuses students' attention on words and letters in a fun, motivating way, it allows all students to participate at all times, and it has something for students at all different levels of phonic development.

One final note, some children will benefit more than others from phonics. While phonemic awareness is related to reading achievement, the evidence is not clear that direct instruction in phonics is necessary for reading success for all children. We subscribe to two beliefs when it comes to phonics. First, if it isn't broken, then don't fix it. That is, if students are already reading successfully and comprehending what they are reading, then teaching phonics as an aid to reading is a waste of time—both yours and the students'. (For these students, you might point out some phonic generalizations as an aid to conventional spelling, however.) Our second credo is that if a strategy is not working for a student, more of the same is not likely to help. Thus, if a student has considerable difficulty with phonics, it is up to you, as the teacher, to find other ways to facilitate reading for this student. Such ways include focusing on visual features of words such as length and shape, using much more repeated reading, focusing more attention on learning whole words, and using word structure as a clue to unknown words. We will now turn to a discussion of word structure as a clue to unknown words.

USING STRUCTURAL ANALYSIS TO DECODE WORDS

In using structural analysis, students first break up an unknown word into its component parts. Once the word is broken into its parts, students may be able to recognize the parts without further analysis and simply reassemble them to form the whole word. Alternately, once they have broken a word into its component parts, they may use their phonics skills to sound out one or more of the parts. Finally, after they have identified each of the parts of the word, they can reassemble the parts and identify the whole word.

Suppose, for example, that students did not at first recognize the word *football*. Using structural analysis, they might first recognize the word *foot* and mentally separate it from the rest of the word. Then, they might recognize the remaining word *ball*. Finally, they would need to reassemble the two words to form the compound word *football*. At this point, assuming that *football* was in their oral vocabulary, they would simply recognize it. Alternately, students might not at first recognize the word *dragonfly* but might recognize the word *fly* and separate it from the rest of the word. Then, they might sound out the remainder of the word *dragon*, recognize *dragon* as a word, put the two parts back together, and recognize the whole of the word *dragonfly*. Again, this assumes that *dragonfly* is a word in their oral vocabulary.

Here, we consider using structural analysis to decode compound words, suffixed words, prefixed words, and words with both prefixes and suffixes. Work with structural analysis is best begun after students have mastered the basic consonant letter-sound correspondences. So within the early, intermediate, and advanced levels discussed relative to phonics, structural analysis fits into the intermediate and advanced levels.

More specifically, work with compound words and a few suffixes is appropriate for the intermediate level. Instruction in prefixes and the remaining suffixes is appropriate for the advanced level. An advantage of structural analysis is that it can also give students clues as to word meanings in addition to pronunciations. Therefore, we continue our discussion of prefixes and suffixes in Chapter 6, which deals with teaching word meanings. We open the discussion in this chapter by illustrating the use of word structure as a clue to word pronunciation. Defining a few terms will facilitate the discussion.

Roots are units of meaning that can stand alone and cannot be broken down without changing or losing their meaning. For example, the word *want* is a root, while the word *wanted* is a root plus a suffix. Although English employs both English roots and roots from other languages (see Durkin 1981, 1993), in this book we deal only with English roots. There are tens of thousands of English roots. Some roots likely to be familiar to primary grade students are *school, read, with, home, mother, father, table, answer,* and *winter.*

Prefixes are units of one or more letters that are placed before a root to form a word with a meaning different from that of the root. Prefixes cannot stand by themselves as words; they must be attached to roots. The three most frequently occurring prefixes are *un-* as in *unbelievable, re-* as in *reread,* and *in-* as in *independent.*

Suffixes are units of one or more letters that are placed after a root to form a word with a different meaning or a different grammatical function. Like prefixes, suffixes cannot occur by themselves; they must be attached to roots. There are two types of suffixes: inflectional and derivational. *Inflectional suffixes,* also known simply as word endings, include *-s, -ed, -ing,* and *-er,* as in *talks, talked, talking,* and *talker.* Inflectional suffixes, which will be addressed in this chapter, do not influence the meaning of a word. They merely change a word so that it fits the structure of a sentence. *Derivational suffixes*—such elements as *-ful, -hood,* and *-less*—change the meaning of a root word. These are discussed in Chapter 6.

Compound words are words composed of two or more roots. The roots that go together to make up compound words can, of course, occur by themselves. Some common compound words are *applesauce, afternoon,* and *backyard.*

Like phonics instruction, attention to word structure should take place in meaningful literacy contexts such as with the material students are reading, students' writing, and classroom notes and labels. Because we have already discussed such contexts at length, we will not review them here. Instead, we will focus on the information about various structural components of words that can be conveyed to students within any of these contexts.

STRATEGIES APPROPRIATE FOR THE INTERMEDIATE LEVEL

Working with Inflectional Suffixes: -s, -ed, -ing, -ly, and -er

Thomas White and his colleagues (1989) have compiled a very useful list of the 20 most frequently occurring English suffixes. Here, we deal with the five most frequent suffixes—*-s* or *-es, -ed, -ing, -ly,* and *-er.* These five suffixes—all of which are inflections—appear in over 1,500 words and are the ones students need to learn first, since they are most likely to appear in the texts students read.

To work effectively with inflectional suffixes, students need to know three things:

- Suffixes are word parts that are added to the end of root words.

- Identifying suffixes and mentally setting them aside while looking at the rest of the word can sometimes help us recognize the root word.

- Most of the time, adding a suffix changes the meaning of the word only slightly.

The information is phrased as it might be presented to students. It should be noted that some students will be receptive to the use of the term *suffixes,* while others will benefit from a simpler phrase such as *word endings.*

We recommend beginning instruction in inflectional suffixes by giving students the basic information on suffixes we just listed. After that, put some suffixed words from the students' reading material on the board. These should be words that show no spelling change when the suffixes are removed. Ask a student to identify the suffix in the first word by underlining it. Then, have the volunteer write the suffix next to the suffixed word. After that, ask the student to remove the suffix and write the root word by itself. Finally, have students pronounce the suffixed word. Continue with this procedure for all of the words on the board.

Step 1: coward<u>ly</u>

Step 2: cowardly   ly

Step 3: coward

Step 4: cowardly

After using this procedure a few times with words that require no spelling changes, students need to be made aware that adding suffixes sometimes results in spelling changes. This information is important because the purpose of recognizing and removing suffixes is to find the familiar root word. In order to find the root word, students will need some information on spelling changes. Here are the most useful guidelines for spelling changes. Because these guidelines are fairly complex, they are best presented one at a time in separate lessons.

- Sometimes you need to subtract one of a doubled consonant after you remove a suffix in order to get the correct spelling of a root word (e.g., *bobbing* becomes *bob*).

- Sometimes you need to change an *i* to a *y* after removing a suffix (e.g., *happily* becomes *happy*).

- Sometimes you need to add an *e* after you remove a suffix (e.g., *hoped* becomes *hope*).

Once students have learned these guidelines for spelling changes, they can follow the four steps listed above to work with words that undergo spelling changes when suffixes are added.

A special case arises with students who do not use certain word endings in their speech. It is not uncommon for students who speak a nonstandard dialect of English or who speak English as a second language to omit certain endings when they speak. A student might read, *She jump up and down* for *She jumped up and down,* for example. What is important is that the student sees the *-ed* ending and realizes that it denotes action that took place in the past. Whether the student pronounces the *-ed* is not important to his or her comprehension, and we recommend that you do not attempt to change students' normal speech as a part of reading instruction.

STRATEGIES APPROPRIATE FOR THE ADVANCED LEVEL

Working with Compound Words

Assuming that you have read a book like *The Snowy Day* by Ezra Jack Keats to your class, you might use it to introduce compound words. After reading the book for enjoyment, reread it calling attention to the compound words, such as *snowsuit, snowball,* and *snowman,* that appear in the book. Tell students that these are compound words—words made up of two other words put together. You might then rewrite the two roots that make up each compound word so there is a space between the roots and explain again why these are compound words. To close this introductory session, write the full words and draw students' attention to the meaning of each word, explaining that many times the meanings of the individual words that make up the compound word provide a hint about the meaning of the compound word.

On another occasion, you might carry the instruction further by adding other compound words from the story, such as *everything, outside, something,* and *another.* You might then ask individual students to come up to the board and rewrite each of the compound words leaving a space between the two roots. Finally, put a small set of words on the board that include both compound words and root words from the story and ask students to identify those that are compound words and those that are not. The lesson can be concluded by reminding students when and why they should look for compound words and by rereading the entire story.

Working with Prefixed Words

Teaching the analysis of prefixed words should follow sometime after the teaching of suffixed words. Exactly when you decide to teach students about prefixes will depend on your students' needs and abilities and the material they are reading.

As they did with suffixes, White and his colleagues (1989) have compiled a list of the 20 most frequent English prefixes. We have included this list in Chapter 6 where we consider prefix meanings. Here, it is sufficient to deal with only the most common prefixes—*un-, re-,* and *in-.*

Tell students that there are several prefixes that are worth learning and put the three most frequent prefixes on the board—*un-, re-,* and *in-.* Next, write two or three prefixed words on the board—words such as *unkind, refill,* and *inhuman.* Then, tell students that they are prefixed words, rewrite the prefix and the root that compose each derived word so that there is some space between them, and explain that it is easier to recognize the root now that the prefix is removed. Finally, taking each word in turn, pronounce the prefix, pronounce the root, and pronounce the prefix and the root together, saying something at the end like, "Oh, of course, the word is *unkind.* I know that word; I just didn't recognize it when the prefix and the root were right together."

Following that demonstration, write another set of three or four prefixed words on the board—words such as *unhappy, return,* and *nonsense*—and tell students that they are prefixed words. Next, ask individual students to come up to the board and rewrite each of the words leaving a space between the prefix and the root and then reading the whole of the word aloud. Finally, you might put a small set of words on the board that included both prefixed words and root words and ask students to identify those that were prefixed words and those that were not.

Before ending this lesson, give students one warning. Tell them that some words that look like prefixed words are not prefixed words at all and that, if they remove what looks like a prefix and cannot identify the root, they will just need to try some other method of identifying the word. After explaining this, show a few examples of such words on the board, words such as *invent* and *remain.* Before ending the lesson, remind students when and why they would use structural analysis, and encourage them to consider the possibility that an unknown word they come across is a prefixed word and see if they can break it into its prefix and its root.

After this brief formal instruction on decoding prefixed words, future work with decoding prefixed words should consist of the same sorts of brief activities recommended for suffixed words, that is, occasional reminders to consider the possibility that an unknown word has a prefix and that stripping the word of that prefix may reveal a known root. Later in the curriculum, you can include work on prefix meanings. This work, as we noted, is described in Chapter 6.

Words with Both Prefixes and Suffixes

At some point after teaching students to make use of prefixes and suffixes in words that include only one or the other of these word parts, let them know that many words have both, and give them practice in using structural analysis to analyze such words.

A PROGRESSION OF INSTRUCTION IN PHONIC AND STRUCTURAL ANALYSIS

As noted in Chapter 4, there is no sharp distinction between emergent literacy and beginning reading instruction. Similarly, there is no definite time at which formal instruction in word-recognition strategies should begin. However, by now you may be wondering when, during the early years, you should turn your attention to phonics and structural analysis.

Generally, students who will profit from word-recognition strategies instruction are those who

- Are already interested in books;

- Are aware of the functions of print and purposes for reading;

- Conceive of words as individually speakable, printable, and understandable units;

- Know that printed words consist of letters;

- Know the names of the letters;

- Possess phonemic awareness; and

- Understand school language.

For most children, this will be in the middle of the kindergarten year. However, it is not necessary for all students to possess all of these characteristics in order to profit from instruction. As mentioned in Chapter 4, the key is to help children to develop these characteristics rather than waiting until they show evidence of these characteristics before teaching them to read. As Adams (1990) has noted, formal phonics instruction "should not be an abrupt step—but a further step in a journey already well underway" (71).

Because individual students differ, the duration of instruction varies as well. Some students will profit from instruction in the middle of kindergarten and will have learned all of the important concepts by the middle of second grade. Others will continue to benefit from instruction well into the third and fourth grades. Still others will come to school with a large sight vocabulary and will read without benefit of word-recognition strategy instruction at all. Unfortunately, there will almost certainly be students who experience difficulty learning some of the concepts we've presented in this chapter. In addition to the strategies presented here, we recommend the chapters on reading instruction in *Strategies for Teaching Students with Learning and Behavior Problems* (1998) by Candace Bos and Sharon Vaughn as an instructional resource.

Figure 5–2 shows a progression of word-recognition strategy instruction. We have divided word-recognition strategy instruction into three levels. The early level represents the period of emergent literacy and the very beginnings of reading that most children display in kindergarten and first grade. The intermediate level corresponds to early fluency in reading and occurs for most children in grades one and two. Finally, the advanced level reflects the fairly fluent reading displayed by most children in second and third grade. As indicated previously, some children will continue to profit from word-recognition strategy instruction into fourth grade. Also, all children will benefit from the kind of further work in prefixes and suffixes that leads to enhanced meaning vocabularies. This usually occurs in grades three and above.

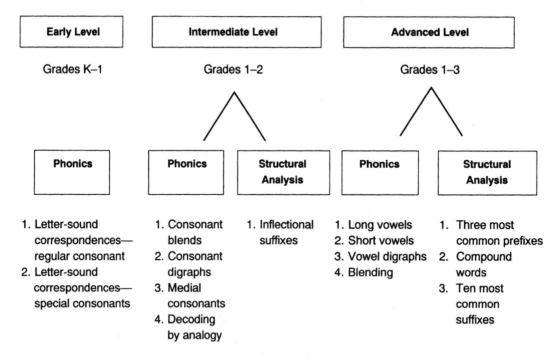

Figure 5–2.   Progression of Word-Recognition Strategy Instruction

Note that each level of development should include practice in the strategies learned at the previous level.

CONCLUDING REMARKS

Because we believe that natural student curiosity coupled with lots of supervised reading will provide opportunities to teach both phonic and structural analysis, our goal in this chapter has been to equip you with the knowledge needed to make wise decisions about when and how to teach these word-recognition strategies. In addition, we suggest the following guidelines:

• *Using word-recognition strategies, not unlike reading in general, is a problem-solving process.* It is a process of trial and error. The first guess is not necessarily correct. Therefore, the classroom must be an environment where students feel free to take risks. In addition, words used to teach strategies should be in students' oral vocabularies so that students are able to determine whether their attempts at pronunciation are accurate.

• *Generalizations about letter-sound correspondences should be thought of as just that—generalizations—and not rules.* This is because they do not work all the time, only generally. Thus, you should teach only the ones that are most often useable, tell children that they are generalizations and not rules, and provide children with alternatives when a particular strategy does not work.

- *The goal of using word-recognition strategies is to arrive at meaning.* Students should always ask themselves whether what they are reading is making sense.

- *Phonic analysis does not in and of itself yield meaning.* Instead, it may provide the information needed to pronounce a word that is in students' oral vocabularies and thus has meaning for them.

- *It is easier to think about a few large chunks of information than it is to think about many small chunks.* Therefore, for most students the larger the group of letters that children can work with, the better. The eventual goal is identification of entire words, not individual letters.

SELF-CHECK

1. What is the purpose of teaching word-recognition strategies?

2. List five types of basic letter-sound correspondences.

3. Describe one method for initially teaching letter-sound correspondences and several ways in which students can practice them.

4. Why is careful observation of students so important in phonics instruction?

5. Explain what is meant by blending and describe a procedure for teaching children how to blend.

6. What is *decoding by analogy?*

7. Discuss the general information children need about any reading strategies they will use.

8. Tell what is meant by *structural analysis* and define compound words, root words, suffixes, and prefixes.

9. Describe a general method of teaching children to decode suffixed and prefixed words.

10. List and explain the five guidelines for teaching word-recognition strategies.

11. Look through some books that you might use with first- or second-grade children, and identify two or three words they might not know. Then consider each of these words and identify and explain the word-recognition strategies that a first or second grader might use in identifying the word.

12. Suppose that you and two other classmates or colleagues were talking about beginning reading instruction. One of them argues that phonics is central to reading and that nothing else should be done until students have mastered phonics. The other argues that the purpose of reading is to construct meaning and that phonics is irrelevant and should not be dealt with at all. Compose an answer to each of them. We suggest that you actually write out your answers so that you really think them through, since these are arguments you are likely to hear with some frequency.

13. In this chapter, we have repeatedly noted that it is crucial that word-recognition strategies be taught in meaningful contexts and that whether particular contexts are meaningful depends on students' cultural and linguistic backgrounds. Thus, contexts that are meaningful to middle-class students who are native English speakers may not be meaningful to students with different backgrounds. In order to appreciate this point, describe some topics that might not be familiar to students who have lived most of their lives in (a) a small hamlet in Appalachia, (b) an inner-city on the east coast, (c) Vietnam, and (d) rural Alaska.

REFERENCES

Adams, M. (1990). Beginning to read: *Thinking and learning about print.* Cambridge, MA: MIT Press. A comprehensive report describing research in beginning reading and the implications for instruction.

Bos, C. S. and Vaughn, S. (1998). Strategies for teaching students with learning and behavior problems (4th ed.). Boston: Allyn & Bacon. Discusses approaches for teaching, across the curriculum, that are appropriate for students who experience difficulty learning.

Cunningham, P. M. (1995). *Phonics they use: Words for reading and writing* (2nd ed.). New York: HarperCollins. Presents straightforward, classroom-tested approaches to teaching about single consonants, consonant blends and digraphs, single vowels, vowel digraphs, and common spelling patterns in meaningful contexts.

Durkin, D. (1981). *Strategies for identifying words.* Boston: Allyn and Bacon. A step-by-step approach to the use of phonics and structural analysis in the identification of words.

Durkin, D. (1993). *Teaching them to read* (6th ed.). Boston: Allyn and Bacon. Chapters 8 and 9 include thorough discussions of syllabication and spelling patterns.

Fountas, I. C. and Pinnell, G. S. (1996). *Guided reading: Good first teaching for all children.* Portsmouth, NH: Heinemann. A thorough presentation of how to manage guided reading in a classroom reading program.

Holdaway, D. (1990). *Independence in reading: A handbook on individualized proce-dures.* Portsmouth, NH: Heinemann. Discusses the reading process and its re-lationship to cognitive development in children as well as various approaches to teaching reading with an emphasis on meaning. Appendices include a list of basic sight words in context and a progression of word-recognition skills.

International Reading Association. (1997). *The role of phonics in reading instruction: A position statement of the International Reading Association.* Newark, DE: In-ternational Reading Association. The official position of the International Reading Association on the role of phonics instruction in the primary grade classroom.

Routman, R. (1994). *Invitations: Changing as teachers and learners K–12* (2nd ed.). Portsmouth, NH: Heinemann. A hands-on approach to becoming a whole-language teacher by a teacher who made the transition. Includes attention to the place of phonics in a whole-language program and several valuable ap-pendices and literary resources for teachers and their students.

Trachtenburg, P. (1990). Using children's literature to enhance phonics instruction. *The Reading Teacher, 43,* 648–654. Provides a list of literature appropriate for the development of various letter-sound correspondences as well as guidelines for the use of literature in conjunction with phonics instruction.

Wharton-McDonald, R., Pressley, M., Rankin, J., Mistretta, J., Yokoi, L. and Etten-berger, S. (1997). Effective primary-grades literacy instruction = Balanced lit-eracy instruction. *Reading Teacher, 50,* 518–521. Presents the results of studies focused on instructional characteristics of teachers who successfully develop literacy competencies in their students.

White, T. G., Sowell, J. and Yanagihara, A. (1989). Teaching elementary students to use word-part clues. *Reading Teacher, 42,* 302–308. Lists the 20 most-frequent prefixes and suffixes and gives suggestions for teaching them.

BOOKS FEATURING LONG AND SHORT VOWEL SOUNDS

There are a number of books that are lively, interesting, and give children opportunities to practice with different vowel sounds. Here is a slightly modified version of Trachtenburg's (1990) list, which is presented with the permission of the International Reading Association.

Short *A*

Flack, M. (1931). *Angus the cat.* New York: Doubleday.

Griffith, H. V. (1982). *Alex the cat.* New York: Greenwillow.

Most, B. (1980). *There's an ant in Anthony.* New York: Morrow.

Nodset, J. (1963). *Who took the farmer's hat?* New York: Harper & Row.

Seuss, D. (1957). *The cat in the hat.* New York: Random House.

Long *A*

Aardema, V. (1981). *Bringing the rain to Kapiti.* New York: Dial.

Bang, M. (1987). *The paper crane.* New York: Greenwillow.

Blume, J. (1974). *The pain and the great one.* New York: Bradbury.

Henkes, K. (1987). *Sheila Rae, the brave.* New York: Greenwillow.

Hines, A. G. (1983). *Taste the raindrops.* New York: Greenwillow.

Short *A* and Long *A*

Slobodkina, E. (1940). *Caps for sale.* Redding, MA: Addison-Wesley.

Short *E*

Byars, B. (1975). *The lace snail.* New York: Viking.

Ets, M. H. (1972). *Elephant in a well.* New York: Viking.

Galdone, P. (1973). *The little red hen.* New York: Scholastic.

Ness, E. (1974). *Yeck Eck.* New York: Dutton.

Thayer, J. (1975). *The blueberry pie elf.* New York: Morrow.

Long *E*

Keller, H. (1983). *Ten sleepy sheep.* New York: Greenwillow.

Martin, B. (1992). *Brown bear, brown bear, what do you see?* Cambridge, MA: Holt.

Thomas, P. (1971). *"Stand back," said the elephant, "I'm going to sneeze!"* New York: Lothrop, Lee, & Shepard.

Short *I*

Browne, A. (1984). *Willy the wimp.* New York: Knopf.

Ets, M. H. (1963). *Gilberto and the wind.* New York: Viking.

Hutchins, P. (1971). *Titch.* New York: Macmillan.

Keats, E. J. (1964). *Whistle for Willie.* New York: Viking.

Long *I*

Berenstein, S. and Berenstein, J. (1964). *The bike lesson.* New York: Random House.

Hazen, T. S. (1979). *Tight times.* New York: Viking.

Short *O*

Benchley, N. (1966). *Oscar Otter.* New York: Harper & Row.

Emberly, B. (1967). *Drummer Hoff.* Englewood Cliffs, NJ: Prentice-Hall.

Seuss, D. (1965). *Fox in socks.* New York: Random House.

Long *O*

Shulevitz, U. (1967). *One Monday morning.* New York: Charles Scribner's Sons.

Tresselt, A. (1947). *White snow, bright snow.* New York: Lothrop, Lee & Shepard.

Short *U*

Carroll, R. (1950). *Where's the bunny?* New York: Henry Z. Walck.

Marshall, J. (1984). *The cut-ups.* New York: Viking Kestrel.

Yashima, T. (1958). *Umbrella.* New York: Viking Penguin.

Long *U*

Lobel, A. (1966). *The troll music.* New York: Harper & Row.

Segal, L. (1989). *Tell me Trudy.* New York: Farrar, Straus, & Giroux.

CHAPTER

6 Developing Vocabulary

At just about the time that you had your first birthday, you probably spoke your first word. It is likely to have consisted of a consonant sound followed by a vowel sound—something like *ma,* or perhaps a repetitive *mama.* You are likely to have followed this first utterance by learning an additional fifty or so words over the next few months. After that, your vocabulary probably grew impressively. In fact, you almost certainly entered school with an oral vocabulary of several thousand words. Then, at about the time you began school, you started acquiring a reading vocabulary, and soon both your reading vocabulary and your oral vocabulary are likely to have been growing impressively. That growth continues for most of us throughout the elementary school years—and, of course, well beyond the elementary school years. To be sure, a good deal of the growth of your vocabulary occurred outside of school and would have occurred whether or not you attended school. Nevertheless, your vocabulary would certainly not be what it is today if you had not gone to school and had teachers who both taught vocabulary and nurtured your interest in words. You have the opportunity to have a similar effect on the vocabularies of the students you teach.

LOOKING AHEAD

This chapter is divided into five parts. In the first part, we begin by considering how many words students know and how many words they learn as they progress through school. After that, we examine how well students are likely to know the words they do know, and suggest a simple metric of depth of word knowledge.

In the second part, we emphasize the importance of wide reading as a major vehicle of vocabulary growth. Wide reading is one of the key activities that allows students to acquire the vocabularies they need to interpret and appreciate what they read and to communicate effectively.

The third part of the chapter addresses the matter of teaching individual words. We first outline the various word-learning tasks students face and then discuss some ways of deciding which words to teach. Finally, as

106

the last and longest topic in this part of the chapter, we describe methods for teaching words.

The fourth part of the chapter examines ways of teaching students to learn words independently. Here, we give procedures for teaching students to use context cues, prefixes, and the dictionary to determine the meanings of unknown words. The fifth and concluding part of the chapter discusses ways to foster students' *word consciousness*, which we define as their interest in words and the pleasure they take in using them well and seeing others use them well.

KEY CONCEPTS

- The size and growth of elementary students' vocabularies
- Levels of word knowledge
- Components of a comprehensive program of vocabulary instruction
- Importance of wide reading to vocabulary growth
- Different tasks students face in learning vocabulary
- Identifying words students may not know and selecting specific words to teach
- Teaching methods for the various word-learning tasks
- Teaching students to use context cues to reveal word meanings
- Teaching students to use word parts to reveal word meanings
- Guidelines for using the dictionary effectively and efficiently
- Word consciousness

THE VOCABULARY LEARNING TASK

Most students enter school with relatively large oral vocabularies—perhaps 5,000 words—and quite small reading vocabularies—perhaps numbering only a few words. Ahead of them lies a sizable task. The materials likely to be read by third- to ninth-grade students contain well over 100,000 words (Anderson and Nagy 1992), and the average sixth-grade student has a vocabulary of something like 20,000 words that she can both read and understand (Nagy and Herman 1987). Even first-grade children are likely to have reading vocabularies ranging between 2,000 and 5,000 words, and their reading vocabularies are likely to grow by something like 3,000 to 4,000 words each year (White, Graves and Slater 1990).

Obviously, students learn many more words each year than we can teach directly. However, students do not have deep and rich meanings for many of the words they know. Instead, they often have only partial and incomplete meanings for words, meanings that are not sufficient to promote full comprehension of reading materials that contain the words.

Isabel Beck and her colleagues (1987) have distinguished three levels of word knowledge: the *unknown, acquainted,* and *established* levels. A word at the *unknown* level is, as the name indicates, unknown. The word *repel* is likely to be unknown to most fourth graders. A word at the *acquainted* level is one whose basic meaning is recognized but only with some deliberate attention. The word *resident* would probably be understood by most fifth graders but only after a moment's thought. A word at the *established* level is one whose meaning is easily, rapidly, and automatically recognized. For most second graders, the word *house* would be at an established level.

Of course, students do not need to know *all* words at the established level. They do, however, need to know the vast majority of words they encounter in their reading at the established level because, as we noted in Chapter 5, words that are not recognized automatically will thwart the process of comprehending text.

A comprehensive vocabulary program must reflect these facts about children's word knowledge and how it grows, and the one we describe here does so. The program has three major thrusts. First, it emphasizes the importance of wide reading because students learn much of their vocabulary from reading. Second, it includes instruction on individual words because such instruction can assist students in learning some words, improve comprehension of selections from which the words are taken, and show students the value you place in words. Third, it provides instruction in learning words independently because students must learn much of their vocabulary on their own.

THE IMPORTANCE OF WIDE READING

If you consider that students learn to read something like 3,000 to 4,000 words each year, it quickly becomes clear that most of the words students learn are not taught directly. With a 180-day school year, teaching 3,000 to 4,000 words would require teaching approximately 20 words each and every school day. Obviously, this does not happen. Instead, as we have already noted, students learn many words from silent reading. Thus, as Richard Anderson (1996) has convincingly shown, if you can substantially increase the amount of reading students do, you can markedly increase their vocabularies. Moreover, wide reading can foster automaticity and provide knowledge about a variety of topics and literary forms, and leave students with a habit that will make them lifelong readers. In brief, wide reading is both tremendously important and tremendously powerful for vocabulary development and for a number of other goals.

Unfortunately, many students do very little reading. For example, Linda Fielding and her colleagues (1986) found that on an average day fifth graders spent only about 10 minutes of their out of school time reading books. Clearly, children need to be encouraged to do more reading. Here we offer several suggestions.

As a starting point, we encourage you to learn about as many interesting and engaging books for your students as you possibly can. Sources such as *The Reading Teacher*'s annual Children's Choices and Teachers' Choices and compilations such as *More Kids' Favorite Books* (International Reading Association 1995) offer one way of doing this. Additionally, both *The Reading Teacher* and *Language Arts* have columns and articles on children's literature, and children's literature is an increasingly popular topic at reading and English education conferences. We also suggest having a host of books readily available in the classroom and making the classroom a place where books are regularly discussed and traded. Of course, these books should be diverse both in the cultures reflected and in their reading levels. For second-language learners and students experiencing difficulty, wide reading is especially critical for building both word knowledge and world knowledge. Thus, it is particularly important to have interesting and readable books available for these students. Once books are available, sustained silent reading—extended time periods during which students read books of their own choosing (McCracken 1971)—should be a frequent activity. Add to this effort frequently reading to students, modeling your enthusiasm for reading, and getting parents involved in securing good reading materials and in promoting reading at home.

Taken together, approaches such as these and those you develop out of your classroom experience will indeed promote wide reading.

TEACHING INDIVIDUAL WORDS

Here, we first discuss the various word-learning tasks students face and ways of identifying words to teach. Then, we discuss teaching procedures for each of these word-learning tasks.

The Word-Learning Tasks Students Face

As we noted in the introduction, all word-learning tasks are not the same. Word-learning tasks differ depending on such matters as how much students already know about the words to be taught, how well you want them to learn the words, and what you want them to be able to do with the words afterwards. Here we consider six tasks students face in learning words.

Learning to Read Known Words
Learning to read known words, words that are already in their oral vocabularies, is the major vocabulary learning task of beginning readers. Such

words as *surprise, stretch,* and *amaze* are ones that students might be taught to read during their first three years of school. By third or fourth grade, good readers will have learned to read virtually all the words in their oral vocabularies. However, the task of learning to read all of the words in their oral vocabularies remains for many less-able readers and for some second-language learners.

Learning New Words Representing Known Concepts

A second word-learning task students face is learning to read words that are in neither their oral nor their reading vocabularies but for which they have an available concept. For example, the word *pant* would be unknown to a number of third graders, but almost all students have seen dogs panting and know what it is like to be out of breath. All students continue to learn words of this sort throughout their years in school, and this is one of the major word-learning tasks for intermediate-grade students. It is also a major learning task for second-language learners, who, of course, have a number of concepts for which they do not have English words.

Learning New Words Representing New Concepts

Another word-learning task students face, and a very demanding one, is learning to read words that are in neither their oral nor their reading vocabularies and for which they do not have an available concept. Learning the full meanings of such words as *equation, impeach,* and *mammal* is likely to require most elementary students to develop new concepts. All students continue to learn words of this sort throughout their years in school and beyond. Once again, learning new concepts will be particularly important for second-language learners. Also, students whose backgrounds differ from that of the majority culture will have internalized a set of concepts that is at least somewhat different than the set internalized by students in the majority culture. Thus, words that represent known concepts for some groups of students will represent unknown concepts for other groups.

Learning New Meanings for Known Words

Still another word-learning task is learning new meanings for words that students already know with one meaning. Many words have multiple meanings, and thus students frequently encounter words that look familiar but are used with a meaning different from the one they know. Students will encounter such words throughout the elementary grades and beyond. Teaching these words occupies a special place in content areas such as science and social studies because words often have different and important meanings that are critical to comprehension in particular content areas. The meaning of *product* in mathematics and that of *legend* in geography or history are just two examples of such words.

Clarifying and Enriching the Meanings of Known Words

The next word-learning task we consider is that of clarifying and enriching the meanings of already known words. The meanings students originally attach to words are often imprecise and only become fully specified over time. For example, students initially might not recognize any difference between *brief* and *concise*, not know what distinguishes a *cabin* from a *shed*, or not realize that the term *virtuoso* is usually applied to those who play musical instruments. Although students will expand and enrich the meanings of the words they know as they repeatedly meet them in new and slightly different contexts, some more direct approaches to the matter are warranted.

Moving Words into Students' Expressive Vocabularies

The last word-learning task we describe is that of moving words from students' receptive vocabularies to their productive vocabularies, that is, moving words from students' listening and reading vocabularies to their speaking and writing vocabularies. Sixth graders, for example, might know the meaning of the word *ignite* when they hear it or read it, yet never use the word themselves. Most people actively use only a small percentage of the words they know. Direct methods of getting students to use the words they do know are called for. This is particularly true of second-language students, who are likely to have small expressive vocabularies as they begin learning English and who need a lot of practice and encouragement to use the words they know.

Identifying and Selecting Vocabulary to Teach

Once you have considered the levels of word knowledge that you want your students to achieve and the word-learning tasks students face, you still have the task of selecting specific words to teach. We recommend a two-step process in which you first get some idea of which words are likely to be unknown to your students and then follow several criteria for selecting the words.

Identifying Unknown Words

The most useful source of information about what words students know is the students themselves. One easy way to find out which words students know is to simply list words on the board and have students raise their hands if they do not know a word. This approach is quick, easy, and risk free for students; and it gives students some responsibility for their word learning. Moreover, research (White, Slater and Graves 1989) indicates that students can be quite accurate in identifying words that they do and do not know.

Selecting Words to Teach

Once potentially difficult vocabulary is identified, criteria for identifying the most important words to teach need to be established. The answers to four questions should be helpful.

- "Is understanding the word important to understanding the selection in which it appears?" If the answer is, "No," then other words are probably more important to teach.

- "Are students able to use context or structural-analysis skills to discover the word's meaning?" If they can use these skills, then they should be allowed to practice them. Doing so will both help them consolidate these skills and reduce the number of words you need to teach.

- "Can working with this word be useful in furthering students' context, structural analysis, or dictionary skills?" If the answer here is, "Yes," then your working with the word can serve two purposes: It can aid students in learning the word and it can help them acquire a strategy they can use in learning other words. You might, for example, decide to teach the word *regenerate* because students need to master the prefix *re-*.

- "How useful is this word outside of the reading selection currently being taught?" The more frequently a word appears in material students read, the more important it is for them to know the word. Additionally, the more frequent a word is, the greater the chances that students will retain the word once you teach it.

As a final comment on these four questions, we need to add that they are not independent. In fact, the answer to one question may suggest that a word should be taught, while the answer to another suggests that it should not. In such cases, you will need to use your best judgment about which words to teach.

Methods of Teaching Individual Words

How might you go about teaching words representing each of the six word-learning tasks described? As you will see, the instruction needed for some word-learning tasks is much more complex than that for others. Note, too, that instruction appropriate for some of these tasks will promote deeper levels of word knowledge than others.

Learning to Read Known Words

In learning to read known words, the basic task for the student is to associate what is unknown, the written word, with what is already known, the spoken word. The most appropriate method for teaching these words is the sight-word method described in Chapter 4. To establish the association between the written and spoken forms of a word, the student needs to see the word at the same time that it is pronounced, and once the association is established, it needs to be rehearsed and strengthened so that the relationship becomes automatic. We have listed these steps below to emphasize just how straightforward the process is.

1. See the word.

2. Hear the word as it is seen.

3. Rehearse that association a myriad of times.

Technology

Of course, there are a number of ways in which each of these steps can be accomplished. Students can see the word on the board, on a computer screen, or in a book that they are reading or you are reading to them. They can hear the word when you say it, when another student says it, or when a voice simulator on a computer says it. They can rehearse the association by seeing the word and pronouncing it a number of times, writing it, and playing games that require them to recognize printed versions of it. However, wide reading in materials that contain many repetitions of the words and that are enjoyable and easily read by students is by far the best form of rehearsal for these words and an essential part of students' mastering them.

Finally, one very important point to remember when teaching these words is that there is no need to teach their meanings. By definition, these are words students already know and understand when they hear them; they simply cannot read them. Time spent "teaching" students the meaning of words they already know is time wasted.

Learning New Words Representing Known Concepts

Here we present three approaches to teaching new words representing known concepts. These require differing amounts of teacher time, differing amounts of class time, and differing amounts of students' time and effort; and they are likely to yield different results.

The first method, Context Plus Use of the Dictionary, takes the least amount of preparation on your part while taking a fair amount of students' time. It will provide students with a basic understanding of a word's meaning and give them practice in using the dictionary. This method consists of giving students a word in context and then asking them to look up the word in a dictionary. For example,

> *excel* (ic SEL)
>
> To get into the Olympics, a person must really *excel* at some Olympic sport.

The second method, Definition Plus Rich Context, takes a fair amount of preparation time on your part, but it takes very little class time. It, too, will provide students with a basic understanding of a word's meaning. This method consists of giving students both a definition of a word and a rich context. For example,

> *vital* (VI tle)—extremely important, perhaps even necessary
>
> In areas in which water is very scarce, it is *vital* that everyone takes extra care to ensure that no water is wasted.

The third method, the Context-Relationship Procedure (Graves & Slater, 1996), takes quite a bit of preparation time on your part. However, presenting words in this way takes only about a minute per word, and we have repeatedly found that students remember quite rich meanings for words taught in this fashion. To use this procedure, you create a brief paragraph that uses the target word three or four times. Then, follow the paragraph with a multiple-choice item that checks students' understanding of the word. A sample paragraph and multiple-choice item and the steps for presenting each word are shown below.

Conveying
The luncheon speaker was successful in *conveying* his main ideas to the audience. They all understood what he said, and most agreed with him. *Conveying* has a more specific meaning than *talking*. *Conveying* indicates that a person is getting his or her ideas across accurately.

Conveying means

_____ A. putting parts together.

_____ B. communicating a message.

_____ C. hiding important information.

1. Explain the purpose of the procedure.

2. Pronounce the word to be taught.

3. Read the paragraph in which the word appears.

4. Read the possible definitions and ask students to choose the best one.

5. Pause to give students time to check a definition, give them the correct answer, and answer any questions students have.

6. Read the word and its definition a final time.

Learning New Words Representing New Concepts
Because the two methods we describe in the next section can also be used to teach new concepts, here we consider only one method. It was developed by Dorothy Frayer and her colleagues (1969). The major steps of our version of the method and examples with the word *globe* are shown below.

1. Define the new concept, giving its necessary attributes. When feasible, it is also helpful to show a picture illustrating the concept.

   A *globe* is a spherical (ball-like) representation of a planet.

2. Distinguish between the new concept and similar but different concepts with which it might be mistaken. In doing so it may be appropriate to identify some accidental attributes that might falsely be considered to be necessary attributes of the new concept.

   A *globe* is different from a *map* because a map is flat. A *globe* is different from a *contour map,* a map in which mountains and other high points are raised above the general level of the map, because a contour map is not spherical.

3. Give examples of the concept and explain why they are examples.

   The most common *globe* is a globe of the earth. Globes of the earth are spherical and come in various sizes and colors.

   A much less common *globe* is a globe of another planet. A museum might have a spherical representation of Saturn.

4. Give nonexamples of the concept and explain why they are nonexamples.

   A map of California

   A map of how to get to a friend's house

5. Present students with examples and nonexamples and ask them to distinguish between the two.

   An aerial photograph of New York (nonexample)

   A red sphere representing Mars (example)

   A walking map of St. Louis (nonexample)

   A ball-shaped model of the moon (example)

6. Have students present examples and nonexamples of the concept, have them explain why they are examples or nonexamples, and give them feedback on their examples and explanations.

   Teaching concepts in this way takes a good deal of your time and a good deal of students' time. The method also requires a good deal of thought on the part of both you and your students. However, the fruits of the labor are well worth the effort, for with this method students can gain a new idea, another lens through which they can interpret the world.

Learning New Meanings for Known Words

New meanings for known words may or may not represent new concepts for students. If the new meanings do not represent new and difficult concepts, the procedure for teaching new meanings for known words is fairly simple and straightforward. The approach shown below is one appropriate method.

1. Acknowledge the known meaning.

2. Give the new meaning.

3. Note the similarities between the meanings (if any).

   Product
   something made by a company
   the number made by multiplying other numbers
   The similarity is that in both instances something is produced or made by some process.

If the new meanings to be learned represent new and difficult concepts, then Frayer's approach to teaching concepts or the methods described in the next section are more appropriate.

Clarifying and Enriching the Meanings of Known Words

Here, we present two methods of clarifying and enriching the meanings of known words. These methods are also useful in preteaching unknown words to improve comprehension of a selection. And they can be used to teach new concepts, if the concepts are not too difficult and students have at least some information related to them.

The first method discussed, termed *possible sentences,* is one Steven Stahl and Barbara Kapinus (1991) have shown to be very useful for teaching words from informational texts. With this procedure, the teacher begins by choosing six to eight words that might cause difficulty for students from an upcoming selection. These should represent key concepts and related words. Next, the teacher selects an additional four to six words that are likely to be familiar to students. These familiar words are used to help students generate sentences.

Once the 10 to 12 words are selected, they are put on the board. If some students in the class know the definitions, they can define them. If not, you should provide short definitions. Following this, students are told to create sentences that use at least two of the words and that are *possible sentences* in the selection they are about to read. The sentences students created are then put on the board and students are instructed to read the selection.

Following the reading of the selection, you return to the sentences on the board and the class discusses whether each of them could or could not be true given the content of the reading selection. Sentences that could be true are left as they are. Sentences that could not be true are discussed by the class and modified so that they could be true.

Shown below are some of the words Stahl and Kapinus selected from some science texts they worked with and a few of the possible sentences students might generate with the words.

Potentially difficult words: *front, barometer, humidity, air mass, air pressure,* and *meteorology*

Familiar words: *clouds, rain,* and *predict*

When a *front* approaches it is quite likely to *rain.* (could be true)

Most people don't like days with a lot of *humidity* or with a lot of *clouds.* (could be true)

When a *front* approaches, it is very unlikely to *rain.* (could not be true)

The second method of clarifying and extending the meanings of known words, and of introducing vocabulary in a way that is likely to improve comprehension of a selection, is called *semantic mapping* (Heimlich and Pittleman 1986). With this method, the teacher puts a word representing a central concept on the chalkboard; asks students to work in groups listing as many words related to the central concept as they can; writes students' words on the chalkboard grouped in broad categories; has students name the categories and perhaps suggest additional ones; and discusses with students the central concept, the other words, the categories, and their interrelationships. Shown below is a semantic map of the word *tenement* that students might create before or after reading a social studies chapter on urban housing.

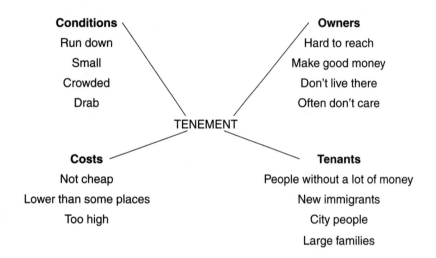

Moving Words into Students' Expressive Vocabularies

Students can be encouraged to move words into their expressive vocabularies by your providing a model of precise word use, your encouraging students to employ precise and mature words in their speech and writing and recognizing appropriate diction when they display it, and your providing time and encouragement for various sorts of word play that prompt students to work with words they might otherwise not speak or write.

A more direct approach to fostering expressive vocabulary has been developed by Ann Duin (Duin and Graves 1988). The major features of the instruction are shown below.

- Words are taught in groups of 10 to 15 related words presented over a three- to six-day period. The words are not necessarily semantically related, but they do lend themselves to writing on a particular topic. A set of words Duin has used with an essay about *space* includes *feasible, accommodate, tether, criteria, module, retrieve, configuration,* and *quest.*

- Students work extensively with the words, spending about half an hour a day with the 10 to 15 words taught during the three to six days of instruction and doing 5 to 10 activities with each word.

- Instruction is deliberately varied in order to accomplish various purposes. Students define words, use them in sentences, do speeded trials with them, make affective responses to them, compare them to each other and to other concepts, keep a written record of their work with them, are encouraged to use them outside of class, and do several short writing assignments with them.

Examples of the tasks Duin has used include the following: Students discussed how *feasible* space travel might soon be for each of them. They were asked if they thought their school could find a way to better *accommodate* handicapped students. They distinguished between new words, such as *retrieve,* and related words, such as *return,* by filling in sentence frames with the more appropriate of the two words. They wrote brief essays called "Space Shorts" employing the words in dealing with such topics as the foods that would be available in space and judged each others' use of the words.

Duin's work has indicated that students working with this sort of instruction use a substantial proportion of the taught words in essays targeted to using the words and that the essays of students who have received the instruction are judged markedly superior to those of students who have not received it. Equally important, her work has shown that students thoroughly enjoy learning and using words in this way. These findings can be taken as a recommendation for helping and encouraging students to experiment with new, precise, and vivid vocabulary in their writing.

TEACHING STUDENTS TO LEARN WORDS INDEPENDENTLY

As we noted at the beginning of the chapter, students learn something like 3,000 to 4,000 words each year, many more words than could be directly taught. Thus, even when instruction in individual words is as frequent and rich as one could possibly make it, students need to learn much of their vocabulary independently. In this section, we consider three strategies that students need to become independent word learners: using context, using prefixes, and using the dictionary.

Using Context Cues to Unlock the Meanings of Unknown Words

It is almost certainly the case that most words are learned from context. No other explanation seems capable of accounting for students' learning 3,000 to 4,000 words each year (Anderson and Nagy 1992). At the same time, it is important to realize that gleaning a word's meaning from most contexts is not an easy task. However, wide reading exposes students to a huge number of unknown words, many of which will occur more than once; and, given a typical amount of reading over a year's time, average students might acquire over 1,000 words from meeting them in the context of their reading. Additionally, students learn a large number of words from oral contexts— conversations, lectures, films, and even television. Of course, students who have better than average skills in learning words from context will acquire more words from context than will students with only average skills.

In this section, we discuss teaching students to use context cues—words, phrases, and sentences that surround an unknown word and provide clues to its meaning—to learn word meanings. The instruction we suggest includes two steps: First, we present a carefully constructed unit on using context. Then, we provide students with ongoing reminders of the value of using context to learn word meanings, encouragement to use context, and opportunities to get feedback on their efforts.

Step One: An Introductory Unit on Using Context
We would begin our work on context with a three- to four-day unit. This concentrated effort seems necessary to get students off to a solid start. Begin the instruction by telling students what you are going to be working on, why the strategy is important, and when and where they should use it. Also, if students are likely to have had previous experience working with context, acknowledge that. Your introduction might look something like this, although you would modify what you say to fit your class and your style of talking with children.

> "Today, we're going to begin working with using context cues to figure out the meanings of words we don't know or aren't sure of. Context cues are cues and hints that the words and sentences surrounding an unknown word give us about the meaning of the unknown word.
>
> "Learning to use context cues is important because much of the time when we read we will come upon at least some words we don't know. And learning words we don't know is important because knowing the words in something we're reading helps us understand it. Also, learning more words and using them helps us speak and write clearly."

At this time, put several sentences containing unknown words or nonsense words and some fairly rich context on the board or overhead and talk through the cues that context provides to the words' meanings. It is important to include some nonsense words so you can be certain students deal with at least some unfamiliar words.

> <u>The buttery and salty odor of the *zeemee* filled the theater lobby, and Sara's mouth began to water.</u>
>
> "Let's see. *Zeemee* has an odor, it smells buttery and salty, you get it in a theater, and smelling it makes Sara's mouth water. That's easy. It's popcorn."
>
> <u>Rusty *scowled* angrily at Mary and then stamped out of the room. "I'm never coming back! " he shouted as he left.</u>
>
> "Hum. *Scowled* is something Rusty did at Mary. He was angry, and he did this *scowling* just before he stamped out of the room,

and then he shouted at Mary. I'm not sure what *scowled* means, but it must have something to do with expressing anger. Maybe it means the same thing as *shouted,* or maybe it means *sticking out your tongue,* or maybe it means *giving a mean look.* I'm still not sure what *scowled* means, but I think it's related to anger, that it's a way of showing anger."

After discussing several examples, continue your introductory remarks.

"Using context cues to figure out the meanings of unknown words is something you'll do often. In fact, if you're reading along and come across an unknown word, and if that word seems important to understanding what you're reading, checking the context to see if it will give you a clue to the word's meaning is usually the first thing to do.

"Now I know that some of you have worked with context cues before, and that's good. Why don't you tell me some of the things you've learned about context cues, and then we'll go on to see if there isn't more to know that would be useful in figuring out unknown words."

At this point, let students volunteer what they know about context cues, being as accepting as you can with their answers but at the same time clearing up misconceptions. The most likely misconceptions are that context always yields a word's meaning, that it yields exact meanings, and that the important thing to know about context cues is the names of the various cues.

Following this discussion, say something positive about students' existing knowledge of context cues, but then say that there is more to be learned, that you are going to be taking a little different approach with context cues, and that learning to use context cues, like learning to play a musical instrument, requires repeated practice.

Next, introduce the basic facts students need to know about context cues. These could be initially presented on an overhead or the board, but they should also be put on a chart that could be left up and referred to occasionally over a period of a few weeks or so.

- Most words are learned from context. Therefore, it is really important to learn to use context well.

- Sometimes, context clearly tells us a word's meaning. More often, however, it only hints at a word's meaning.

- Context cues include words, phrases, and sentences that tell us something about the unknown word.

- Cues can occur both before the unknown word and after it, and often there is more than one cue to a particular unknown word.

- The most useful cues are usually close to the unknown word, generally in the same sentence. However, we sometimes get cues in other sentences and even other paragraphs.

Don't have students memorize these points, but do discuss them, clear up any confusion there seems to be, and give examples where appropriate. Also, tell students that eventually you do want them to learn these facts about context, and that you will bring them up from time to time in discussions about how context provides cues to unknown words they come across.

This would conclude the first day of the context unit. On the following day, present students with the procedure for using context shown below. As is the case with the major points about context, present the procedure on an overhead or the board and also put the steps on a chart so that they can be left up and referred to occasionally. As was not the case with the major points, ask students to learn the steps of the procedure at this time, and call on several students to state the steps before going on with the lesson.

- Identify the unknown word.

- List the words or phrases which tell us something about its meaning.

- Start at the beginning of the sentence containing the unknown word and list all the cues in that sentence. Then, if you think you need more cues, look at other sentences before and after the one containing the word.

- Guess the unknown word's meaning based on what you have found in the context.

Now comes a crucial part of the instruction. It consists of your modeling the procedure and then gradually transferring the task of using the procedure to students so that in time they can use the procedure independently. What you are attempting to do in modeling the procedure is to reveal to students the mental processes that you employ when using context to figure out word meanings. Prompted by your modeling, students will begin to use similar processing.

Your first attempt at modeling would be very similar to what you did with the examples used in introducing the concept of context cues. However, slow down a bit here, emphasizing the steps you are going through. Begin by putting a sentence containing an unknown word and some rich context on the board. Then, model the procedure, asking students to follow along and record the cues on paper as you put them on the board.

> As Byron stood in the valley, the snow began falling thickly, quickly covering the ground and *obliterating* the view of the mountain that he had seen clearly only moments before.

> "First, I find the word I don't know. It's *obliterating*. . . .

> Second, I look for cues to its meaning in the sentence.

> It's snow that does the *obliterating*. . . . And it's thickly falling snow. . . . And it's the view of the mountains that got *obliterated*. . . . And I know that Byron could see the mountain clearly before the snow began."

Once the cues have been listed, synthesize them to get the unknown word's meaning.

> "Third, I try to add it all up and get a meaning for *obliterating*.
>
> "Let's see. Thickly falling snow *obliterates* the view that Byron could see before. *Obliterating* must mean something like *covering up*.
>
> "And, fourth, I'll try my meaning in the sentence to see how it works. 'As Byron stood in the valley, the snow began falling thickly, quickly covering the ground and *covering up* the view of the mountain that he had seen clearly only moments before.' That makes sense, so for now at least I'll assume that *obliterating* means 'covering up.'"

In order to transfer responsibility for this task to students so that they internalize the procedure and use it independently, use it with additional sentences, gradually letting students do more and more of the task. With the next sentence, for example, volunteer some cues and let students volunteer others. Then, let students volunteer some of the cues and have them try to put the cues together to get a meaning for the unknown word. Next, still working from the board, have students volunteer all of the cues and attempt to add them up to get a meaning.

Finally, give students some sentences as seatwork or homework. At first, have students work on these in pairs; later, they can work on them independently. In both cases, review the work as a group activity, praising students when they are correct, trying to figure out what went wrong and how it could be avoided in the future when they are incorrect, and reteaching as necessary.

The process of your modeling, getting responses from student volunteers as you work at the board, having students practice using context in pairs and independently, and discussing their work and reteaching as necessary should continue over several days. Conclude this concentrated instruction once you think students have internalized the basic procedure, typically in three or four days.

Step Two: Further Work with Context

After this introductory unit on teaching context, most work with context should take place when students need to figure out unknown words in their reading. Of course, you might at some later point teach another unit on context, either as a review or as an extension activity working with longer and more difficult contexts. Through periodic incidental instruction in context and some additional short instructional units, you can maintain and extend students' ability to use context.

Using Prefixes to Unlock the Meanings of Unknown Words

As Jeremy Anglin (1993) and William Nagy and his colleagues (1994) point out, about half of the "new" words that students meet in their reading are related to familiar words and can be understood if students see these relationships. In Chapter 5, we took up the matter of using structural analysis to decode words, and there we defined the three sorts of word parts—suffixes, prefixes, and roots—and discussed teaching students to use suffixes and prefixes in decoding words that are in their oral vocabularies. Here, we discuss students using prefixes as part of learning the meanings of words that are not in their oral vocabularies. We do not advocate attempting to teach students to use suffixes to uncover word meanings because most suffixes have grammatical meanings that are tacitly understood by students or abstract meanings that are very difficult to teach. We do not advocate systematically teaching non-English roots to elementary students because non-English roots are relatively rare in elementary reading materials. However, you might occasionally introduce students to particular roots that occur frequently in selections they are reading. The Greek root *tele*, for example, might appear frequently in a chapter on communication.

English contains a substantial number of prefixes. Fortunately, a small number of them are extremely frequent and thus particularly worth teaching. Table 6–1, based on the work of Thomas White and his colleagues (1989), shows the 20 most frequently occurring prefixes and the number of prefixed words in written school English. As can be seen, the material read by school-age children contains about 3,000 prefixed words; the four most frequent prefixes account for about 60 percent of these words; and the 16 most frequent prefixes account for about 90 percent of them. The most frequent prefixes are, of course, the ones students should learn first.

Most prefixes have a clear meaning, which is attached to the base in a fairly straightforward way. Thus, students can use their knowledge of prefixes not only to decode words but also to unlock the meaning of unknown words. Also, prefixes tend to be consistently spelled, and they occur at the beginning of words. Thus, they are relatively easy for students to recognize. For both of these reasons, knowing and being able to use a relatively small number of prefixes can be a powerful aid in learning vocabulary.

As is the case with learning to use context, learning to use prefixes requires some basic knowledge. This is shown below.

- Prefixes are meaning-bearing units that are attached to the beginnings of words to change their meaning.

- Knowing the meanings of prefixes and how to use that knowledge in unlocking the meanings of new words is a powerful way of increasing our vocabularies.

- Although prefixes are very useful, they can present some problems: Some prefixes have more than one meaning. Also, some letter sequences that look like prefixes are not.

Perhaps the most important point to keep in mind when teaching prefixes is that you are not just teaching prefixes, you are teaching students to

Table 6–1.   Most Frequently Occurring Prefixes

PREFIX	WORDS WITH THE PREFIX
un-	782
re-	401
in-, im-, ir-, il- ("not")	313
dis-	216
en-, em-	132
non-	126
in-, im- ("in" or "into")	105
over- ("too much")	98
mis-	83
sub-	80
pre-	79
inter-	77
fore-	76
de-	71
trans-	47
super-	43
semi-	39
anti-	33
mid-	33
under- ("too little")	25
All others	100 (estimated)
TOTAL	2,959

use their knowledge of the prefixes to unlock the meanings of unknown words. That is, you are teaching strategies. As with all strategies, we suggest that as part of your instruction you explain to students what the strategy is, why they should learn it, how to use it, when and where to use it, and how to evaluate its success.

As part of instruction on prefixes, include the basic knowledge about prefixes listed above. We recommend putting this information on an overhead or the board and discussing it with students before teaching specific prefixes. For teaching prefixes themselves, we have found the following simple and straightforward procedure based on one recommended by Judith Irvin (1998) to be very effective.

1. Write two familiar words containing the prefix on the board or overhead, and have students define them.

   Suppose you wanted to teach the prefix *dis-*, meaning "not," to a group of fourth graders. Virtually all students know the words *disobey* and *disbelieve*, so these are appropriate words to use here.

2. Underline the prefix and note its spelling. Then, point out its meaning, or have students give its meaning.

   Dis-, of course, means "not."

3. Write a novel word that contains the prefix in a sentence on the board or overhead.

   You might write the word *disapprove* in a sentence such as "Certainly, most people *disapprove* of cooking too much food and then throwing it away." Ask students to use their knowledge of *dis-*, the element that remains when the prefix is removed (*approve*), and the context of the sentence to arrive at a meaning of the word. *Disapprove* means to not approve.

4. Give an example of a word students know in which the letter group just taught does not represent the meaning taught, and caution them that letter groups that look like prefixes are sometimes just groups of letters. Also point out that if an element is a prefix, there will be a recognizable word left when the prefix is removed and that the combination of a prefix and the rest of the word must make sense.

   The letter group *dis-* does not have the meaning "not" in *distant;* the letter string *tant* is not a word, and the idea "not tant" makes no sense.

Using the Dictionary to Define Words

Recent investigations have shown that elementary students frequently have difficulty using the dictionary to define unknown words. Perhaps this should not be surprising. Students often receive instruction in alphabetizing, in using guide words, and in using pronunciation keys. However, instruction usually does not go much beyond this, and such instruction is not sufficient for teaching students to effectively work with a tool that they will use throughout their schooling and that most adults continue to use almost daily after completing school.

Two guidelines are particularly important if students are to use the dictionary effectively. First, students need to learn that many words have multiple meanings and that they cannot just take the first meaning listed and assume it will be the one they want; they need to choose meanings appropriate for the context in which they found the word. Second, students need to learn to consider the full definition given and not just a part of it.

Explaining these guidelines and giving students opportunities to practice using them is a straightforward matter. Begin by telling students that many words have multiple meanings and that they need to pick the definition most appropriate to the context in which the word is used. Then, emphasize that they need to consider the whole of each definition and not just one or two words in the definition. Next, demonstrate how you would look up the meaning of an unknown word. Think aloud, sharing your thinking with students as you come across the unknown word in a text. Show students how you look through the dictionary and find the word, find the definition that seems to fit, consider all of that definition, and then mentally check to see if the meaning you chose makes sense in the context in which the unknown word occurred.

Another important thing students need to learn about dictionaries is which dictionaries are appropriate for them. As you know, dictionaries come in a variety of levels, from primary-grade dictionaries to those suitable for middle-grade students, junior high students, and so forth. Show students several dictionaries, talk about their advantages and disadvantages, and discuss why they might want to use one or the other. Students also need to know the characteristics and features of the particular dictionary they use—what the entries for individual words contain and how they are arranged, what aids to its use the dictionary provides, and what features beyond the basic word list the dictionary includes. Much of the important information appears in the front matter of the dictionaries themselves, but students seldom read it on their own. Thus, explicit instruction in how to use specific dictionaries is usually needed.

FOSTERING WORD CONSCIOUSNESS

Thus far, we have described three approaches to vocabulary development —wide reading, teaching individual words, and teaching word-learning strategies. Here we describe a fourth approach—fostering word consciousness. Word consciousness is a disposition toward words that is both cognitive and affective (Anderson and Nagy 1992). The student who is word conscious knows a lot of words, and she knows them well. Equally importantly, she is interested in words, and she gains enjoyment and satisfaction from using them well and from seeing or hearing them used well by others. She finds words intriguing, recognizes adroit word usage when she encounters it, uses words skillfully herself, is on the look out for new and precise words, and is responsive to the nuances of word meanings. She is also well aware of the power of words and realizes that they can be used to foster clarity and understanding or to obscure and obfuscate matters.

Fostering such attitudes is something to be achieved across the elementary school years—and, of course, in the years beyond the elementary grades—and there are a myriad of ways of developing and nurturing such positive attitudes. These include modeling and encouraging adept diction, promoting word play such as the use of rhymes and puns, using word play books and playing word games, and providing intensive and expressive instruction in vocabulary. We have described these and other approaches in some detail elsewhere (Graves and Watts 1997; Watts, Graves and Harrison in press). Here, we list a few word books and word games and consider some ways of modeling and encouraging adept diction.

BOOKS ABOUT WORDS AND WORD GAMES

Authors who particularly value words have written a host of books that feature words and word play. Here, we include just a small sample. Your school and local library will have many others.

Fred Gwynne. *A little pigeon toed.* New York: Simon & Schuster, 1988. A marvelous collection of ambiguous phrases and amusing illustrations depicting the wrong interpretations of those phrases. Similar books by Fred Gwynne include *Chocolate Moose for Dinner* (Windmill Books, 1976) and *The King Who Rained* (Simon & Schuster, 1970).

Richard Lederer. *Pun and games.* Chicago: Chicago Review Press, (1996). A terrific introduction to word play—including jokes, riddles, puns, and spoonerisms—for grades 4 and up.

Peggy Parish. *Thank you, Amelia Bedelia.* New York: Harper-Collins, 1964. Amelia has a repeated problem with homophones and often confuses literal and figurative meanings. Asked to make a jelly roll, for example, she scoops a jar full of jelly onto the floor and tries to roll it around. Other books in the series include *Play Ball, Amelia Bedelia!* (Harper, 1972) and *Come Back, Amelia Bedelia.* (Harper, 1971).

Arnold Shapiro. *"What's new?" Asked the gnu.* New York: Dial, 1995. A book of colorful pop-up and rhyming couplets like "I ate a cake, said the snake" to draw younger children into the world of words.

Another excellent way to spur children's interest in words and give them a chance to engage in various manipulations with words is provided by words games. Here we list two examples.

Articulation. Word Origins, 1993. In this commercial board game, players move toward the finish line and victory by rolling the dice, drawing cards, and answering questions about slang, jargon, and word origins. One slang card, for example, asks if a *clay pigeon* is an escaped convict, a substitute teacher, or a fool. One jargon card asks if a critic who refers to a film as a *B movie* means that it is a low budget movie, a Big movie with many stars, or a movie shot in a foreign country. And one word origin card asks if the word *food, discuss,* or *money* comes from the Greek word meaning "to throw." With the cards provided, *Articulation* is most appropriate for students in grades five and above. However, with the game board and rules in hand, it is easy for students to make alternative slang, jargon, and word origin cards; and doing so is both a challenging language activity for the students creating the cards and an activity that allows you to tailor the game to the needs of the students who will be using it.

Fictionary. (Also sold commercially as Balderdash, Gameworks Creations, 1984). Playing *Fictionary* is a great way for students to develop their sense of what characterizes a dictionary definition, and it is a game they really enjoy. To play, each member of a group of four to six players needs several 3 × 5 cards or slips of paper. One student (the leader) thumbs through the dictionary looking for a word that is sure to be unknown to the rest of the group. She then writes the word on a card, says it to the group, and spells it for the group. During the next few minutes, each group member writes the word and a made-up definition for the word on a card, and the leader writes the real definition of the word on her card. After all definitions have been written, the leader collects all of the cards and mixes them up. She then reads each definition as seriously as possible as the group members try to figure out which definition is the real one. After all definitions have been read, the students vote for the definition they believe to be correct. The leader earns one point for each player who does not select her correct definition, while each player earns one point for each other player who does select his or her incorrect definition. Leadership then rotates to the next person in the group until each person has had a chance to lead.

Modeling and Encouraging Adept Diction

The starting point, we believe, in encouraging and nurturing word consciousness lies in our attitude toward words and the attitude we project to students. We want children to feel that adept diction—the skillful use of words in speech and writing—is something worth striving for. We want them to see that, by using the right word themselves and recognizing the adept word choices authors make, they can both communicate more effectively and more fully appreciate an author's message. Several conscious efforts can be useful in promoting skillful diction. One is to model adept word usage in your classroom talk, deliberately using and perhaps explaining words that at least some of your students might not yet know. Thus, in describing how you were startled by a low-flying jet on the way to school, you might tell your fourth graders that the jet made a *thunderous* noise and point out that *thunderous* is sometimes an excellent word for describing a really loud noise because it reminds us of the great booming sound of thunder.

Another way to very effectively focus students' attention on words is to include a "word-of-the-day" activity in daily plans. Appropriate for all ages, word-of-the-day can take a number of forms. In a first-grade classroom, word meaning can be linked to word recognition and general language facility by sharing with students a particular word of interest and paying special attention to the way it sounds, the way it looks, and what it means. Words-of-the-day can be added to a bulletin board each day until, at the end of the month, the entire board is filled. Words-of-the-day can also be acted out, used in a game of charades, or drawn. They can also be made part of a song, riddle, pun, poem, or some other form or artistic expression.

You might designate a period of five minutes every day to introduce a new and interesting word. At the beginning of the year, you could choose the word and present it to the class by telling what it means, explaining why you selected it, and giving one or two examples of how it relates to either your life or their lives. Students often have questions and comments, so this period of time is spent thinking deeply about one particular word. After the first month of school, students take the responsibility for selecting a word and introducing it to the class, either individually or in pairs.

Students can select words from any number of sources—books, newspapers, another classroom, their parents, and teachers, to name a few. You can also suggest that students find their special words in particular sources in order to complement particular classroom activities. For example, during a unit on the newspaper, you might suggest that students find words in the newspaper; and during a unit on weather, you might suggest that students choose "weather words." More often, however, it is worthwhile to let students find their words wherever they wish. In this way, they tend to view the words as their own, take greater pride in sharing them, and more readily see learning new words as an enjoyable experience.

Another opportunity for recognizing and promoting adroit word usage comes from children's own writing. Thus, you might compliment a third grader for describing banana slugs as *gigantic* and give a little recognition to a sixth grader who noted that the odds of winning the lottery are *astronomically small.* During writing conferences, you might also encourage students to re-think word choices in an effort to make their writing more colorful and precise.

CONCLUDING REMARKS

In this chapter, we have described the vocabulary-learning task students face, noted the importance of wide reading, described six word-learning tasks and ways of selecting vocabulary to teach, and presented teaching procedures that are appropriate for each of the word-learning tasks. We also suggested approaches to teaching students to use context, prefixes, and the dictionary so that they can become independent word learners. Finally, we suggested several approaches to fostering students' word consciousness.

Of course, no one teacher is expected to cover all facets of vocabulary instruction. You can choose which words to teach, which level of word knowledge you expect your students to achieve, and what teaching procedure or procedures are most appropriate for the words in a particular selection your students are reading. Also, no one teacher needs to take major responsibility for teaching students to use context, word parts, and the dictionary. You and the other teachers in your school can work together to decide who is responsible for these various teaching tasks. Every teacher, however, should share in the responsibility for fostering word consciousness. All in all, by teaching some words, fostering word consciousness, and working with your colleagues to teach students to learn words on their own, you will be helping all of your students develop rich and powerful vocabularies.

SELF-CHECK

1. About how large is an average third-grade student's reading vocabulary? About how many words do elementary students learn each year?

2. Describe the three levels of word knowledge listed.

3. Identify the four major parts of a comprehensive program of vocabulary instruction.

4. What part does children's reading play in the growth of their vocabularies?

5. Name the six word-learning tasks students face.

6. Describe several ways of identifying words students may not know and some criteria for selecting specific words to teach.

7. Describe at least one teaching method for each of the six word-learning tasks.

8. Explain how you would teach students to use context cues to figure out the meanings of words they do not know.

9. Explain how you would teach students to use word parts to figure out the meanings of words they do not know.

10. Note the two guidelines students need to follow in order to use the dictionary effectively.

11. Describe several of the approaches we gave for fostering word consciousness, and suggest any approaches of your own that you might use.

12. Suppose that your third-grade students were about to read a story with half a dozen difficult words that did not represent new concepts. How might you teach them?

13. Suppose your fifth graders were going to read a science chapter that includes a single difficult concept. What procedure might you use here? About how long might you spend on the concept?

14. Assume that you are a fourth-grade teacher and the third-grade teacher has already taught students to use context cues to unlock word meanings. What sort of review on context cues would you provide? What would you do with your students who were new to the school?

REFERENCES

Anderson, R. C. (1996). Research foundations to support wide reading. In V. Greaney (ed.), *Promoting reading in developing countries*. New York: International Reading Association. A lucid presentation of the data and arguments supporting wide reading.

Anderson, R. C. and Nagy, W. E. (1992). The vocabulary conundrum. *American Educator*, Winter, 14–18, 44–47. A convincing argument for the size of the vocabulary learning task students face.

Anglin, J. M. (1993). Vocabulary development: A morphological analysis. *Monographs of the Society for Research in Child Development, 58* (10, Serial No. 238). A technical report on the growth of children's vocabularies.

Beck, I. L. and McKeown, M. G. (1983). Learning words well. A program to enhance vocabulary and comprehension. *The Reading Teacher*, 36, 622–625. This article describes a program for developing rich and deep word meanings and inspired the Duin and Graves program described in the chapter.

Beck, I. L, McKeown, M. G. and Omanson, R. C. (1987). The effects and uses of diverse vocabulary instructional techniques. In McKeown, M. G. and Curtis, M. E. (eds.), *The nature of vocabulary acquisition*. Hillsdale, NJ: Erlbaum, pp. 147–163. Describes various sorts of vocabulary instruction that are useful.

Duin, A. H. and Graves, M. F. (1988). Teaching vocabulary as a writing prompt. *Journal of Reading*, 22, 204–212. An interesting program for building students' expressive vocabulary.

Fielding, L. G., Wilson, P. D. and Anderson, R. C. (1986). A new focus on free reading: The role of trade books in reading instruction. In Raphael, T. E. (ed.), *The contexts of school-based literacy*. New York: Random House, pp. 149–160. Research and theory on the importance of free reading.

Frayer, D. A., Frederick, W. D. and Klausmeier, H. J. (1969). *A schema for testing the level of concept mastery* (Working Paper No. 16). Madison: Wisconsin Research and Development Center for Cognitive Learning. A detailed presentation of a powerful approach to teaching concepts.

Graves, M. F. and Prenn, M. C. (1986). Costs and benefits of different methods of vocabulary instruction. *Journal of Reading, 29,* 596–602. Examines the results of different vocabulary teaching methods and the time taken to implement them.

Graves, M. F. and Slater, W. H. (1996). Vocabulary instruction in content areas. In Lapp, D., Flood, J. and Farnan, N. (eds.), *Content area reading and learning: Instructional strategies* (2nd ed.). Needham Heights, MA: Allyn & Bacon. Includes the description of the context-relationship procedure and a number of other vocabulary-teaching techniques.

Graves, M. F. and Watts, S. M. (1997). Spotlight on words. *Teaching K–8, 28*(1), 66–67. Some brief and easily implemented ideas for fostering word consciousness.

Heimlich, J. E. and Pittelman, S. D. (1986). *Semantic mapping: Classroom applications.* Newark, DE: International Reading Association. A detailed description of semantic mapping along with lots of examples.

International Reading Association. (1995). *More Kids' Favorite Books.* Newark, DE: International Reading Association. A compilation of *The Reading Teacher's* Children's Choices lists for 1992–1994.

Irvin, J. L. (1998). *Reading and the middle school student.* (2nd ed.). Needham Heights, MA: Allyn and Bacon. Contains a number of excellent teaching methods.

McCracken, R. A. (1971). Initiating sustained silent reading. *Journal of Reading,* 14, 521–524, 582–583. Suggests six rules to follow when implementing sustained silent reading in the classroom.

Nagy, W. E. and Herman, P. A. (1987). Breadth and depth of vocabulary knowledge: Implications for acquisition and instruction. In McKeown, M. G. and Curtis, M. E. (eds.), *The nature of vocabulary acquisition.* Hillsdale, NJ: Erlbaum, pp. 19–36. Emphasizes the importance of incidental learning of vocabulary.

Nagy, W. E., Winsor, P., Osborn, J. and O'Flahavan, J. (1994). Structural analysis: Some guidelines for instruction. In Lehr, F. and Osborn, J. (eds.), *Reading, language, and literacy* (pp. 45–58). Hillsdale, NJ: Erlbaum. Excellent and very practical guidelines for structural analysis instruction.

Stahl, S. A. and Kapinus, B. (1991). Possible sentences: Predicting word meanings to teach content area vocabulary. *The Reading Teacher,* 45, 36–43. An explanation and study of the possible sentences method.

Watts, S. M., Graves, M. F. and Harrison, C. (in press). Fostering word consciousness. *Reading.* A detailed look at ways of promoting word consciousness.

White, T. G., Graves, M. F. and Slater, W. H. (1990). Growth of reading vocabulary in diverse elementary schools: Decoding and word meaning. *Journal of Educational Psychology,* 82, 281–290. Details on the size of first through fourth grade students' vocabularies.

White, T. G., Slater, W. H. and Graves, M. F. (1989). Yes/no method of vocabulary assessment: Valid for whom and useful for what? *Cognitive and social perspectives for literacy research and instruction.* Chicago: National Reading Conference, pp. 391–398. Presents clear evidence of students' ability to indicate which words they do and do not know.

White, T. G., Sowell, J. and Yanagihara, A. (1989). Teaching elementary students to use word-part clues. *The Reading Teacher,* 42, 302–308. A useful examination of which word parts to teach and how to teach them.

BIBLIOGRAPHIES OF CHILDREN'S BOOKS

The books reviewed in each of the following journals are recent trade books, published in the year prior to the reviews. The review and selection processes used by the journals are thorough and very carefully done, resulting in excellent book lists. As noted in the chapter, wide reading in books such as those in these bibliographies will both foster vocabulary development and yield a host of other benefits.

Children's Choices. (annually, in October). *The Reading Teacher.* Fiction and nonfiction books elementary and middle school children have identified as some of their favorites.

Notable Children's Trade Books in the Field of Social Studies. (annually, in April/May). *Social Education.* Short reviews of notable social studies trade books for kindergarten through eighth-grade children.

Outstanding Science Trade Books for Children. (annually, in March). *Children and Science.* Short reviews of outstanding science trade books for prekindergarten through eighth-grade children.

Teachers' Choices. (annually, in November). *The Reading Teacher.* Fiction and nonfiction books teachers have identified as among their favorites for kindergarten and elementary age students.

7 Fostering Comprehension of Specific Selections

Imagine you get a call from a rich uncle saying he wants you to take a trip to Bolivia to investigate his landholdings there. The plane leaves in an hour. He will pay for everything. All you need to do is answer a few questions and write up a short report when you return. Your passport and inoculations are current and, being the adventurous person you are, you decide to go. But the trip is a disaster—no one is there to greet you, you brought the wrong clothes, you can't understand the language, the culture is confusing, and, what's worse, you can't even locate the landholdings. When you return, you scribble a note to your uncle. "The trip was a disaster. I was a failure. You may give me an 'F' as nephew."

What went wrong? For one thing, you weren't prepared to go to Bolivia. For another, no one was there to show you around once you got there. Consequently, and not surprisingly, when you returned all that you could recall of your trip was your failure.

Reading a story or expository text is something like taking a trip into the unknown. Sometimes the territory may be quite familiar, other times very new. Whatever the case, one of our tasks as teachers is to help ensure our students a successful, meaningful journey. We can do this by sufficiently preparing students before reading, guiding them where necessary during reading, and providing them with meaningful experiences after reading.

LOOKING AHEAD

In the previous chapter, we talked about teaching students individual words and teaching them strategies for unlocking the meanings of unknown words on their own. In this chapter, we consider what you can do to help students successfully read specific texts, in other words, what you can do to help students comprehend the text, achieve their purposes for reading it, and enjoy the experience.

In the first part of this chapter, we briefly discuss the roles that *purpose*, the *selection*, and the *students* play in planning and designing reading activities. In the second part of the chapter, we take a closer look at the reading activities themselves. We describe various kinds of *prereading, during-reading,* and *postreading* activities you might use to prepare and engage readers. In the last part of the chapter, we present a detailed example of taking students through the three phases with a specific selection.

The general approach taken in this chapter relies heavily on an instructional framework two of us have described elsewhere as a Scaffolded Reading Experience, an approach that is discussed in detail in *Scaffolding Reading Experiences to Promote Success* (Graves and Graves 1994).

KEY CONCEPTS

- Factors to consider in planning reading activities
- The role of purpose in planning reading activities
- How specific reading selections influence the purposes for students' reading
- Three categories of reading activities
- Functions of prereading activities
- How activating readers' background knowledge helps them read effectively
- Activities that activate prior knowledge
- Functions of prequestioning and predicting activities
- Situations in which oral reading is appropriate
- Cuing activities
- Types of postreading activities
- The value of postreading activities

THE PURPOSE, THE SELECTION, AND THE STUDENTS

Three elements come into play when considering the kinds and number of activities needed to foster successful reading experiences—the *purpose* for reading, the *selection,* and the *students*. The purpose, the reading selection, and the students will dictate what sorts of activities you design to foster a successful reading experience.

The Purpose

Let us first talk briefly about purpose. In the scenario we used at the beginning of the chapter, there was at least one explicit purpose for your journey to Bolivia—to find out about your uncle's landholdings there.

Purpose is what motivates us, helps focus our attention, and gives us a goal, something tangible to work toward.

Without purpose, we have no way to measure our success. "Open your science books and read pages 16–20." "Why?" the student might ask. In this instance he might answer, "Because the teacher told me so. If I don't want to get into trouble, I'd better do it." This is not a very good purpose in our estimation. "Read pages 16–17 to find out three interesting facts about Pluto" is a slightly more focused purpose, and you can measure students' success in achieving this purpose.

Purposes for reading are nearly as numerous and varied as the seashells along the beach. They might be singular or multiple, straightforward or complex. One reading purpose might be to simply enjoy a well-told tale, another to discover a story's theme or the differences and similarities between characters, and another to find out the ten ingredients needed to make chocolate pinwheel cookies. Whatever the purpose for reading, you want to ensure your students' success in achieving it.

Purposes are determined by a number of factors. Among these are the students reading the selection, the selection itself, and what it is your students need to know, want to know, or will be empowered, enriched or enlightened by knowing.

Purposes can be student generated or teacher generated. A student-generated purpose may begin with a student telling you, "I'm getting a guinea pig for my birthday, but I don't know what to feed it and I need to know." You pull a book on guinea pigs from your library shelf. "I don't know what they eat either. Will you tell me when you find out?" By embracing student-generated purposes for reading, you will heighten interest in reading among all of your students, particularly those whose cultural experiences lead to purposes for reading that may be different from your own.

A teacher-generated purpose begins with a purpose in the mind of a teacher. Perhaps your social studies curriculum includes the study of California and Japan. You want your students to learn how to compare and contrast. Focusing students' attention on looking for similarities and differences between these two places while they read will help you achieve your teacher-generated purpose.

The Selection

Of course, before you begin to create activities for a particular text, you will have read it and become acquainted with its topics and themes, its potentially difficult vocabulary or other potential stumbling blocks, and the opportunities it presents for instruction. The reading material itself will dictate how you want your students to approach it and what you want them to take away from it. A science chapter, for instance, will require a different kind of reading than a folktale; thus, the activities you set up to prepare, guide, and enrich the reading experience will be quite different for each.

Say, for instance, a science chapter has a number of difficult concepts that your fourth graders will need to understand if they are to comprehend the thrust of the chapter. In this case, you will probably want to do some preteaching of these concepts before students begin reading on their own and encourage students to attend to these concepts while they are reading.

You may also decide to provide alternatives to independent reading for students in your classroom who are not reading on the fourth-grade level and would, thus, be unable to comprehend much of the chapter on their own. You might pair students for reading or have students work in groups where there is one reader who reads the text paragraph by paragraph, stopping after each paragraph for the group to discuss what was read and, as a group, write a one-sentence summary.

After all of your students have finished reading, in order to ensure depth of processing, you will want them to work with these concepts in yet another way, perhaps by having students make a chart listing the concepts and illustrating them. Providing opportunities for students to work with concepts in a variety of ways—through listening, writing, drawing, watching, and touching, to name a few—will be of particular benefit for students who may have missed some of the important concepts in their initial reading.

Suppose, as another example, that the class is reading a folktale. A folktale will most likely suggest other, perhaps quite different, kinds of activities. For instance, after you read the folktale, you may realize it has a wonderfully straightforward story line, one that would work perfectly into your curriculum for fostering understanding of story grammar. In this case, your prereading, during-reading, and postreading activities would focus on the elements of the story that you found were well illustrated in the tale. Before students read the story, you might tell a simplified story similar to the folktale using flannel board props, focusing on the elements of character, the problem, attempts to solve the problem, and the solution. When students read the folktale, you could have them look for these elements. As a follow-up, you might let them retell the folktale using flannel board cutouts you have prepared that represent the characters, problem, attempts at solution, and resolution of the folktale. This approach would ensure that students whose primary literacy experience is with other story structures gain a clear understanding of the structure of folktales.

As explained by Louise Rosenblatt (1978), the purposes for reading informational texts and literature are often quite different. In the first instance, we are usually reading to extract information we can do something with. In the second, our purpose is most often aesthetic; our primary purposes for reading literature are usually to enjoy, appreciate, and respond to it. In planning reading activities for students, we need to keep these differences in mind.

The Students

When you are thinking about purposes and analyzing reading material, there is another factor that will be uppermost in your planning—your students. Certainly, you want to do everything possible to guarantee their success, both in school and in their lives outside of school. Therefore, whatever decision making you are involved in, your students' needs, concerns, and interests will be uppermost in your mind.

Say, for example, you are teaching a class of low-income fifth graders who are average-to-poor readers living in a midwestern city. Your social studies curriculum includes a unit on Australia, and one of the reading selections is an article on the Great Barrier Reef. Although your students may have heard of Australia and seen pictures of it in the media, you know they have not visited there; nor, for the most part, have they actually been to an ocean. To read this article successfully, these students will need prereading experiences that provide them with background information that helps fill the gaps in their repertoire of concepts about Australia, and about oceans, reefs, and other topics central to the article. Students from other countries might provide some of this information. If your class includes students from Cuba, Puerto Rico, or Haiti, for example, they could provide information on their experiences with the Atlantic Ocean. Both the Atlantic and Pacific oceans could then be discussed in preparation for the reading on Australia. Also, suppose the reading level of the article is about sixth grade; some of your students may need further assistance in understanding it. This may include preteaching potentially difficult vocabulary, then suggesting a reading strategy—such as recommending students read the article quickly once to get its main thrust, then again slowly to pick up the details.

If, on the other hand, the class reading the selection on the Great Barrier Reef is from an affluent suburb on the west coast, your prereading activities will be quite different. These may include having students discuss what they know about the topic before reading it, perhaps even writing down what they know about Australia, reefs, and their experiences and knowledge of the ocean. After reading the article, the students might discuss what new information or ideas they discovered from the reading, what questions were brought to mind while they read, and where they might go to find the answers to those questions.

THE ACTIVITIES

As we mentioned earlier, the activities you provide to foster students' comprehension of specific texts can be divided into three categories—*prereading, during reading,* and *postreading.* As we also indicated, although you will want to provide students with something in each of these categories, such activities can range from something extremely brief to something quite complex. A straightforward short story might only require your saying, "This is a terrific story. Read and enjoy," then having students read the entire story silently and afterwards discussing whether they enjoyed the story, and if so why. A difficult expository piece, however, might require several pre-, during-, and postreading activities. For prereading, you might provide activities that relate the reading to the students' lives and activate background knowledge. You might also preteach potentially troublesome vocabulary. As students are reading, you might have them write summaries of each section of the text. Postreading activities might include discussion, chart making, and demonstrations. In the next three sections, we discuss some of the components of each of these three categories— prereading, during reading and postreading. After that, we provide sample activities for each.

Before we discuss these activities separately, there is one very important point to keep in mind. As we have discussed in detail elsewhere (Graves and Graves 1994), prereading, during-reading, and postreading activities are interrelated; that is, each will affect and be affected by the others and each will be determined by the selection, the purpose or purposes for reading it, and the students. Figure 7–1, showing the two phases of a Scaffolded Reading Experience, illustrates this relationship.

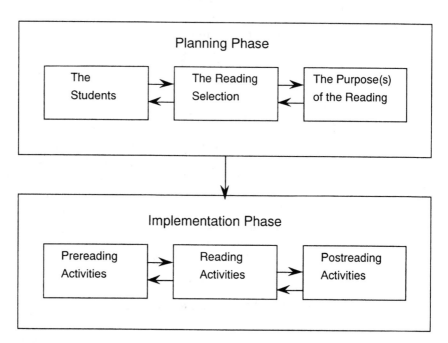

Figure 7–1.   Two Phases of a Scaffolded Reading Experience

Prereading Activities

Obviously, prereading activities are those things you do with students prior to their reading a selection. Prereading activities serve multiple purposes. Prereading activities can function to

- motivate and set up purposes for reading.
- activate background knowledge.
- build text-specific knowledge.
- teach vocabulary and concepts.
- relate the reading to students' lives.
- help focus the reading process.
- suggest strategies.

We will now briefly consider the nature of each of these activities—what they are and why and when you might use them—and then give an example of each. Remember, although we deal with each of these kinds of activities separately, as you read about them, you will notice overlap among them. For example, a motivating activity may also activate prior knowledge, introduce a new concept, and relate reading to the students' lives. Similarly, a prereading activity targeted at teaching vocabulary may also activate prior knowledge.

Motivating and Setting Up Purpose

As you well know, most of the time we need to be motivated to do something —reading is no exception. Getting students to *want* to read is sometimes easy, sometimes not, but it is always essential. Think about yourself and the reading you are doing right now. What is motivating you to read this? In an ideal world, our motivation would be intrinsic, stemming from an internal need or desire that is fulfilled when we read. However, that is not always the case, particularly in school. We might hope that all students are intrinsically motivated to read what we feel is important and worthwhile for them to read, but the truth is that they sometimes are not. We need to motivate them to want to read, to light their fire, so to speak, so they feel that need and desire. Motivating activities, then, are any kinds of activities that help students delve into reading material willingly, even eagerly, knowing there is some sort of reward at the end—new knowledge, experiences, discoveries, excitement, laughter. It is there for them if they will but read.

Activating Background Knowledge

In Chapter 2, we explained that having appropriate background knowledge —*schemata*—is absolutely crucial to understanding text. By activating background knowledge we mean calling up from students' memory information they already have on a particular subject, information that will help them make connections between what they already know and what they glean from the text. We do this informally all the time. Before a party, your friend might say to you, "You remember my Uncle Pete, don't you? He's kind of short and tells jokes." You think for a minute and then say, "Sure. He's the one with the bald head and the belly laugh." At the party, when you hear a boisterous laugh and Uncle Pete calls to you from across the room, you can answer confidently, "Uncle Pete, hi!" Your background knowledge was sufficiently activated to make the connection.

For students, activating background knowledge before they read a story means providing activities that prompt them to bring to consciousness information they already know that will help them understand the upcoming text. The more a student knows about the topic of a text before reading it, the more he can understand from it. Moreover, as Richard Anderson (1984) has pointed out, prior knowledge not only enables us to comprehend a text, it also helps us organize and remember what we have learned.

Given the vital importance of prior knowledge to comprehension and memory, it is critical to recognize that different students bring different stores of prior knowledge into the classroom and are thus differentially prepared to read some selections. Recognizing and accommodating to these differences in today's culturally and linguistically diverse classrooms is one of the major challenges teachers face. Yet it is a challenge that teachers must face in order for all students to reach their potential as readers.

Building Text-Specific Knowledge
Building text-specific knowledge is motivated by the same reasoning as activating background knowledge; that is, having background knowledge or schemata for something prior to reading about it greatly facilitates comprehension. In this case, the information you give students will be information they do not have in their storehouse of knowledge. Say, for instance, your fifth graders are going to read *The True Confessions of Charlotte Doyle* by Avi. The story takes place on a sailing ship in the early 1800s and knowing how a ship is rigged is crucial to appreciating and understanding the plight of Charlotte, the main character in the story. You can probably be quite certain that most fifth graders will not have a rich schema for this kind of ship's rigging. Providing them with this information by way of models, diagrams, or illustrations will give them something to attach new information to when they read and help them to better understand Charlotte's emotions when she has to climb up the various riggings to trim the sails. In addition, you might share a short picture book such as *The Wretched Stone* by Chris Van Allsburg with your students. The brilliant illustrations in this book will give students an opportunity to locate various components of the ship and to learn a bit about the role of the ship's captain and crew while, simultaneously, providing recreational reading for students who are not reading on the fifth-grade level.

Relating Reading to Students' Lives

Like activating background knowledge and building text-specific knowledge, activities that relate reading to students' lives also activate prior knowledge. In this case, however, your goal is to draw students into the text by helping them recall situations in their lives that are similar to those found in the selection. These types of activities are of a more personal nature than the other two. For example, before they read a biography on Martin Luther King, Jr., you might have students think about and discuss times in their lives when they felt that they were not treated as well as others, when they felt they were mistreated or treated unfairly. Having students think about these times and talk about them will help students understand better the concept of discrimination, a central theme in the biography. In addition, minority students may have stories that their parents have told them about being discriminated against in the United States, while students who have recently moved from other countries may have recent memories of discrimination. Helping build bridges between the students' lives and the text will facilitate their understanding as well as their appreciation and enjoyment of what they read.

Preteaching Vocabulary and Preteaching Concepts

The issue of preteaching vocabulary and preteaching concepts also comes under the umbrella of prior knowledge. The more words a student knows, the more he can learn. Also, a student's vocabulary knowledge is a good predictor of comprehension. Children who know the word *tree* can more easily learn the words *maple, elm, sycamore,* and so on. Because vocabulary is so important to comprehension and learning, we need to pay attention to the vocabulary in reading selections. We do not want students to read material containing too many unknown words; they simply will not understand the material. However, we want to stretch students somewhat, to offer them some challenges for vocabulary growth. So, ideally, the selections students read should be composed primarily of words they know but include some words they do not know—words that will provide opportunities for expanding their vocabulary and the depth of their knowledge of individual words.

In Chapter 6, we considered six word-learning tasks. Here we return to three of those—teaching students to read words that are in their oral vocabularies, teaching words that are new labels for known concepts, and teaching words that represent new and potentially difficult concepts. For example, let us say your high achieving second graders are reading *Camper of the Week* by Amy Schwartz. After reading the story, you decide some students might have problems decoding the words *continued, courteous,* and *considerate* and might have trouble understanding the meanings of *mess hall* and *burl plaque.* They have *continued* in their oral vocabularies and *courteous* and *considerate* represent words that are new labels for known concepts. However, while they may be able to decode *mess hall* and *burl plaque,* they will have trouble understanding the terms. These words represent new, although not particularly difficult, concepts.

Showing students the words *continued, courteous* and *considerate* in print, pronouncing them, and having students talk about their meanings may be sufficient for making these words accessible to students when they meet them in the text. However, *mess hall* and *burl plaque* may not be in your students' oral vocabularies, and you will need to provide additional work with these words, perhaps by describing orally or with visuals what a mess hall and burl plaque are and having children work with these words in context. Sometimes, as you preteach vocabulary and central concepts, it will become apparent that your students will require much more support for a text than you had anticipated. You may even find that the text you were planning to use is simply inappropriate for them at this point in time. Thus, there will be occasions when you will need to drastically alter your approach to a text or put it off for another time instead of forging ahead when it is clear that your students will not benefit from reading it—even with a great deal of support.

Prequestioning and Predicting
Prequestioning and predicting activities are ones which focus students' attention on what to look for as they read. These activities begin as prereading activities, are carried out during reading, and are wrapped up after the reading. Prequestioning and predicting activities are important because without them students may not know what to attend to, and it is simply impossible for a reader to attend to everything in a reading selection.

Prequestioning activities are those in which you ask students questions or students themselves pose questions about the upcoming text—questions they would like to find answers to. To give an example of teacher-generated prequestioning, let us say you have been studying nutrition in your sixth-grade class and one student brings in an article from the Sunday paper, which includes a stir-fry dish that is touted as being "healthful." Before students read the article, you might ask them to think about the question, "Is this a healthful recipe, or not?" as they read. In such an activity, you would ask them to be ready to defend their answers, and this defense would be carried out in the postreading discussion. Student-generated questioning occurs whenever the students are asking their own questions about a selection and reading to discover the answers. For example, suppose that during the nutrition unit, students are asked to create a puppet play to teach the kindergarten and first-grade classes good eating habits. When they read material to prepare for their play, they will need to ask all sorts of questions in order to create an appropriate script: "What are good healthful foods that five and six year olds will like?" "What are foods that are unhealthful that children should avoid?" "Why are these foods unhealthful?" The answers to questions such as these will provide students with the raw material for their play.

Predicting activities are those in which students make predictions about the text and read to find out whether their predictions are accurate. Predicting upcoming story events leads children to construct interconnected representations of stories. Before reading, students need some idea of what to expect in order to compare their expectations to what they encounter as they are reading. Reading to confirm or refute predictions makes reading an active process, a process that will engage students and facilitate their understanding and memory of what they read.

For example, let us say your first graders are going to read *Mouse Soup* by Arnold Lobel. Before they begin reading, you show them the cover illustration, which shows a mouse standing up in a bowl. Then you write on the chalkboard *Mouse Soup by Arnold Lobel—mouse, book, weasel, cooking pot, stories.* After reading the book's title and author and pronouncing the words, you ask the students to use the words to make up sentences that they think might tell something about the story (Moore and Moore 1990). For instance, "A *mouse* was looking at a *book*. A *weasel* came up and put him in a *cooking pot* and told him *stories*." Write the sentences students suggest on the chalkboard and then have the students read the story to see whether any of their predictions are correct.

Suggesting Strategies

Suggesting strategies is a somewhat different kind of prereading activity than those discussed thus far in that the focus here is on suggesting ways in which students themselves might effectively approach the text to achieve their reading purposes. We cover this topic in depth in the next chapter, so we just briefly touch on it here.

The strategies that you suggest that your students employ while reading a selection will have been taught sometime prior to your suggesting they use them. A strategy that would be appropriate for an expository selection might include studying a selection's illustrations, graphs, headings, and subheadings prior to reading; reading the piece once quickly to get the gist of it, and then reading more slowly and taking notes on a second reading. Another strategy, one that can be used for any type of text, might be for students to pause at the end of a paragraph or section and ask themselves if they have understood what they have read. If the answer is "no," they would probably go back and reread that paragraph or section before going on. Of course, there are many other strategies you can suggest students use while reading, and some students will require a great deal of support in their use of strategies. As we just noted, we discuss teaching strategies at length in the next chapter.

Wrapping Up Prereading

By now, you are probably aware that the possibilities for prereading activities are almost limitless. But there is a common thread to all of them—each serves in one way or another to build a bridge from the student to the selection. So, when you think about prereading activities in general, think about building bridges, helping students cross from the known to the unknown. Think about what students need to know to understand and appreciate a particular reading selection and how you can help launch them on a successful reading experience each and every time they read.

When you begin to plan your prereading activities, think about your students, the material they are to read, and their purpose for reading it. Think about the entire reading experience, how the prereading activities you use will integrate with the during- and postreading activities you employ. Then, decide what sort of prereading activities will best accomplish your goal.

Here is a sample prereading activity. As you read through it, think about what it attempts to accomplish in preparing the reader to read with understanding and enjoyment. Does it motivate? Activate prior knowledge? Build text-specific knowledge? Relate reading to students' lives? Preteach vocabulary or concepts?

SAMPLE PREREADING ACTIVITY

QUESTIONNAIRE/OPINIONNAIRE

The students: Fourth-grade students of high reading ability in an ethnically diverse urban class that includes three ESL students.

The selection: *Journey* by Patricia MacLachlan. When their mother goes off, leaving Cat and Journey with their grandparents, they feel as if their past has been erased until Grandfather finds a way to restore it for them by taking family photographs. This is a short novel, 83 pages, of high literary quality. Because it is a story that students may not select on their own, *Journey* is an ideal choice for in-depth reading in school.

The purpose: To engage students in the kind of thinking that will help them focus on the main themes in the story by connecting them with similar themes in their own lives.

The procedure: Before students begin reading *Journey,* create a display of cameras and photographs (Graves and Graves 1994). Then, just prior to students' reading the novel, hold up the book and tell them that *Journey* is a wonderful story written by Patricia MacLachlan. Explain that the story tells about a boy whose mother has left him and his sister to live with their grandparents and that two things are very important in the story—a camera and photographs. Ask students to describe the items you have displayed and to think about and discuss how and why photographs might be important in the story.

Next, explain that because of the significance of cameras and photographs in *Journey,* you want students to think about what parts these items play or have played in their own lives. Tell them that to help them focus their thinking, you have made up a questionnaire/opinionnaire (Reasoner 1976) that you want them to answer. Before distributing the questionnaires, read the questions on it aloud. Then, give the questionnaire/opinionnaires to students and let them complete them. Have one of your students help the ESL students complete their questionnaires. After all of the students have finished their questionnaires and before they begin reading the story, give them an opportunity to share their ideas.

Questionnaire/Opinionnaire

Do you have a camera? _____ yes _____ no _____

If you do have a camera, what do you like to take pictures of? _____
_____

When do you use your camera most? _____

Do you have family photographs at home?   yes _____ no _____

What do these photographs show? _____

What do your *favorite* photographs show? _____

   Why do you like these photos the best? _____

Which are your least favorite photographs? _____

   Why don't you like these photos? _____

What do you think family photographs can tell us about ourselves?
_____
_____

Why can we sometimes see things in photographs that we don't notice in real life?
_____
_____
_____

During-Reading Activities

Now that you have built the bridge with prereading activities, students are ready to get into the act itself. During-reading activities include both things that students do themselves as they are reading and things that you do to assist them—activities that facilitate or enhance the actual reading process.

As we explained in Chapter 2, reading is a constructive process; that is, readers build meaning as they read, combining what they know with the author's words and coming up with meaning. One of our jobs as teachers is to make sure this meaning building is taking place, to foster active involvement in thinking and reasoning about the text. You have already begun this process with prereading activities, but there are additional opportunities for supporting students' efforts as they are reading.

Silent Reading and Oral Reading

Reading is carried out most often and most efficiently by reading the words silently. Most of the time, this is what students will be doing. However, oral reading is also an important option and should not be overlooked. Oral reading can be done either by you or by students. Oral reading by students is usually left as a postreading activity so that students have had the opportunity to become familiar enough with the material that they do not have to process ideas and sound out unfamiliar words at the same time. However, having students read orally may be appropriate in some during-reading situations. Although silent reading is recommended prior to oral reading, if you know a student is a competent reader and can easily handle the material on the first reading, you might ask that student to read a selection aloud to another less-competent reader while he or she follows along in the text.

Many times, you will want to read *to* your students—a novel, story, poem, informational book, article, or textbook chapter. Doing this sort of reading not only provides a model for good oral reading and a very enjoyable experience, but it can also provide experiences and knowledge some children might not otherwise get. As Bill Martin, Jr., storyteller and author, once said, "A blessed thing happened to me as a child. I had a teacher who read to me" (Martin 1992). As a kindergarten or primary grade teacher, you would, of course, be doing a great deal of reading to your students, but middle and upper elementary students need to have the pleasure of being read to as well. Even as adults we like to be read to.

Sometimes it is appropriate to read only the beginning of a story or piece of exposition aloud. By doing this, you are easing readers into text that might otherwise seem difficult and uninteresting. Also, a well-read excerpt might prove the perfect catalyst to entice students to read a story or novel on their own.

Providing Cues to Students as They Are Reading

For the most part, during-reading activities will involve just the reader and the text, with little interruption. However, there are times when it may be appropriate to guide the students as they journey through the text by providing them with cues—matters to attend to while they read. Perhaps you want them to become aware of the structure of a story: setting, plot, and character. Or, you may want them to react personally to the material. Or, you may want them to focus on certain concepts, topics, or events. If you think students might benefit from cues and suggestions as to how to approach and interact with the material, then give them some cues.

For example, if your fourth-grade students are reading a chapter in their social studies text on the establishment of missions in California and you think that seeing a graphic display of names and dates will help them understand and retain the main ideas of the chapter, you might have them develop a time line that shows the date that each of the missions was established. As they read about each mission, they can record its name and the date it was founded on their time line.

As a focusing activity for your third graders, you might have students write journal entries after each of the chapters in *Sarah, Plain and Tall*, explaining what they think the main character, Anna, is feeling at the close of each chapter. Having students record information on charts or graphics of various kinds is another way you can prompt them to interact with the text as they read. For example, in reading a biography with several major characters, they might make a data matrix in which they listed the major characters in one column, and their goals, concerns, and values in other columns (Graves and Avery 1997). Or in reading a novel or history text, they might create a time line of major events.

Modifying the Text

Sometimes because of what is either required by the curriculum or what is available, students will be reading selections that present too much of a challenge due to their length or difficulty. In these cases, modifying or shortening the selections is a viable option. For example, suppose your second-grade class contains a number of ESL students and the social studies curriculum includes a chapter on families. After reviewing the material, you realize the chapter will present too much of a challenge to your ESL students. Pair these students with sixth-grade students, and have the older students help the second graders write personal booklets about their families. Then, let each of the second graders read one or two of their classmates' booklets. After they finish reading these, hold a large-group discussion on families in which students share the information they know and have learned from reading each others' booklets. Of course, the students who prepared personal booklets will not have dealt with exactly the same topics as did those who read the commercially produced chapter, but the ideas will be similar and all students will be reading and learning. Moreover, both groups of students will be able to learn from each other and thus both groups will have a richer experience than the text alone could have provided.

Another way to modify the text is to shorten reading selections. As an example of shortening reading selections, let us say the chapter on electricity in your sixth-grade science text is quite lengthy. After reading through it, you decide it is too much for your average to low readers to handle. In this case, you might have students read only selected portions of the chapter—the topics you feel are most important for them to understand. Assuming students can and will read the complete selection, will they get as much out of reading part of it? Of course not. But, assuming they cannot or will not read all of it, success in reading part of it is certainly preferable to failure in reading all of it.

Still another way to make difficult material accessible to students is to tape record a selection for students to listen to as they read along silently with the text. You, or competent students, can make the recordings or you can purchase commercial tapes. Recordings can make material accessible to less-able readers as well as provide a model for good oral reading.

Wrapping Up During Reading

As was true with prereading activities, there are many different kinds of during-reading activities and many ways of varying individual activities. Once again, the three factors that will always determine the make-up of the reading experiences you provide for students are the selection, the students, and the purposes. Because the purposes for reading literature and reading expository materials are often different, during-reading activities for these two types of reading will also often be different. However, some activities can be modified to work for both literature and expository text.

Also, during-reading activities will overlap with both prereading and postreading activities. In other words, during-reading activities require both stage setting and follow-up. For example, if you want students to write journal entries as a during-reading activity, they need to know what to do, how to do it, and why they are doing it. The explanations and modeling used to prepare students to write takes place before they begin reading. Then, after students read the selection and write in their journals, postreading activities generally include a chance for them to share their entries with each other or with you.

Here is a sample during-reading activity designed to follow the questionnaire prereading activity we described earlier. As you read through this activity, think about how it relates to the prereading activity and how it helps students interact with the material. Also, think about the techniques used to engage the reader. Is the selection read orally or silently? Are cues being provided? Is the material being modified in any way to accommodate varying abilities?

SAMPLE DURING-READING ACTIVITY

JOURNAL WRITING

The students: Fourth-grade students of high reading ability in an ethnically diverse urban class that includes three ESL students.

The selection: *Journey* by Patricia MacLachlan. When their mother goes off, leaving Cat and Journey with their grandparents, they feel as if their past has been erased until Grandfather finds a way to restore it to them by taking family photographs.

The purposes: To engage students with the text and to focus their attention on primary themes.

The procedure: At the completion of the prereading activities, read the preface, which introduces the characters, the setting, and the problem of the novel aloud to students. Before students begin reading silently on their own, refer to the prereading questionnaire they completed and remind them to think about how a camera and photographs are used in the story. Tell them you will be interested in hearing their ideas during the postreading discussion.

Explain to students that in order to help them focus on the role photographs play in helping Journey deal with his mother's abandonment, after they have finished reading each chapter, you want them to jot down in their journals a few sentences that describe the incidents that take place regarding photography or photographs. Ask them to write about how Journey felt about them as well as their own reactions to them. Model this activity by initially reading the first page and a half of the novel aloud. These pages describe Grandfather "belly down in the meadow with his camera taking a picture of a cow pie." Have students suggest what they might write in their journals that describes the incident, explains how Journey felt, and gives their own reactions. Write their suggestions on the board. For example, "Chapter One: Grandfather took a picture of a cow pie and Journey was pretty disgusted by it. He can't understand why Grandfather would want a picture of a cow pie. I can't either!"

Distribute the novels and have students read the rest of the book silently, making journal entries after each chapter. Since the language in *Journey* may be a challenge for some of your ESL students, have some competent sixth graders available to read aloud to these students as they follow along in the text. Also, since some of your ESL students are likely to lack some of the background knowledge necessary to understanding and appreciating this novel set in mid-America, have these same sixth graders meet with the ESL students in small groups and discuss various characteristics of the place where Cat and Journey live and the life they lead there.

Postreading Activities

Postreading activities are those that students engage in after they read a selection. These kinds of activities grow out of prereading and during-reading activities and will involve students in various kinds of synthesizing, analyzing, evaluating, applying, or simply savoring or sharing what they have read. These kinds of activities may include questioning, discussion, writing, artwork, drama, music, and various kinds of outreach activities.

What you hope to accomplish with postreading activities is for students to better understand the material and to realize and appreciate the greater implications of a piece of literature or expository text, to take away from the experience not only new knowledge but a positive attitude regarding the beauty and power of written language.

Questioning

Asking students to answer questions about certain aspects of the text is a natural outgrowth of what has taken place in the prereading and during-reading phases and will serve as the final link in the comprehension and engagement chain. For example, suppose as a prereading activity for the chapter book *No Copycats Allowed!* by Bonnie Graves, you and your third-grade students working in groups of 4–5 created "tall tales" using five key words from the story—*copycat, Gabrielle, name, allowed,* and *friend* (Towell 1997–1998). For the during-reading phase, to guide their thinking as they read the text, students focused on how these words are used in the story. After students have finished reading the book, a logical question for them to answer—orally, in writing, or by drawing illustrations—would be, "What does the title *No Copycats Allowed!* mean?" Such a question requires that students take what they know about the concepts *copycat* and *allowed* and compare these notions with what they find in the text. To extend the students' concept of *copycats* and the ideas presented by the author, you might ask the questions, "Why is it sometimes not a good idea not to be a copycat?" and "Can being a copycat ever be a good thing?" These kinds of questions help students understand how ideas they read about in stories can relate to their lives.

When questioning students, try to encourage thinking beyond literal understanding and being able to state explicit details about the story toward interpretive thinking—making inferences or perceiving relationships between and among ideas. Then, encourage students to examine how these ideas might apply to their own lives.

One way to ensure that you ask various types of questions is to deliberately consider three types of questions, which David Pearson and Dale Johnson (1978) have termed *text explicit, text implicit,* and *script implicit.* Assume that your fifth-grade students are reading a brief biography of S. Scott Momaday, the Pulitzer Prize-winning, Native American author (Globe 1993). Text-explicit questions are directly answered in the reading selection. One text-explicit question you might ask after students read the Momaday biography is "When did he win the Pulitzer Prize?" The biography specifically states that he won the Pulitzer Prize in 1969. Text-implicit questions are answered in the reading selection, but they require that at least one inference be made. One text-implicit question you might ask about Momaday is "How did Momaday's winning the Pulitzer Prize influence his writing career?" The biography contains a good deal of information that answers this question, but it does not explicitly answer it. Script-implicit questions, as opposed to text-implicit questions, require the reader to use his prior knowledge in formulating answers. One script-implicit question you might ask after students have read the Momaday biography is, "How would you feel if, like Momaday, you often found yourself in situations in which your background and experiences were very different from those of others?" Obviously, this question is prompted by the Momaday biography, but much of the answer must come from the reader's schemata.

Another way to look at questions is in terms of who creates them. As we have noted, questions can be either teacher generated or student generated. The questions we posed for *No Copycats Allowed!* and for the Momaday biography are examples of teacher-generated questions. Student-generated questions evolve from students' interests and their need or desire to know. After reading Avi's *The True Confessions of Charlotte Doyle,* students might ask, "I wonder what Charlotte's parents will do when they find she's run away?" or "I wonder if a girl like Charlotte really could become a sailor? Would men allow her on the ship? Would she pretend she's a man?" Good readers often ask these kinds of questions without teacher prompting. Through your repeated modeling and with the modeling provided by students who are active questioners, readers who do not initially ask these kinds of questions may begin to.

Discussion

Discussion gives students an opportunity to share their views and listen to the opinions of others. It is a chance to extend students' thinking about the ideas, characters, events, or topics presented in the text and to promote connections between the text and students' lives.

Discussion must always take place in an atmosphere of trust. In order for students to take risks in expressing their thoughts, they need to feel secure in doing so. As we just noted, students should be encouraged and challenged to think about a text, not just to cite facts and figures, but to delve more deeply into meanings and implications. Discussion, which involves speaking and listening, is one way to accomplish this goal.

Of course, good discussions do not just happen. As a number of the authors in *Lively Discussions* (Gambrell and Almasi 1996) explain at length, good discussion requires planning and effort on both your part and your students' part. To become proficient in discussion, students need explicit instruction, modeling, and many opportunities for practice. Students also need feedback from you and their peers on what has been learned in a discussion and on the process of the discussion itself. That is, you and your students need to talk about such matters as all students participating, students listening to each other and respecting each others' opinions, and the group's success in dealing with the topic.

In our previous example, before students read *No Copycats Allowed!,* they wrote tall tales using 5 key words in the story. During reading, students focused their attention on how these words were used in the story. Postreading discussion, then, might focus on what part the ideas represented by some of these words played in the story, and what part they might play in students' lives. For example, they might discuss what part being a copycat played in the story, and they might discuss the sorts of things that sometimes tempt students to become copycats and how they might avoid such temptations.

Writing

Writing is another way to help students become actively involved with the reading selection they have just read, whether for the purpose of better comprehending it or for possible applications of its themes. Writing requires that students really think about what they know. In prereading activities, you might have students write to engage their prior knowledge on a topic, as we suggested in the example on questioning. Postreading activities that involve writing will let them take the new information and ideas they have gleaned from the reading and synthesize or apply them in a new way.

Postreading writing activities should, as is the case with any of the other activities we have been talking about, relate to the initial purposes set for reading the material. If your purpose in having students read a chapter on electricity is for them to understand and remember what they read about electricity, then having them write a summary for each of the sections of the chapter is a useful writing activity. If your purpose is to have students respond personally to a text, you might ask them to write a paragraph telling how a certain poem made them feel.

Reading selections can be the springboard for many kinds of creative writing activities. Say, for instance, before your third graders read the story *Amazing Grace* by Mary Hoffman, you have them brainstorm and write down all they know about heroes. During reading they focus on the heroic qualities of the main character, Grace. At the end of the story, you might ask them to compose a Haiku poem about heroes. As another example, perhaps before reading *The True Confessions of Charlotte Doyle* by Avi, you discuss with students the elements that make for a good adventure story. After students have finished reading the novel, you might suggest that they write a play based on a new adventure for the protagonist, Charlotte.

Dramatics

Because most children love to get into the act, dramatics of all kinds are often popular and they provide a wonderful way to actively involve students in the material they read. Plays, skits, storytelling, pantomimes, and readers' theater are all examples of dramatic activities in which students use their bodies and their voices as well as their minds. Postreading dramatic activities can serve as a welcome break from the quieter, more cerebral sitting-at-the-desk type activities.

Dramatizing an event or portraying a character in a story requires that students not only understand that event or character but make judgments on what to dramatize and how to portray various events and characters. In doing this the student must focus on what are the most important features about that event or character. After they read *Danger Marches to the Palace: Queen Lili'uokalani* by Margo Sorenson, you might have your sixth-grade students get into small groups and prepare skits that show some of the more important and exciting events in this biography. Not only will planning such an activity help students better understand this particular piece of history, it will also give them the opportunity to learn from their classmates' skits. Also, students can write and perform their own plays. As mentioned previously, for example, after reading *The True Confessions of Charlotte Doyle,* students might write a play that illustrates Charlotte's next adventure. Or, you might have groups of students get together and create puppet plays for the folktale *The River Dragon* by D. S. Pattison or for folktales they choose.

Readers' theater, in which students take the role of one of the characters in a story and read that part aloud, is yet another way to get students involved with a text. Good choices for readers' theater are those stories that have several characters and a lot of action and dialogue.

Retelling stories is an excellent way for students to learn about the structure of stories and to encourage literal, interpretive, and creative thinking. Retelling stories can be great fun, but we suggest that you do a good deal of modeling of storytelling before your students make their storytelling debuts. Students do their best retelling and gain the most in terms of understanding the structure of stories when they are very familiar with the story's sequence, characters, problem, and resolution before they attempt to retell it. Certainly, students may want to alter stories when they retell them, and storytelling offers some excellent opportunities for creativity; but students will profit from knowing what changes they are making and why they are making them.

Artistic and Nonverbal Activities

Technology

A myriad of activities are included in this category. Media productions such as videos, slide shows, and photographic displays are examples of artistic postreading activities. For instance, after your fifth graders read the biography *Lincoln: A Photobiography* by Russell Freedman, they might create their own photo biographies of contemporary celebrities by clipping photos from magazines and newspapers, pasting them in a booklet, and writing simple texts to go with them.

Drawing, painting, cutting and pasting, working with clay or play-dough, weaving, and making collages are other sorts of artistic activities that can be used to enhance or extend a reading selection. After you read *The River Dragon* by D. S. Pattison to a kindergarten or first-grade class, students might enjoy a cooperative effort in which they paste colored paper "scales" onto a dragon that you have outlined on a large sheet of butcher paper and paint or draw the details of the dragon's face.

Another frequently used activity in this category involves some sort of graphic presentation—constructing charts, trees, maps, diagrams, schematics, and the like. For instance, after reading one or more of Beverly Cleary's *Ramona* books, third graders might draw family trees of the families portrayed in the books as well as the students' own family trees, or they might make a chart that lists family members and their relationships to each other.

Other artistic and nonverbal activities involve bringing in artifacts or specimens or constructing models that are relevant to the reading selection. For example, after reading the informational book, *Insect Metamorphosis* by Ron and Nancy Goor, fourth graders might begin a class insect collection; and, after reading a chapter on the California missions, they might draw a mural or diorama, or construct models of the missions.

Application and Outreach Activities

The final class of postreading activities we list here is application and outreach activities. These include concrete and direct applications—cooking something after reading a recipe—and less direct ones—attempting to change something after reading about it in a story. For example, after third graders read *Brother Eagle, Sister Sky* written by Chief Seattle and illustrated by Susan Jeffers, they might decide they want to work out a plan to change students' attitudes and behavior with regard to the environment— at school, at home, and in the community.

Application and outreach activities can take students beyond the school setting—to a field trip or a museum after reading *From the Mixed-up Files of Mrs. Basil E. Frankweiler* by E. L. Konigsburg, for example, or collecting food or clothing after reading a newspaper article about a homeless family. Moreover, the more you can tie reading to the world outside of school, the more you will give purpose to reading and to school itself.

Wrapping Up Postreading

Again, postreading activities are those things you do to help students go beyond the text, to do something with the material they read, something that will help them see the relevance of reading, how it relates to their own lives and to the wider world around them. These activities will also help them remember better what they read, provide opportunities to express themselves in a variety of ways, and give them opportunities to see how others interpret selections. As was true with prereading and during-reading, postreading activities are determined by your students, the selection, and your purposes, and will grow out of and complement the prereading and during-reading activities.

The range of postreading options is limited only by you and your students' imagination and enthusiasm. Below are sample postreading activities designed to follow the prereading and during-reading activities we have presented for *Journey*. As you read through the samples, think about what kinds of activities the students are involved in, what function these activities serve in helping students understand and appreciate the text, and how the activities relate to the students, the selection, and the purposes, as well as to the prereading and during-reading activities.

SAMPLE POSTREADING ACTIVITIES

DISCUSSION, JOURNAL SHARING, AND PHOTOGRAPHY PROJECT

The students: Fourth-grade students of high reading ability in an ethnically diverse urban class that includes three ESL students.

The selection: *Journey* by Patricia MacLachlan. When their mother goes off, leaving Cat and Journey with their grandparents, they feel as if their past has been erased until Grandfather finds a way to restore it for them by taking family photographs.

The purposes: To connect story themes to students' lives and extend these to the classroom and beyond, and to give students an opportunity to express themselves in an artistic way.

The procedure: After students have finished reading the novel, discuss the ways in which cameras, photographs, and photography were used in the story and how these uses were similar to those that students described in responding to the prereading questionnaire. For example, some students may have been given a camera that someone else in the family didn't want, as happened with Cat and Grandfather in the story. Students may also have found, as Journey did, that photos sometimes reveal things they didn't notice at the time the picture was taken. Then, discuss how picture taking in the novel and the students' own experiences are different. For example, students may take pictures only at special occasions, while Grandfather and Journey took pictures of seemingly ordinary occurrences. Next, encourage students to share some of their journal entries. Finally, after they have read and talked about their entries, discuss the question, "How did Grandfather's photographs help Journey?"

As a culminating activity, encourage students to bring cameras to school to take candid photos of their classmates as they go about their normal daily activities. (If students don't have cameras, provide one for their use and allow each student to take one or two pictures.) After the photos have been developed, have students create a photo history or profile of the class, either by displaying the photos in an album or on a bulletin board. Such displays of students' work provide them with real audiences for what they have created and can be a very important part of any activity in which students generate a product.

PUTTING IT ALL TOGETHER

On the following pages, we present a sample Scaffolded Reading Experience that takes students through the three phases of reading activities with a single selection. As you read the prereading, during-reading, and postreading activities, think about what is being accomplished in each. Does it pique student interest? Does it build prior knowledge? Are students given a chance to work with concepts or vocabulary before they meet them in the text? Do students know why they are doing a particular task? Are students being led to consider how a selection might relate to their lives? Are students being read to, or are they reading orally or silently? Are students focusing on certain elements in the text as they read? Are students given opportunities to respond to and interact with the text? Do the activities extend students' thinking about ideas, events, or characters? Are students being encouraged to make connections between text ideas and real life? Are students being given a chance to express themselves in a variety of ways—through art, writing, discussion, drama, outreach?

SAMPLE OF PRE-, DURING-, AND POSTREADING ACTIVITIES FOR A SINGLE SELECTION

The students: Low to average second graders, heterogeneous class, suburban setting.

The selection: *Nate the Great* by Marjorie Weinman Sharmat. Nate solves the mystery of Annie's missing picture.

PREREADING: MOTIVATING AND SETTING PURPOSES

The purposes: To pique students' interest in reading the selection, and to introduce or build on students' concept of a detective. (This particular prereading activity was adapted from Graves and Graves 1994.)

The procedure: When you have the children's attention, without saying anything, place several items on a table in students' view. (Items might include a book, chalkboard eraser, hat, marker, and other small objects.) Next, write the word *detective* on the chalkboard. (If you're a bit of a ham, you might even dress the part of a detective, perhaps donning a fedora.) Point to the word *detective* and ask, "What is a detective?" Let children give their answers. Then, ask, "What must a detective be?" Before they have a chance to answer, take out a magnifying glass and act out being observant. If children don't guess *observant,* explain that detectives must be observant. They must look very carefully at things, people, and places—searching for clues to help solve the cases that people hire them to solve.

   After you have made this point, put the items you have placed on the table into a grocery bag and have the children see how observant they were by naming as many items as they can. When they name an item, ask them to tell as many things as they can about that item, and then remove it from the bag and set it on the table. Do this until children have identified all the items and the bag is empty. Explain that the reason you are talking about detectives and being observant is because they are going to read a story about a detective named Nate the Great. Show children the book and the cover illustration, which shows Nate wearing a Sherlock Holmes type hat and jacket and carrying a magnifying glass. Tell students that when they read the story you want them to think about all the things Nate does to show he is observant, that is, a good observer. Remind students that good detectives are observant. They notice details about who, what, when, where, how, and why.

DURING READING: PROVIDING CUES TO STUDENTS AS THEY ARE READING—QUESTIONING

The purpose: To help students develop questioning techniques in order to better understand and enjoy a detective story.

The procedure: Before students begin reading the story on their own, read the first few pages of the book, which introduces Nate and the other main character, Annie, and the problem (Annie has lost a picture and wants Nate to find it).

Next, tell students you are going to play the reporter game. This activity, a modified version of Mary Shoop's Inquest Procedure (1986), is one in which students become news reporters who interview the characters in the story. This procedure encourages students to ask and answer questions during reading. For purposes here, we are assuming students have done this activity before and are quite familiar with how it works.

Appoint students to assume the roles of the two main characters, Nate and Annie, and several reporters who will take the roles of Reporter Who, Reporter What, Reporter Where, Reporter When, Reporter How, and Reporter Why. Depending on how many students are reading the story, you may assign more than one student to assume the roles of the various reporters. Reporter Who will ask a *who* question of the characters. Reporter What will ask a *what* question of the characters, and so on. Also, as students read through portions of the story and conduct their interviews, you can have them change their roles for the next section. Here are some questions the reporters might ask Nate after they read the first few pages of the story.

Reporter Who: Nate, who did you get a call from?

Nate: Annie.

Reporter What: What did Annie ask you?

Nate: To find her missing picture.

Reporter Where: Where did Annie call from?

Nate: Her house.

Reporter When: When did Annie call?

Nate: In the morning.

Reporter How: How do you know it was morning?

Nate: Because I had just eaten breakfast! And I eat breakfast in the morning.

Reporter Why: Why do you think Annie called you about her missing picture?

Nate: Because I'm Nate the Great. I have found lost balloons, books, slippers, chickens, even a goldfish.

Have students read through the story silently, stopping twice more to conduct their interviews. At the end of the story, have students evaluate their questions and answers. Remind them that asking good questions while they read will help them enjoy the story because they will have a better understanding of the story and its characters.

POSTREADING: QUESTIONING AND DISCUSSION

The purposes: To follow up on the initial concept that detectives are observant and to provide an opportunity for students to analyze a story character.

The procedure: After students have read the story (probably the day following the Inquest Procedure), discuss whether Nate was observant and why they think he was or was not. What did he observe that helped him solve the case?

Explain to students that now they are going to get the chance to give Nate a report card as a character. Doing this will help them see how we learn about characters through the things they do and say in a story. On the chalkboard or overhead projector, display a Literary Report Card (Johnson and Louis 1987) tailored to fit the story *Nate the Great.*

As a group activity, have students decide on grades for each of the qualities listed and give examples supporting the grades from the story. Write students' comments on the board or overhead. We have included a sample report card here. Examples students might come up with are shown in italics.

Morningside Elementary School

Student: Nate

G—Good   S—Satisfactory   N—Needs to Improve

Area	Grade	Comments
is observant	G	watched Fang bury a bone
		saw Rosalind had cat hair all over her
		noticed Rosalind had cat pictures on her walls
		noticed Annie's brother was covered with red paint
		noticed one of the painting's on Annie's brother's wall was orange
is smart	G	knew that red and yellow make orange
is thoughtful	G	left his mother a note
is obedient	G	puts on his rubber boots because he knows his mother wants him to

---

CONCLUDING REMARKS

When it comes to planning reading activities that are going to prepare, guide, and enrich your students' reading experience with a particular selection, you need remember only six things.

Students	Prereading Activities
Selection	During-Reading Activities
Purpose	Postreading Activities

Once you have identified your *students'* concerns, interests; become familiar with the *selection*—its topics, themes, and vocabulary; and know your *purpose*—what you expect students to know, feel, or do as a result of reading the selection; then, you can begin selecting and planning *activities.*

Be enthusiastic and excited about the selection as well as the activities you have planned for fostering a successful reading experience for your students. Your enthusiasm will be contagious. Let your students in on why they are doing the activities, how these activities will help them learn something new, interesting, or exciting from their reading material, and how the activities will help them read for meaning and pleasure. Reading is a wonderful lifelong activity; and it is lifelong readers we are trying to make of our children.

SELF-CHECK

1. Name three factors that will influence your thinking as you plan reading activities for your students.

2. Describe the role that purpose plays in planning reading activities.

3. Explain how a specific reading selection might influence purposes for reading.

4. Name the three categories of reading activities considered in this chapter.

5. Name the seven types of prereading activities listed in this chapter.

6. Explain what it means to activate readers' background knowledge and how this helps them read effectively.

7. Describe an activity you might use to activate prior knowledge.

8. Explain the functions of prequestioning and predicting activities.

9. Describe when and how you might use oral reading in your classroom.

10. Describe a during-reading cuing activity you might use with fourth-grade students.

11. Name the seven categories of postreading activities listed in this chapter.

12. Explain the value of discussion as a postreading activity, and discuss some of the steps you can take to foster students' discussion skills.

13. Suppose your fifth-grade students were about to read a biography of Abraham Lincoln. Describe two prereading activities you might engage your students in.

14. Assume your class has two ESL students. Describe what sorts of during-reading activities you might provide to accommodate these students' special needs.

15. Suppose your second graders have read a number of folktales. Describe three different types of postreading activities they might engage in.

REFERENCES

Alvermann, D. E., Dillon, D. R. and O'Brien, D. G. (1987). *Using discussion to promote reading comprehension.* Newark, DE: International Reading Association. A very useful introduction to discussion techniques.

Anderson, R. C. (1984). Role of the reader's schema in comprehension, learning, and memory. In Anderson, R. C., Osborn, J. and Tierney, R. J. (eds.), *Learning to read in American schools.* Hillsdale, NJ: Lawrence Erlbaum, pp. 243–258. A concise and very readable discussion of schema theory.

Baker, L., Afflerbach, P. and Reinking, D. (eds.). (1996). *Developing engaged readers in school and home communities*. Mahwah, NJ: Lawrence Erlbaum. This collection deals with important affective considerations in reading, such matters as engagement and motivation.

Beach, R. W. (1993). *A teacher's introduction to reader-response theories*. Urbana, IL: National Council of Teachers of English. A sophisticated look at modern response theories.

Gambrell, L. B. and Almasi, J. F. (eds.). (1996). Lively discussions: *Fostering engaged reading*. Newark, DE: International Reading Association. The chapters in this collection present many perspectives on discussion.

Graves, M. F. and Avery, P. G. (1997). Scaffolding students' reading of history. *The Social Studies, 88,* 134–138. Description and rationale for a scaffolded reading experience for a history chapter.

Graves, M. F. and Graves, B. B. (1994). *Scaffolding reading experiences to promote success*. Norwood, MA: Christopher-Gordon. A flexible framework for designing reading activities and the model behind the general approach taken in this chapter.

Hogan, K. and Pressley, M. (eds.). (1997). *Scaffolding student learning: Instructional approaches and issues*. Cambridge, MA: Brookline Books. A rich and varied collection of articles about scaffolding students' efforts.

Johnson, T. and Louis, D. (1987). *Literacy through literature*. Portsmouth, NH: Heinemann. Champions the role of literature in promoting literacy.

Langer, J. A. (1995). *Envisioning literature: Literacy understanding and literature instruction*. Newark, DE and New York: International Reading Association and Teachers College Press. Presents Langer's views on reading literature, thinking about it, and teaching it growing out of her research at the National Research Center on Literature Teaching and Learning.

Martin, B., Jr. (1992). Afterword. In Cullinan, B. (ed.), *Invitation to read: More children's literature in the reading program*. Newark, DE: International Reading Association. A telling statement by a well-known author and educator.

McMahon, S. E. and Raphael, T. E. (eds.). (1997). *The book club connection: Literacy learning and classroom talk*. Newark, DE and New York: International Reading Association and Teachers College Press. Describes and critiques a well-planned and extensively researched approach that makes student-led groups the center of reading instruction.

Moore, S. A. and Moore, D. W. (1990). Possible sentences. In Dishner, E. K, Bean, T. W. and Readence, J. E. (eds.), *Reading in the contents areas: Improving classroom instruction* (3rd ed.). Dubuque, IA: Kendal Hunt. An engaging approach to teaching vocabulary from informational selections.

Pearson, P. D. and Johnson, D. D. (1978). *Teaching reading comprehension*. New York: Holt, Rinehart and Winston. The first text to present the contemporary approach to teaching reading comprehension.

Reasoner, C. (1976). *Releasing children to literature* (rev. ed.). New York: Dell. Presents a variety of ideas for involving children in literature.

Rosenblatt, L. M. (1978). *The reader, the text, the poem: The transactional theory of the literary work.* Carbondale, IL: Southern Illinois University. A classic book by the originator of the response approach to literature.

Saul, E. W. (ed.). (1994). *Non-fiction for the classroom: Milton Meltzer on writing, history, and social responsibility.* Newark, DE and New York: International Reading Association and Teachers College Press. Much of the reading done in schools is of fiction. This collection of essays by a widely respected writer discusses the importance and place of non-fiction.

Shoop, M. (1986). Inquest: A listening and reading strategy. *The Reading Teacher, 39,* 670–675. Describes an approach that puts students in a very active role.

Towell, J. (1997–1998). Fun with vocabulary. *The Reading Teacher, 51,* 356–358. Presents 10 strategies and activities for enjoyable vocabulary activities.

Watts, S. M. and Graves, M. F. (1997). Fostering middle school students' understanding of challenging texts. *The Middle School Journal, 29*(1), 45–51. Detailed example of a scaffolded reading experience for a non-fiction example.

CHILDREN'S BOOKS CITED

Avi. (1990). *The true confessions of Charlotte Doyle.* New York: Orchard.

Carlson, J. (1989). *Harriet Tubman, call to freedom.* New York: Fawcett Columbine.

Chief Seattle. Illus. by Jeffers, S. K. (1991). *Brother eagle, sister sky.* New York: Dial.

Freedman, R. (1987). *Lincoln: A photobiography.* New York: Clarion.

Globe. (1993). *Native American biographies.* New York: Globe.

Goor, R. and Goor, N. (1990). *Insect metamorphosis: From egg to adult.* New York: Atheneum.

Graves, B. (1998). *No copycats allowed!* New York: Hyperion.

Hoffman, M. Illus. by Birch, C. (1991). *Amazing Grace.* New York: Dial.

Konigsburg, E. L. (1967). *From the mixed-up files of Mrs. Basil E. Frankweiler.* New York: Atheneum.

Lobel, A. (1977). *Mouse soup.* New York: Scholastic.

MacLachlan, P. (1985). *Sarah, plain and tall.* New York: HarperCollins.

MacLachlan, P. (1991). *Journey.* New York: Delacorte Press.

Pattison, D. S. Illus. by Tseng, J. and Tseng, M. (1991). *The river dragon.* New York: Lothrop, Lee & Shepard.

Schwartz, A. (1991). *Camper of the week.* New York: Orchard.

Sharmat, M. W. (1972). *Nate the great.* New York: Dell.

Sorenson, M. (1997). *Danger marches to the palace: Queen Lili'uokalani.* Logan, IA: Perfection Learning.

Van Allsburg, C. (1991). *The wretched stone.* Boston: Houghton Mifflin.

8 Teaching Comprehension Strategies

Suppose you are reading the newspaper and you come to a sentence you do not understand. What do you do? Perhaps you read on, hoping that the next sentence or two will make the meaning clear. Or, perhaps you reread the sentence or go back to the sentences preceding it.

Or, suppose it is Saturday and you have two tests coming up on Monday. You need to read a novel, three textbook chapters, and four journal articles. What do you do? You know you won't have time to read and study each in depth, so you must use some efficient approaches to understand and remember what you read. The novel you read quickly, skipping over lengthy descriptions and dialogue and concentrating on the basics of setting, plot, and characters. As you read, you look for recurring themes. When you finish, you might ask questions like, "Why was the protagonist so driven?" and "What was the author's main theme?" Before you read the chapters and articles, you might think about points your instructor emphasized; while you read, you might take notes or underline material relevant to these points; and, after your first reading, you might reread those sections that are most relevant to the course.

What you have done in both of these cases is to use reading strategies —deliberate plans that help you understand and recall what you read.

LOOKING AHEAD

In Chapter 7, we dealt with ways in which you can help students understand, enjoy, and learn from specific selections they are reading. In this chapter, we deal with ways in which you can assist students in internalizing strategies that they can use independently in understanding the variety of texts they will read in the future. To use the terms of Robert Tierney and James Cunningham (1984), the topic of the last chapter was "learning from text," while that of this chapter is "learning to learn from text."

This chapter is divided into five parts. In the first part, we define reading-comprehension strategies, note some of their characteristics, and describe eight key comprehension strategies and give a brief example of each. In the second part, we consider some central concepts underlying the approach to strategy instruction suggested here.

In the third part, we describe a specific approach to teaching comprehension strategies and present an example of instruction that follows that model. In the fourth part, we describe three sequences of strategies that have been widely recommended.

Finally, we consider the matter of your deciding which strategies to teach.

KEY CONCEPTS

- Characteristics of reading-comprehension strategies

- The distinction between instruction designed to help students deal with specific selections and instruction in comprehension strategies

- Key comprehension strategies

- Instructional concepts to consider in designing strategy instruction

- The time required for effective strategy instruction

- Possible steps for the first day of instruction in a new strategy

- How comprehension strategy instruction changes over time

- The constructive nature of good comprehension strategy instruction

- Review and follow-up procedures to be used after initial instruction in a strategy

- Some widely recommended sequences of comprehension strategies

READING-COMPREHENSION STRATEGIES

As defined by David Pearson and his colleagues (Pearson, Roehler, Dole and Duffy 1992), reading-comprehension strategies are "conscious and flexible plans that readers apply and adopt to a variety of texts and tasks." They are processes readers engage in for the purpose of better understanding and remembering what they read. One strategy, for example, is determining what is important. Particularly when reading informational material to gain knowledge they need to use, readers must determine just what it is they need to learn. In the opening scenario of the chapter, we suggested that one way you might identify the important information in a chapter you are reading for a course is to consider which points in the chapter the instructor has emphasized. Another way would be to read the chapter introduction and summary, and still another way would be to skim through the chapter seeing what was highlighted in the headings and subheadings. Readers who are adept at determining what is important in a reading selection have these and a variety of other strategies available, and they employ whichever strategies best fit each reading situation they encounter. For all students, including ESL students and students with special educational needs, strategies lead to independence in reading. And a large and robust body of literature has clearly demonstrated that strategy instruction can be effective (see, for example, Pearson et al. 1992, Pressley and Woloshyn 1995, Rosenshine 1995).

Characteristics of Comprehension Strategies

In this section, we consider several characteristics of comprehension strategies, some of which are identified in Pearson's definition and some of which are not. As the discussion will reveal, these characteristics are not absolutes but vary from one situation to another.

Strategies Are Conscious Efforts

At least when they are initially taught, the strategies discussed here are conscious efforts that you ask students to deliberately engage in. For example, after teaching students how to make inferences while reading, you will sometimes ask them to make inferences about specific aspects of material they are reading, and they will sometimes deliberately pause as they are reading and realize that they have come to a point at which they need to make an inference. With practice and experience, however, some strategies are likely to become increasingly habitual and automatic; for example, readers will frequently make inferences without realizing they are doing so. Nevertheless, even well learned strategies can be brought to consciousness and placed under the control of the reader.

Strategies Are Flexible

Flexibility and adaptability are hallmarks of strategies. The very essence of teaching students to be strategic is teaching them that they need to use strategies in ways that are appropriate for particular situations. For example, the strategy of rereading can be used in a variety of ways: A student can reread the whole of a selection immediately after first reading it; she can reread *parts* of a selection immediately after first reading it; or she can reread the whole of a selection a week after first reading it. Whether one or another of these approaches to rereading is most useful will depend on the student, the selection she is reading, and her purpose in reading it.

Strategies Should Be Applied Only When Appropriate

Part of teaching students strategies is teaching them to apply a strategy only when the reading situation makes the use of a particular strategy appropriate. For example, the strategy we just mentioned, rereading, is often useful. However, if a student is reading a straightforward short story, understands it perfectly well, and is not preparing for a test of some sort, she certainly does not need to reread it. In fact, unless the student had some specific reason for rereading the story, rereading would probably be an inappropriate activity here.

Strategies Are Widely Applicable

Many strategies can be used across a wide range of ages, abilities, and reading material. For example, it is appropriate for a first grader to orally summarize something like Stephen Kellogg's *Best Friends.* It is appropriate for a fifth grader to summarize the major events leading up to the Boston Tea Party. It is appropriate for a graduate student to summarize the major tenets of the reader response approach to literature as they appear in something like Louise Rosenblatt's *The Reader, the Text, the Poem.*

Strategies Can Be Overt or Covert

Some strategies involve readers in creating some sort of observable product, while others involve mental operations that cannot be directly observed. Summarizing, for example, is a strategy that often results in a written record of what was read. Determining what is important, on the other hand, is a strategy that frequently does not result in the reader's writing down anything. When you are initially teaching a strategy, you may frequently want students to produce an observable record of their use of the strategy so that you know that they are able to use it. However, much of the time, the strategies students use will be solely mental processes.

Key Comprehension Strategies

In defining comprehension strategies and discussing some of their characteristics, we have mentioned several specific strategies. Here, we define and give an example of each of eight strategies that are particularly worth teaching. Fortunately, there is substantial agreement on a core of key strategies that students need to master (Pearson et al. 1992; Pressley, Johnson, Symons, McGoldrick and Kurita 1989), and these key strategies are the ones we describe here.

These strategies include using prior knowledge, asking and answering questions, determining what is important, summarizing, making inferences, dealing with graphic information, imaging, and monitoring comprehension. Each of these strategies involves readers in actively constructing meaning as they read. Additionally, many of them result in readers transforming ideas from one form to another or in their generating relationships among ideas, activities that support comprehension and memory. For example, when readers summarize they must transform the author's text into something more concise, and when they make inferences they must relate information in the text to information they already know.

Using Prior Knowledge

When using this strategy, readers purposely bring to consciousness information that relates to what they are going to read or what they are reading. What readers are doing here is putting a set of schemata into place, establishing a framework for the new information they will encounter in the text.

Let us say, for instance, a second grader is perusing the library shelf and picks up a book titled *Mistakes That Worked* by Charlotte Foltz Jones. Before she begins reading the book, she thinks about what she knows about mistakes. As she thinks, she recalls mistakes she's made and mistakes others have made. But she really can't think of any "mistakes that worked." Thus, she begins to read the book with the realization that most mistakes don't work and that the book is going to present something different, some information on mistakes that have worked. What the student is doing is using her prior knowledge to set up expectations about what she might encounter in the text. When she reads about one of the mistakes that worked, she will be able to contrast it to her own mistakes, and making that contrast will help her both understand what she is reading and remember what she has read.

Asking and Answering Questions

Using this strategy, the reader poses questions prior to reading a selection or as she is reading the selection and then attempts to answer the questions while reading. Employing this strategy virtually guarantees that reading is an active process. It also serves to focus the reader's attention. A reader who has asked a particular set of questions will be particularly attentive to the information that answers those questions.

Consider a sixth grader preparing to read a chapter on nutrition in a health text. As the first step, she might survey the chapter and find these headings: Nutrients and the US RDA, The Seven Dietary Guidelines, Shopping for Groceries, and Preventing Disease through Proper Diet. Then, she might pose one or two questions about each heading: "What are nutrients?" "What is the US RDA?" "What are the seven dietary guidelines?" "Do I follow them in my diet?" "Should I follow them?" "How is shopping for groceries related to nutrition?" and "Can a proper diet prevent all disease?" As she reads, the student will get answers to some of her questions, find that others are not answered in the chapter, and pose and answer additional questions. As a result of this active involvement, she is likely to learn a good deal.

Making Inferences

When they apply this strategy, readers infer meanings by using information from the text and their existing knowledge of the world, their schemata, to fill in bits of information that are not explicitly stated in the text. No text is ever fully explicit, and thus readers must constantly make inferences to understand what they are reading. By teaching students to make inferences, you are helping them learn to use their existing knowledge along with the information in the text to build meaning.

Suppose that a fifth grader is reading a science text and learns that woodchucks build deep burrows and huddle in them in large groups during the winter. Knowing that a fair number of animals hibernate, she might infer that woodchucks hibernate in their burrows. Knowing that ground temperature remains stable and reasonably warm at depths greater than three or four feet, she might further infer that woodchucks make their burrows deep in order to take advantage of this warmth.

Determining What Is Important

Making use of this strategy requires that readers understand what they have read and make judgments about what is and is not important. As Marilyn Chambliss and Robert Calfee (in press) explain in detail, most texts contain much more information than a reader can focus on and learn. Consequently, determining what is important is a crucial and frequently required strategy. Among other things, determining what is important is something students need to learn to do before they can summarize a selection. Only by determining what is important can students know what to include and what to exclude in a summary.

Sometimes, texts include direct cues to what is important—overviews, headings, summaries, and the like. In many cases, however, students need to rely on their prior knowledge to infer what is important in a particular selection.

For instance, while reading the short story "The Kite" by Arnold Lobel, a first grader might think about the most important characters and events in the story and come up with the following set of important points:

Frog is helping Toad fly a kite.

The kite doesn't fly on the first try.

Toad wants to give up, but Frog tells him to try again.

The kite doesn't fly.

Frog tells him to try a third time and still the kite won't get off the ground.

Frog tells Toad to make one more try.

This time the kites flies.

Together, these important points constitute the essence of the story.

Summarizing

As we just noted, using this strategy requires students to first determine what is important and then condense it and put it in their own words. Ann

Brown and Jeanne Day (1983) have suggested some basic rules for summarizing. Slightly modified, these include

- Deleting trivial or irrelevant information
- Deleting redundant information
- Providing a superordinate term for members of a category
- Finding and using generalizations the author has made
- Creating your own generalizations when the author has not provided them

The above list of important ideas from "The Kite" constitutes a good summary of the story. By dropping less important details and focusing on the most important aspects of the story, the student was able to understand what was taking place. An even briefer summary, one that focuses on the theme of the story, is also possible: "Frog was trying to help Toad. By listening to Frog and doing what he said, and by continuing to try instead of quitting, Toad was able to get his kite into the air."

Dealing with Graphic Information

When they employ this strategy, readers give conscious attention to the visual information supplied by the author. Before youngsters learn to read, they are drawn to and fascinated by the visual material books offer. Teaching them when, how, and why to use the illustrations, graphs, maps, diagrams, and other visuals that accompany selections will enable them to make optimal use of the visual aids texts often provide.

History texts, for example, almost always contain maps that include a legend to the symbols they employ. Students need to learn that maps usually have legends, the kind of information legends normally contain, where legends are typically placed, and how to interpret them.

Imaging and Creating Visual Representations

Using this strategy, readers create visual representations of text either in their mind or by reproducing them on paper or other tangible forms. One kind of imaging occurs when readers visualize people, events, and places. Another kind of imaging consists of visually organizing key ideas in text in a way that graphically displays their relationships. The former type of imaging tends to be used with narrative material, while the latter works particularly well with expository text.

One imaging technique appropriate for intermediate-grade students is constructing semantic maps of key concepts. For example, a semantic map for a chapter on mountains in a geography text might look like that shown in Figure 8–1.

Monitoring Comprehension

Good readers are metacognitive; that is, they monitor their comprehension. Monitoring comprehension is a more general strategy than any of those

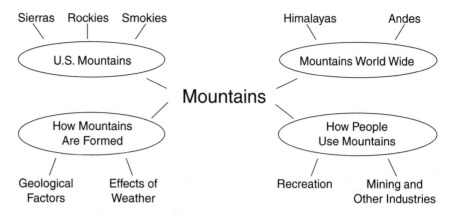

Figure 8–1.   Semantic Map of Mountains

discussed thus far. In monitoring comprehension, readers keep track of what they wish to gain from a text and of their understanding—or lack of understanding—of the text as they are reading. They then use whatever strategies they need to maintain or improve comprehension. You might think of monitoring strategies as the employer and the other sorts of strategies as the employees.

Readers who monitor their comprehension are asking these kinds of questions: "Am I understanding what the author is saying? What do I do if I don't understand something I'm reading? What could I be doing to understand better what the author is saying? Can I do something that will help me remember the material better?"

If, for example, you were reading along and realized that you did not really understand what you were reading, what would you do? What fix-up strategy would you use? In most cases, you would probably reread as much material as necessary in order to build meaning. While you were reading, if you realized there are words whose meanings are unclear to you, you might choose to look them up. If there were illustrations or other graphic material, you might look at those. At some point, you might consciously check your prior knowledge to see how what you already know fits information gleaned from the text. You might try to reproduce a visual image of the material in your head. In brief, you would do whatever is necessary to arrive at a satisfactory understanding of what you were reading. This, of course, is precisely what you want to prepare students to do.

The strategies described here—using prior knowledge, asking and answering questions, determining what is important, summarizing, making inferences, dealing with graphic information, imaging, and monitoring comprehension—will help students reach the goal of understanding and learning from what they read. In learning these strategies, students are internalizing a way of reading and thinking that is active, critical, and reflective. Having learned this mode of thinking, students will be both able and inclined to engage in a variety of reading and learning strategies to understand, appreciate, and learn from what they read. It should be noted that students will differ in the rate at which they learn the strategies that have been described. We believe it is more important for students to have a thorough understanding of fewer strategies than to have a superficial understanding of a larger number of strategies. While the ultimate goal is for students to have several strategies to apply, what is most important is that they are able to effectively use the strategies they have.

CONCEPTS UNDERLYING OUR APPROACH TO TEACHING STRATEGIES

Up to this point, we have discussed a variety of characteristics of reading-comprehension strategies and eight key strategies. In this section, we describe a number of concepts that underlie the approach to strategy instruction we suggest. We emphasize these concepts based on our own experiences and the work of a number of educators, including Donald Deshler and Jean Schumaker (1993), Janice Dole and her colleagues (Dole, Brown and Trathen 1995), Pearson et al. (1992), and Pressley and Woloshyn (1995). Four important concepts—direct explanation, cognitive modeling, scaffolding, and the gradual release of responsibility—were discussed in the Instructional Considerations section of Chapter 3. We encourage you to reread that section of the Chapter to refamiliarize yourself with them. Here we discuss eight additional concepts crucial to success in teaching comprehension strategies. As you will realize as you study these concepts, they are also important to consider when teaching word-recognition strategies—which we discussed in Chapter 5—and when teaching vocabulary-learning strategies—which we discussed in Chapter 6.

The Teacher's Mediational Role

Because learning is a constructive process in which much of what the learner understands is actually constructed by the learner, it often happens that you explain or demonstrate one thing, but some students understand something quite different. In teaching a strategy, you must constantly be alert to how students are interpreting your instruction and be ready to assist students who get a bit off track. This means that after you discuss a strategy or demonstrate it to students, you need to question them or ask them to demonstrate their use of the strategy so that you can see whether they have appropriately interpreted the strategy and understand how to use it. If this reveals any misunderstandings, these should be cleared up before students internalize them.

Cooperative Learning

Cooperative learning puts students with varying abilities and knowledge bases together so that they can provide scaffolding for each other as they work toward mastering strategies. In initially teaching a strategy, it usually makes sense to let students work together on the strategy before requiring them to deal with it individually. Thus, after you have explained and modeled a strategy such as summarizing, you might have students work in pairs or in groups of three or four as they make their first few attempts at summarizing material.

Authenticity and Quality of Texts

It makes good sense to have students learn to use strategies with the kinds of selections they will typically read. At the same time, during the initial stages of instruction, it will be useful to work with fairly short texts in order to focus students' attention. For example, it is often convenient to put a paragraph of text on an overhead so that you and the students can all see it as you discuss the strategy and how to apply it to the text. Later, of course, students need to work with increasingly lengthy texts. Regardless of whether shorter or more lengthy texts are used, remember that students will have difficulty applying strategies to text that they cannot adequately decode and read with some fluency. It is impossible to draw inferences, for example, from text that is not first comprehended at the literal level. Since the focus of instruction is strategy use, students should be working with texts that are not so difficult for them to decode that they will have no mental energy left for strategy application.

Multifaceted and Long-Term Instruction

Strategy instruction needs to be multifaceted and long term. What you are introducing, building, and nurturing are complex procedures, behaviors, and attitudes. These take time to develop and develop differently in different students. If one approach does not work with a particular student or group of students, then another approach needs to be tried. Good strategy instruction also takes patience, commitment, flexibility, and a good dose of perspective and humor. Like many things that are worth having, strategies are often not easily acquired.

Promoting Positive Attitudes and Behaviors

As we just mentioned, strategy instruction promotes certain attitudes and behaviors. If you want your students to use strategies, they need to be motivated to use them. They must understand how using strategies will help them achieve their goals. You can achieve this in part by frequently specifying the utility of the strategy you are teaching and of those that students have already mastered. Students must also learn that, although strategies do require substantial amounts of time and effort, they do not require unreasonable amounts of time and effort. You can help them learn this by thoroughly preparing them to use the strategies you ask them to use and by allowing a good deal of class time for them to work with strategies, particularly with strategies they are just learning.

Connecting Success to Strategy Use

Strategy instruction should also include prompting students to connect their performance gains to their having used strategies. Let us say that a second grader, Julie, comes up to you one morning quite excited. She has just read *Nothing Ever Happens on My Block* by Ellen Raskin.

Prepared for Julie's usual lengthy, rambling retelling you are surprised when she says, "This guy, Chester Filbert, sits on his stoop, see. He says that nothing ever happens on his block. But everything does happen! Witches, fires, robberies. All sorts of stuff. But Chester never even notices!"

"Julie, that's wonderful," you tell her. "Do you know what you have just done? You've used the summarizing strategy. You've told everything important about the story in just a few sentences. Summarizing can help you better understand and remember a lot of what you read."

Practice and Feedback

If students are going to get better at a strategy, they need to practice it in a way that allows you to evaluate their use of the strategy and give them feedback about how they are doing on it. Moreover, they need many opportunities for practice and feedback.

Review

When learning something complex such as comprehension strategies, students need to be given many opportunities to review and solidify what they have learned. Thus, part of your plan for strategy instruction should include systematic review of the strategies you teach. Ideally, students need opportunities to review in the days, weeks, months, and even years that follow their initial experiences with a strategy.

AN APPROACH TO TEACHING STRATEGIES

In this section, we present a specific approach to teaching comprehension strategies. In illustrating the approach, we first describe the components that make up the first day of instruction. Next, we consider how instruction proceeds over the course of a three-week unit. After that, we explain the constructive nature of good strategy instruction. Finally, we discuss the types of review and follow-up activities that are needed to make a strategy a tool that students spontaneously use. Although instruction will vary somewhat with different strategies, different students, and different age groups, the general plan presented is widely applicable.

Components of a Day's Instruction

The activities described in this section are those used on the first day of instruction on a new strategy. In order to make the description concrete, we will deal with a particular strategy—determining what is important—with a class of fourth-grade students. The students may have had some experience with the strategy in previous grades, but we are assuming that this is the first time it is formally taught. We are providing instruction on this particular strategy because these students have recently been having difficulty sifting out less important details and focusing on more important ideas in their science and social studies books. The first day's instruction includes six different components.

Motivation and Interest Building (5 minutes)

To capture students' attention and build interest, introduce the strategy by having students guess the categories represented by various sets of words you write on the board. Choose categories and words of interest to the particular group of students being taught. We have chosen fastfood restaurants, sports that use balls, and sports that don't use balls. Write the word sets on the board underneath unlabeled umbrellas—an idea suggested by James Baumann (1986)—as illustrated in Figure 8–2. Tell students that these words are examples of more general ideas, have them guess what those more general ideas are, and write them in the umbrellas above the sets of examples.

Teacher Explanation (5 minutes)

After students have determined the more general ideas represented by several sets of examples, explain that identifying these ideas is part of a strategy you are going to teach them. At this point, ask students about the reading they have been doing in science and social studies, and discuss some of the challenges they have faced. One of the challenges that is likely to come up is that these books cover a lot of information and it is hard to remember all of it. Explain that the strategy they will learn—determining

What ideas cover each of these?

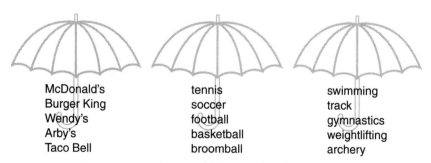

McDonald's	tennis	swimming
Burger King	soccer	track
Wendy's	football	gymnastics
Arby's	basketball	weightlifting
Taco Bell	broomball	archery

Figure 8–2.   First Graphic Used in Determining What Is Important

what is important—will help them to better understand and remember what they read.

Next, explain that what they do when they use this strategy is focus on the most important information and let the less important details fade into the background. Much of the social studies and science material they read contains a great deal of information, and concentrating on only the most important information cuts down on what they need to learn and remember. Tell students that knowing how to determine what is important can make understanding and remembering what they read much easier.

Teacher Modeling (5 to 10 minutes)

Reveal more about how the strategy works by writing a sentence on the board such as, "Matthew Blaine, a fourth-grade student at Ridgeview Elementary School, won first prize in the Rotary Speech Contest with his essay titled, 'What Freedom Means to Me.'" Read the sentence aloud and model the thought processes you might go through in identifying the most important information in the sentence.

> Let's see, what is the main idea the author is communicating in this sentence? The topic seems to be Matthew Blaine. And what is the most important information about Matthew? Winning first prize sounds pretty important. [Circle the phrases *Matthew Blaine* and *won first prize in the Rotary Speech Contest*.] The other information—that he's a fourth-grade student at Ridgeview Elementary School and the title of his essay—are interesting, but not as important. [Cross out *a student at Ridgeview Middle School* and *with his essay titled, "What Freedom Means to Me."*]

Use the umbrella analogy from the previous activity to illustrate that "Matthew Blaine won the Rotary Speech Contest" is more important than the other information in the sentence as shown in Figure 8–3.

Once you have explained the strategy and modeled it, check to see if students were following you by asking a few students to explain the strategy and tell why it is worth knowing.

*Matthew Blaine won
the Rotary Speech Contest*

a student at Ridgeview Middle School
essay titled, "What Freedom Means to Me"

Figure 8–3.   Second Graphic Used in Determining What Is Important

**Large Group Student Participation
and Teacher Mediation (10 to 20 minutes)**
Put a paragraph from one of the students' social studies or science texts
on the overhead and read it aloud. The paragraph should be one in which
the important information stands out. The sample paragraph below is
taken from *Scaly Babies: Reptiles Growing Up* by Ginny Johnson and Judy
Cutchins.

> For many people, the word *reptile* describes an ugly, slippery,
> and sometimes dangerous animal. But reptiles are not slimy, and
> most are not dangerous. There are nearly six thousand different
> kinds of these scaly-skinned animals in the world today. It is true
> that some are large and scary-looking and a few are venomous,
> but most reptiles are harmless to humans. Like many wild ani-
> mals, reptiles may strike or bite to defend themselves. But they
> rarely bother a person who has not disturbed or startled them.
> (Johnson and Cutchins 1988, 1)

Ask students what the paragraph is mainly about. (reptiles) Next, ask
them how they determined this. (Everything in the paragraph is about
reptiles.) Have students supply the details about reptiles that are given in
the paragraph and write these on the board as shown in Figure 8–4.

After you have written the details students supply on the board, ask
them which information in the paragraph is the most important? Explain
that all of these details say something about reptiles, but that one is the
most general and important idea, the idea that the author really wants to
get across. Help students determine the most important idea by asking
questions such as these about each of the details: "Is this the most important idea in the paragraph?" "Do the other ideas support this one?" "Do
you think this is the main thing the author is trying to tell you?"

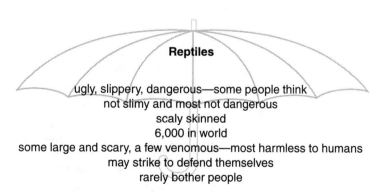

Figure 8–4.   Third Graphic Used in Determining What Is Important

After students have agreed on the most important idea, rewrite the chart on the board to show the most important idea with its supporting details underneath it as shown in Figure 8–5.

Next, work together with students to determine the most important idea in several additional paragraphs in the same book. Call on students to determine what is most important in each paragraph and to explain how they determined that the information they selected is the most important. On the board, create a visual display similar to the one you did for the first paragraph. If students seem to understand the strategy, move to the next step. If not, do some further explaining and modeling.

Cooperative Group Work (10 minutes)

Once large-group questioning indicates that students have a basic understanding of the strategy, they need a chance to practice it. Initially, they can practice in pairs. Remember, this is the first day of instruction and a lot of scaffolding is appropriate. You want to ensure that students are successful and feel successful at this point. Since they have worked only with paragraph-length selections thus far, they should continue with paragraph-length selections in this practice session. Also, since the selections used thus far have been ones in which the important information stood out clearly, the practice paragraphs should also clearly reveal the important information. Two or three such paragraphs might be a good number for this part of the lesson.

Sharing Group Work and Teacher Response and Mediation (10 minutes)

Once students have had an opportunity to use the strategy in pairs, they should share their work with the class. Call on pairs to present the important information they found in the passages and discuss how they deter-

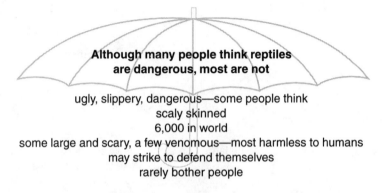

Although many people think reptiles
are dangerous, most are not

ugly, slippery, dangerous—some people think
scaly skinned
6,000 in world
some large and scary, a few venomous—most harmless to humans
may strike to defend themselves
rarely bother people

Figure 8–5.   Fourth Graphic Used in Determining What Is Important

mined this was the crucial information. Monitor their responses carefully and provide feedback and clarification as necessary.

This would conclude the first day's instruction and practice with the strategy. Subsequent days are discussed in the following section.

Overview of a Unit

A typical unit might last three weeks. Although instruction should continue to include a number of the features of the first day's instruction, it should gradually change as students become increasingly competent with the strategy. Here are some of the major ways in which it would change.

Subsequent Instructional Periods Become Shorter
During the first few days of instruction, the instructional periods should be quite lengthy, perhaps lasting 45 minutes or so. After the first few days, the periods of instruction get shorter, with those at the end of the unit perhaps lasting 20 minutes.

Instruction Becomes Less Concentrated Each Week
During the first week, students should work on the strategy nearly every day; then, with each successive week, they should work on it less frequently. For example, during the first week there might be four days of instruction, during the second week three days, and during the third week two days.

Students Do More of the Work
Particularly on the first day of instruction and to a lesser extent in the first few days of instruction, the teacher bears the burden of much of the work. In other words, the teacher heavily scaffolds instruction. Teacher explanation, teacher modeling, and teacher response and feedback occupy a significant amount of the time. Increasingly, however, the teacher should gradually release responsibility for completing the strategy to students. More and more time is spent on students actually working with the strategy. Also, perhaps after the first week or so, students move from working in pairs to working independently at least some of the time.

Texts Become Longer and More Challenging
In addition to students doing more of the work themselves, over time they need to work with increasingly lengthy and more challenging texts. On the first few days of instruction, students might work with paragraphs; next they might work with one-page texts; then, eventually, they will work with typical chapter-length texts. Similarly, on the first few days, students would work with selections in which the important information stands out prominently, that is, selections in which important information is cued

by titles, headings, or topic sentences. Later, they would work with material in which the important information is less obvious, material more typical of much of what they will read.

Strategies Are Used on Authentic Tasks

Since the purpose of students learning strategies is for them to use the strategies as part of their normal reading experiences, they need to be given increased opportunities, prompts, and encouragement to employ the strategies outside of the context of specific strategy instruction. Such opportunities can be pointed out during class time devoted to reading; during class time devoted to other subjects, such as social studies and mathematics; and when the strategies are likely to be useful for work done outside of class. For example, almost any written report requires that students determine what is important in the material they read for the report.

Students Are Encouraged to Use the Strategies Independently

Once students reach the point where they can routinely use the strategies when you prompt them to do so, you need to repeatedly encourage them to use the strategies without your prompting them. Much of the time, when students set out to read something or encounter a comprehension problem in what they are reading, you will not be there to suggest what strategy they can use to read effectively or to remedy the problem.

The Constructive Nature of Good Strategy Instruction

Conveying the constructivist, interactive, flexible nature of good strategy instruction is difficult on paper, and we want to be certain that our description of strategy instruction thus far has not left some of you thinking of it as rather rigid and teacher centered. Good strategy instruction is neither rigid nor teacher centered. In Figure 8–6, we emphasize this by presenting a set of guidelines for good strategy instruction and a comparison of teacher-dominated instruction to constructivist instruction.

Review and Follow-up Activities

If students are to become permanent strategy users, their use of the strategy needs to be encouraged and nurtured beyond the initial unit of instruction. Three types of follow-up are important.

One- or Two-Day Formal Reviews

It seems appropriate to have one or two formal reviews of the strategy following initial instruction. By formal reviews, we mean 30- to 45-minute instructional sessions in which renewing students' understanding and competency with the strategy is the main topic of the lesson. Assuming that initial instruction in the strategy took place early in the school year, the first

A PORTRAIT OF TEACHER-DOMINATED INSTRUCTION	A PORTRAIT OF CONSTRUCTIVIST INSTRUCTION
The teacher lectures and the students listen.	The teacher and the students interact, with modeling, explanation, and discussion prominent.
Children assume the role of passive, rather than active, participants.	Children assume the role of *active* participants.
It is as if the knowledge the teacher has can be transmitted directly to the students; the metaphor is that of pouring information from one container (the teacher's head) to another (the student's head).	It is understood that the knowledge the teacher has cannot be transmitted directly to the students; the metaphor is that of an instructional conversation between teacher and students.
There is little discussion and give and take.	There is a great deal of discussion and give and take.
Teachers do very little on-the-spot diagnoses of individual students' understanding and progress.	Teachers frequently make on-the-spot diagnoses of individual students' understanding and progress.
The instruction proceeds at a predetermined rate and sequence that is dictated by the curriculum employed in the particular classroom.	The instruction proceeds at a rate and sequence that is dictated by the students' needs and progress.
Teachers appear to follow a script and students are expected to proceed at the same rate.	Lessons are not scripted. Students are expected to proceed at their own rate, with teacher and peer scaffolding facilitating progress.
Skills are emphasized at the expense of understanding.	Understanding is emphasized as strategies are developed.
Students are rarely told about why they practice the activities they do or taught how to monitor and self-regulate their use of the strategies.	Students are always informed about the purposes of the skills they are taught and helped to develop monitoring and self-regulation of the strategies.

Figure 8–6.   Teacher-Dominated and Constructivist Strategy Instruction
The comparison here is from Graves, Juel and Graves (1998) and is modified from descriptions written by Pressley et al. (1992).

review might be given in November and the second review in February or March.

More Frequent Mini-Lessons
In addition to the 30- to 45-minute formal reviews, occasional 5- to 10-minute mini-lessons should be given when the materials students are

working with seem applicable to use of the strategy and a short review seems needed.

Frequent Suggestions to Use the Strategies

Finally, whenever the materials students are using lend themselves to use of a strategy that has been taught, students can be given a brief reminder that the strategy may prove useful.

WIDELY RECOMMENDED SEQUENCES OF STRATEGIES

As we noted earlier in this chapter, in addition to using individual strategies such as those discussed thus far, good strategy users employ sequences of strategies—several individual strategies routinely used as a set—to understand and remember what they read. Three sequences of strategies—the SQ3R Method, the K-W-L Procedure, and Reciprocal Teaching—have been widely recommended for students to use when their goal is to learn from and remember informational material. In the next several sections, we briefly describe each of these sequences and then discuss procedures for teaching them.

The SQ3R Method

The SQ3R Method was originally described by Francis Robinson in 1946 and is probably the best known and most frequently recommended sequence of strategies. The sequence consists of five steps: surveying, questioning, reading, reciting, and reviewing. This sequence is certainly not something students should use with all material, and it is only appropriate for older students, probably those in grade 5 and up. However, for serious study of informational material students want to learn and remember, it is a very useful technique.

Surveying

The first step of the SQ3R method is to survey the article or chapter, considering the title, introductory paragraphs, headings and subheadings, and concluding paragraphs. Any graphic overview and other pictorial information should also be surveyed. As a result of their survey, students should have a good idea of what types of information the selection contains and how it is organized.

Questioning

The second step is to return to the first section of the selection and formulate a question that is likely to be answered in that section. If the selection contains section headings, then this step consists largely of turning the headings into questions. The purpose of posing questions is to give students a definite purpose for reading.

Reading
The third step is to read the first section attempting to answer the question posed. If that question is not answered in the section, then students need to formulate another one and answer it.

Reciting
The fourth step is to recite the answer to the question posed. If possible, the question should be answered in the students' own words and without looking back at the selection. At least with difficult or lengthy material, it is a good idea to have students write out their answer. After questioning, reading, and reciting with the first section of the selection, students repeat these steps with each of the remaining sections.

Reviewing
The last step is to review the material learned, that is, again answer the questions posed. This should initially be done as soon as the article or chapter is concluded. Then, in order for the material learned to be remembered over time, it should be periodically reviewed.

The K-W-L Procedure

The K-W-L Procedure, developed by Donna Ogle (1986), can be used as a teacher-directed procedure for guiding students through a particular selection or taught to students as a strategy for them to use independently (Carr and Ogle 1987). Since this chapter deals with strategies, here we are primarily concerned with teaching K-W-L as a strategy that students can use independently. Used as a strategy, this three-step procedure is somewhat similar to SQ3R, but differs from SQ3R in that it is less complex and puts more emphasis on learners' prior knowledge and what they want to learn from the selection. The procedure consists of three major steps: What I **K**now, What I **W**ant to Learn, and What I Did **L**earn.

What I Know
The first step includes two stages. To begin, students consider the topic of the selection and list what they already know about it. Then, they categorize the information they listed and note other categories of information that they expect to learn something about as they read. For example, if the topic is horses, one student might list that horses are expensive, take a lot of care, are a lot of fun, and are used for racing and recreation. Given this list, she might generate categories for which she has some information—Uses of Horses, Advantages of Owning Horses, and Disadvantages of Owning Horses—and categories in which she expects to find information—Types of

Horses and the Origins of the Modern Horse. Note that this step of listing what is known and identifying categories of information could well be undertaken in small groups. Also, when K-W-L is used as a teacher-led procedure, this is a group brainstorming activity in which the teacher solicits responses and writes them on the board.

What I Want to Learn

The second step follows directly from the first. Based on the information the students already have and the categories in which they expect to find additional information, they list areas in which they would like further information. Even when K-W-L is used as a group or teacher-led activity, students are encouraged to construct personalized lists of what they want to learn from their reading. For example, having considered the issue of how much horses cost and thinking at least vaguely about getting one, the student may decide that getting information on the cost of horses is her major interest in reading the passage.

What I Did Learn

The third step is for students to record what they have learned. Additionally, students are encouraged to consider some things they wanted to learn about the topic but did not learn from this particular selection and to pursue their interest further through additional reading. For example, the student who wanted to know about the cost of horses may find that the selection contained very little information about current costs and that she needs to go to the newspaper in order to find current prices. Again, if the procedure is being used in small groups or by the whole class, individual students are encouraged to create their own lists of what they learned and what they still want to learn and to pursue additional reading in order to gain the information they are seeking.

Reciprocal Teaching

Reciprocal Teaching, developed by Annemarie Palincsar and Ann Brown (1984), is a small group procedure in which students work together to learn how to actively glean meaning from informational texts. The procedure employs five strategies: reading, generating questions, clarifying issues, summarizing, and making predictions. At first, the teacher or some other more experienced reader serves as the leader of the group, taking the primary role in carrying out the strategies and modeling them for others in the group. The central purpose of the strategy, however, is to get all students actively involved in using the strategies. Thus, from the beginning, responsibility is increasingly handed over to the students in the group, and eventually students work without the aid of the teacher.

Reading

The text is divided into short segments, initially a paragraph or so in length, and the leader reads the first segment aloud.

Questioning

Once the segment has been read, the leader or other group members generate several questions prompted by the passage just read, and members of the group answer the questions. For example, after reading the opening paragraph of Seymour Simon's *Oceans*, one question a student might ask is, "How is the earth different from any other planet in the solar system?" to which another student might respond, "It's the only planet with water on its surface."

Clarifying Issues

If the passage or questions produce any problems or misunderstandings, the leader and other group members clarify matters. For example, in continuing to work with *Oceans*, a student might point out that the earth is different from other planets in a number of ways. Other members of the group might agree, but then point out that the book's topic is oceans and therefore the presence of water is being emphasized.

Summarizing

After all the questions have been answered and any misunderstandings have been clarified, the leader or other group members summarize the segment.

Predicting

Based on the segment just read, segments that have preceded it, and the discussion thus far, the leader or other group members make predictions about the contents of the upcoming section. The sequence of reading, questioning, clarifying, summarizing, and predicting is then repeated with subsequent sections.

Teaching Sequences of Strategies

We recommend that these sequences of strategies be taught using the same procedure that we described for teaching individual strategies. Initially, teach each of them in a fairly concentrated unit in which teaching the strategy is the main order of business. Begin with explicit instruction to the class as a whole or a relatively large group of students. Provide motivation, explain the strategies, model them, solicit student participation from the large group and provide mediation as necessary, have students practice them in pairs or small groups, and have the small groups share their work and again provide mediation as necessary. Finally, gradually give students the responsibility for using the strategies independently and provide periodic review and encouragement to use the strategies in a variety of authentic situations.

CONCLUDING REMARKS

Up to this point, we have taken up a number of matters involving teaching comprehension strategies. We have

- Defined comprehension strategies

- Identified eight key strategies

- Explained some instructional concepts underlying our approach to teaching strategies

- Described procedures for teaching strategies

- Described three sequences of strategies and a procedure for teaching them

One very important task remains—that of your deciding which strategies to teach. Which strategies you teach will, in some cases, be determined by your school's curriculum. More often, however, identifying strategies to teach will be left up to you. In this case, we have a definite recommendation: Teach a few strategies well rather than many strategies less well. Comprehension strategies are complex procedures, and they need to be learned well if they are to be of real use to students. Teaching either one or two a year is a reasonable goal. In choosing which one or two to teach, we suggest that you teach those that your students appear ready to learn and that can be used frequently in dealing with the selections students read in your classes. Additionally, where possible, it would be a good idea to coordinate the teaching of strategies with other teachers in the school. Whatever strategy or strategies you teach, remember that learning the strategy itself is not the primary goal of strategy instruction. As with word-recognition strategies, comprehension strategies are a means to an end—the end being students understanding, enjoying, and remembering what they read.

SELF-CHECK

1. Define reading-comprehension strategies.

2. Distinguish between instruction designed to help students deal with a specific selection and instruction in comprehension strategies.

3. List and briefly describe the eight comprehension strategies described in this chapter.

4. Describe the major instructional concepts underlying the approach to teaching strategies presented in this chapter.

5. State how long you would spend on initial instruction in a strategy and give a rationale for spending this amount of time.

6. Outline the steps suggested for the first day of instruction in a new strategy.

7. Explain how your instruction would change during the initial unit of strategy instruction.

8. Describe the constructive nature of good strategy instruction.

9. Explain the review and follow-up procedures you would use in the rest of the school year following the initial unit on a strategy.

10. Name and very briefly describe three sequences of comprehension strategies that have been widely recommended.

11. Suppose you were teaching a fifth-grade class and you had decided to teach two comprehension strategies. Think about the class and the sort of reading they are likely to do. Then select two strategies to teach and give a rationale for teaching these particular strategies.

12. Make a list of the eight comprehension strategies discussed in the chapter. Then interview several students at the grade level that interests you most, and attempt to determine (1) what the students know about the strategies, (2) if they use them, and (3) when they use them. After you gather this information, write a brief statement on the importance of teaching strategies.

13. The strategies discussed in this chapter are among the most important ones to teach, but they are certainly not the only ones you might teach. Based on your experiences with elementary students or on your own experiences as a reader, identify two or three more strategies that might be taught and explain the importance of each.

REFERENCES

Baumann, J. F. (1986). The direct instruction of main idea comprehension ability. In Baumann, J. F. (ed.), *Teaching main idea comprehension*. Newark, DE: International Reading Association, pp. 133–178. Describes a method of teaching a particular comprehension strategy.

Brown, A. L. and Day, J. D. (1983). Macrorules for summarizing text: The development of expertise. *Journal of Verbal Learning and Verbal Behavior*, 22, 1–14. A scholarly article describing the tacit rules summarizers use and how these develop.

Carr, E. and Ogle, D. (1987). K-W-L Plus: A strategy for comprehension and summarization. *Journal of Reading*, 30, 626–631. Describes the basic K-W-L sequence of strategies and two additional strategies that could be added for more able readers.

Chambliss, M. J. and Calfee, R. C. (in press). *Textbooks for learning: Nurturing children's minds.* London: Blackwell Publishers. An in-depth look at what textbooks are, what they can be, and what they should be.

Deshler, D. D. and Schumaker, J. B. (1993). Skills mastery by at-risk students: Not a simple matter. *Elementary School Journal, 94,* 153–167. Summary and discussion of a large body of the authors' work with strategy instruction for at-risk students.

Dole, J. A., Brown, K. J., and Trathen, W. (1996). The effects of strategy instruction on the comprehension performance of at-risk students. *Reading Research Quarterly, 31,* 62–88. A truly excellent example of well planned and thoughtfully presented comprehension strategy instruction.

Graves, M. F., Juel, C. and Graves, B. B. (1998). *Teaching reading in the 21st century.* Boston: Allyn & Bacon. An elementary reading method much like this one but considerably longer, more detailed, and more comprehensive.

Ogle, D. (1986). K-W-L: A teaching model that develops active reading of expository text. *The Reading Teacher, 39,* 564–570. Describes the original K-W-L strategy in more detail than that given here.

Palincsar, A. S. and Brown, A. N. (1984). Reciprocal teaching of comprehension fostering and monitoring activities. *Cognition and Instruction, 1,* 117–175. A detailed account of this powerful sequence of strategies.

Pearson, P. D., Roehler, L. R., Dole, J. A. and Duffy, G. G. (1992). Developing expertise in reading comprehension. In Samuels, S. J. and Farstrup, A. E. (eds.), *What research has to say about reading instruction* (2nd ed.). Newark, DE: International Reading Association, pp. 145–199. Presents an up-to-date view of reading comprehension instruction, with particular emphasis on teaching comprehension strategies.

Pressley, M., Harris, K. R. and Marks, M. B. (1992). But good strategy instructors are constructivists! *Educational Psychology Review, 4,* 3–31. An argument that good strategy instruction is consistent with constructivist principles.

Pressley, M., Johnson, C. J., Symons, S., McGoldrick, J. A. and Kurita, J. A. (1989). Strategies that improve children's memory and comprehension of text. *The Elementary School Journal, 90,* 3–32. An excellent examination and discussion of key comprehension strategies.

Pressley, M. and Woloshyn, V. (1995). *Cognitive strategy instruction that really improves children's academic performance* (2nd ed.). Cambridge, MA: Brookline Books. A detailed look at cognitive strategy instruction in a number of subjects.

Robinson, F. P. (1946). *Effective study.* New York: Harper and Bros. The original source of the SQ3R sequence of strategies.

Rosenblatt, L. M. (1978). *The reader, the text, the poem: The transactional theory of the literary work.* Carbondale, IL: Southern Illinois University. A classic book by the originator of the response approach to literature.

Rosenshine, B. (1995). Advances in research on instruction. *Journal of Educational Research,* 88, 262–268. Presents a strong case for the validity and importance of the findings of research on cognitive strategy instruction.

Tierney, R. J. and Cunningham, J. W. (1984). Research on teaching reading comprehension. In Pearson, P. D. (ed.), *Handbook of reading research.* White Plains, NY: Longman, pp. 609–654. A very well laid out review of the research on learning from text—the topic of Chapter 7—and learning to learn from text—the topic of this chapter.

CHILDREN'S BOOKS CITED

Johnson, G. and Cutchins, J. (1988). *Scaly babies: Reptiles growing up.* New York: Morrow.

Jones, C. F. Illus. by John O'Brien. (1991). *Mistakes that worked.* New York: Doubleday.

Kellogg, S. (1986). *Best friends.* New York: Dial Books for Young Readers.

Lobel, A. (1979). *Days with frog and toad.* New York: Harper & Row.

Raskin, E. (1966). *Nothing ever happens on my block.* New York: Atheneum.

Simon, S. (1990). *Oceans.* New York: Morrow.

9 Classroom Assessment

Tests—the very word may make you cringe, recalling anxious moments of performing under pressure with the weight of a course grade or entrance into a particular college hanging in the balance. American students spend a considerable amount of time taking tests, an activity that many students do not relish. Moreover, in too many cases, these tests do not seem to serve any clear purpose. Nevertheless, there are many legitimate reasons for testing. There are also many legitimate reasons for types of assessment other than the paper and pencil forms most of us think of when we think of testing.

Recently, the two largest professional organizations in literacy, the International Reading Association and the National Council of Teachers of English, collaborated to develop *Standards for the English Language Arts* (1996). These standards call for the ability to comprehend, interpret, evaluate, appreciate, research, and reflect on the ideas and information gleaned from print. They call for the development of the high levels of literacy needed for full participation in today's world. In this chapter, we concentrate primarily on assessment practices that help students and teachers to reach these goals.

LOOKING AHEAD

In this, the last regular chapter in the book, we examine various facets of reading assessment. First, we examine several dimensions of assessment—its ongoing nature, its audiences, its purposes, and its relationship to instruction. Next, we discuss the major types of assessment and the sorts of assessment records to keep. After that, we consider different facets of reading that need to be assessed and how they can be assessed. Then, we discuss student self-assessment and teacher self-assessment. In addition to your assessing students, it is very important that students are taught how to assess themselves and develop a habit of being strategic readers who routinely assess their success in the reading they do. It is also important that you assess your teaching as well as your students' learning. Finally, we present some general guidelines for any assessment you do.

KEY CONCEPTS

- Norm-referenced and criterion-referenced tests, and the uses and values of each

- Informal reading inventories and their uses

- Additional approaches to assessment

- Reading portfolios and their purposes

- Reading skills, competencies, and attitudes to be assessed and recorded in portfolios

- Procedures for assessing specific skills and attitudes

- Student self-assessment

- Teacher self-assessment

- Reflective teaching

- General guidelines for assessing students

DIMENSIONS OF ASSESSMENT

Assessment is an on-going process. As teachers, you will assess your students' learning on a day-by-day and, sometimes, a moment by moment basis. For example, as you address your students, you may scan the group and make a mental note of whether each student appears to be engaged in the lesson. If you see a look of confusion, you will probably restate what you just said or invite questions. This ongoing assessment of the learning situation will allow you to modify your instruction in order to maximize student learning.

Of course, observation is only one of several types of assessment. Assessment can take many other forms—anecdotal records of behavior, audio tapes of reading, and paper and pencil tests. The type of assessment used in any given situation is determined by the purpose of that assessment—that is, what it is you are trying to learn about a student or group of students. If you are trying to learn whether students are comprehending instruction, you might observe their facial expressions and body language or ask them a question. If you are trying to learn about students' decoding strategies, you might listen to them read a passage aloud, making note of the words that cause them difficulty. Once you decide what information you are after —that is, your purposes for assessment—you can decide how to go about collecting that information. Ways of collecting specific types of information are discussed later in this chapter. At this point, we consider how audience and instruction relate to assessment.

The Audience

Just as there are multiple purposes for assessment, there are multiple audiences; and the audience to be reached is another factor influencing the type of assessment appropriate in a particular situation. Students, teachers, parents, principals, and public officials exemplify distinctly different audiences, each with its own interests. Parents, for example, might be most interested in whether their children make progress from the beginning of the year to the end and whether their children work at a level commensurate with their peers. Principals are often concerned with how students in their schools fare compared to students in other schools. Public officials are often concerned with how students in the areas they represent compare to other students across the country. On a national level, those who set educational policy are often concerned with how American students perform relative to students in other countries. In addition, students themselves wish and deserve to know whether they are making the progress they think they should. Finally, teachers' primary concern will be monitoring student progress and finding out how to deliver the best possible instruction.

Instruction

The final point we make in this section is the one we hope you will carry with you as you read the remainder of the chapter. Although some assessment is done for the sake of informing people outside of the classroom about students' performance and has no direct influence on instruction, most of the time the assessment you employ will be inextricably linked with instruction. Information gleaned from various forms of assessment will inform your instruction, and your instruction will inform your decisions about the types and amounts of assessments to conduct. Specifically, classroom assessment can help you to: (1) determine how quickly and in what ways your students are progressing as readers, (2) identify students who are not making adequate progress and pinpoint specific areas of difficulty for these students, and (3) plan instruction that meets the needs and utilizes the strengths of your students.

TYPES OF ASSESSMENT

In this section, we discuss three types of assessment used to collect information about student achievement in reading. The first two, *norm-referenced* and *criterion-referenced tests,* are often used to monitor general reading progress. They may also be used to determine whether a student is eligible for special services such as additional help from a reading specialist. The third type of assessment, *informal measures,* is used to collect more detailed information about specific aspects of reading performance.

Norm-Referenced Tests

Norm-referenced tests provide a way of describing student performance relative to the performance of other students who took the same test. Norm-referenced scores such as grade-equivalent scores and percentile ranks reflect this comparison between the test taker's score and the score of students in the norm group—a group of students whose scores are used as a reference point. Tests such as the Scholastic Aptitude Test and the American College Testing Program are norm-referenced tests that you may have taken before applying for college. The results of such tests are reported in several ways, two of which are discussed here.

Grade equivalent scores describe the average performance of students at various grade levels. A student obtaining a grade equivalent score of 2.9, for example, has scored as well on the test as did the average student in the norm group taking the test in the ninth month of second grade. Unfortunately, grade equivalent scores are not nearly as precise an indicator as they appear to be and are often misinterpreted. *Percentile ranks* are more easily interpreted. *Percentile ranks* describe the relative position of the test taker compared with students in the norm group. A student scoring at the 50th percentile, for example, has performed equal to or better than 50 percent of the students at his or her grade level in the norm group, and a student scoring at the 75th percentile has performed equal to or better than 75 percent of these students.

There are many factors to consider when evaluating scores on norm-referenced tests, and it is important not to overemphasize the value of such tests. Their primary merit lies in the fact that they can usually be given to large groups of students at one time and can give you a *general* idea of how a student is performing relative to other students. The most important thing to remember is that the scores are only helpful if the test is a valid test of reading ability and if the students in the norming group are similar to your students.

Validity is the extent to which a test actually measures what it purports to measure. For example, while most norm-referenced reading tests have a vocabulary section, some consist only of a vocabulary test requiring students to match words with their definitions. Because reading involves the comprehension of phrases and sentences, a test of vocabulary in isolation is a valid test of word knowledge but not of reading performance as a whole.

Norm groups consist of those students on which the norm-referenced scores are based. This group of students should be as similar to your students as possible. If, for example, you are teaching in a suburban school district and your students represent several ethnicities, the tests you give should have been normed on a group that includes suburban students and multi-ethnic students. If you are teaching in a rural school and all of your students are African-American and the test you give was normed on a group of white students in an urban area, the resulting scores will be difficult to interpret. In addition, American tests are generally normed on students whose native language is English. Thus, the performance of an ESL student on such a test would be difficult to interpret.

Criterion-Referenced Tests

Criterion-referenced tests focus on how well students perform specific tasks rather than on how their performance compares to that of other students. These tests use the idea of a cutoff score, or a criterion, set by the test makers, your school district, or you. Students scoring at or above this point are said to be proficient in the particular facet of reading tested, while students scoring below this point are said to require further development in order to reach proficiency. Thus, a criterion-referenced test accompanying a reading series might include a 300-word story and specify a criterion of 98 percent accuracy in oral reading. In this example, students must make no more than six oral reading errors in order to meet the criterion. In another example, a district goal for silent reading comprehension may be 80 percent on a given passage. If there are five comprehension questions, students must answer at least four of the questions correctly in order to demonstrate the criterion of proficiency specified.

Informal Measures

Generally, audiences such as parents, principals, and educational policy makers find commercially produced norm-referenced and criterion-referenced tests more helpful than do teachers. Norm-referenced and criterion-referenced tests can reveal general facts about achievement and provide information on groups of students. In most cases, however, they do not provide information that is specific enough to aid in the planning of instructional goals, methods, and materials for individual students. Further, since they are not designed to match the instructional emphasis of a specific school or district, they are not necessarily good measures of what students are learning on a day to day basis. Finally, there is some concern that these measures may not be sensitive to small increments in growth over time, making it difficult to determine how students who struggle with reading are progressing. The measures described in this section and throughout much of the remainder of this chapter are more useful for making classroom instructional decisions. Because they differ from the types of assessment described previously, which have a securely established place in American education, they are often referred to as informal measures or alternative assessment procedures. Despite these names, the assessments we describe here should be an integral and systematic part of your classroom reading program.

Informal Reading Inventories

Informal reading inventories (often referred to as IRIs) consist of passages that a student reads orally to a teacher. They can be used to assess the appropriateness of specific texts for individual students as well as to investigate areas of strength and weakness for individual students. Informal reading inventories allow you to check student development in such areas as oral reading (fluency, decoding strategies, and types of oral reading errors), reading comprehension (literal and inferential), sight vocabulary, reading rate, and behaviors such as finger pointing and holding the text too close.

The particular IRI described here is teacher-made and individually administered. In order to avoid confusion, we should point out that this version of an IRI differs in some ways from conventional IRIs, which have been described in detail by Marjorie Johnson and her colleagues (1987). To make your own IRI, first select a text. Selecting a text that you might actually use with the student will maximize the applicability of the assessment. After making your selection, follow the steps outlined here.

- Select two passages that seem representative of the book as a whole in terms of sentence length, vocabulary, prior knowledge required, and so on. A 100- to 125-word passage is generally sufficient for beginning readers, and a 200- to 250-word passage is appropriate for higher levels.

- Make sure the student feels at ease, then introduce the passage by saying something such as, "I'm going to have you read this paragraph about whales to me and then I'd like you to tell me what you read about."

- As the student is reading, follow along with a duplicate copy. Circle words that the student has difficulty with or omits during reading, noting in the margin any mispronunciations or substitutions of one word for another. In addition, note any significant behaviors exhibited by the reader, such as lack of expression during reading, finger pointing, holding the text close to the eyes, and markedly slow or markedly rapid rate.

- After the passage has been read, check comprehension by asking the student to retell what he has read. Initially, ask the student to respond without looking back at the passage. However, if he needs to look back in order to give a satisfactory retelling, let him do so. Characterize the retelling using simple descriptions such as "complete, coherent, and shows good understanding," "somewhat sketchy but showing basic understanding" or "sketchy and not showing much understanding." You might also want to ask a question or two, perhaps an inferential question and an application question, and record the student's success with those. Additionally, your notes should indicate whether the student needed to look back to retell the passage.

- If you are uncertain about the student's competency with this and similar texts, you can repeat the IRI with the second passage.

In addition to providing you with information on the student's oral reading, reading comprehension, sight vocabulary, and reading rate, an informal reading inventory will give you a good sense of whether the reading material from which the passages were taken and similar selections are appropriate for the student.

Identifying three levels of students' competence with a particular selection—and, therefore, with other selections much like the one used—is useful when you consider matching students with texts.

- *Independent level.* Material is at a student's independent level when he can read it with fluency and ease, can effectively retell a short passage, and can answer inferential and application questions on the passage. This level of material is suitable for independent reading in the classroom and for reading outside of school. This would also be appropriate material for initially teaching strategies such as those described in Chapter 8.

- *Instructional level.* Material is at a student's instructional level when he can read it but occasionally stumbles over words, can retell some of a short passage but may have to reread to give a fairly detailed retelling, and seems to find answering inferential and application questions challenging. This level of material is appropriate for lessons in which you will aid the student; that is, this level of material is appropriate for classroom instruction in which you would provide some of the types of assistance we describe in Chapter 7.

- *Frustration level.* Material is at a student's frustration level when he reads it somewhat haltingly, pausing or stumbling over 10 percent or more of the words. Another sign that material is at a student's frustration level comes if he can retell little of it, has to reread to retell it, or is confused in his retelling. Still another sign comes if the student cannot answer inferential or application questions. If the inventory reveals any of these characteristics, the material used in the inventory and probably other similar material is too difficult for the student and not something that you want to encourage him to read in or out of school.

In addition to creating your own IRIs for the purposes of selecting appropriate materials for specific students or spot-checking reading progress throughout the year, you may wish to use a published IRI to measure growth from the beginning of the year to the end. There are several good IRIs on the market including the *Qualitative Reading Inventory—II* by Lauren Leslie and Joanne Caldwell (1995).

Observation, Anecdotal Records, and Portfolio Assessment

Observing students as they complete various reading tasks can be a simple, convenient, and very informative means of gaining information. However, observation is useful only if you know what it is you are looking for and have a system for recording what you see. Many opportunities to learn about the development of young readers are lost if you are unprepared for them. Here, we discuss what to observe and recommend some simple ways to keep anecdotal records and other indicators of students' reading development.

It is very worthwhile to prepare a file folder for each child, a portfolio in which you assemble various sorts of information about the student's reading proficiency. Then, when you encounter something to record, you already have a place to put it. You don't risk losing the information by writing it on a stray piece of paper.

Use the inside cover of the folder, or a sheet stapled to the inside cover, to keep track of progress in the areas you deem important. For a kindergarten or first-grade student, you might divide the chart into five sections: enjoyment of reading, comprehension, phonemic awareness, vocabulary, and word-recognition strategies. You might then subdivide each of the five sections into more specific components. For example, enjoyment of reading might consist of subsections such as enjoys listening to stories in a group, enjoys looking at books, self-selects reading as a free time activity. Comprehension might include subsections such as recognizes a printed word has meaning, can predict what might happen next in a story, and can retell a story.

For an older student, comprehension might be broken down into literal comprehension, inferential comprehension, and ability to make judgments. Also, for an older, accomplished reader, the phonemic-awareness and word-recognition sections might be replaced with one for metacognitive strategies.

Another item to include in the folder is the student's own comments on his reading. Periodically, you might ask students to reflect on their growth as readers, asking them to write about what they perceive as their strengths and what goals they wish to work toward. Student self-assessment is an important part of portfolio assessment.

Along with observational and anecdotal information, portfolios of individual student's work can include reading test scores, notes that you periodically make on students' strengths and weaknesses in reading, notes about their attitude and involvement in reading and on the kinds of material they prefer to read, and samples of their written work. Over the year, you should refer to these fairly frequently—to add new information, to check students' progress and perhaps set new goals, and to check your initial perceptions of students' strengths and weaknesses, see if these have proven to be valid, and revise them as necessary. Portfolios are also useful for sharing information about how students are doing with the students themselves and with their parents. Finally, portfolios are particularly useful at the end of the year when you are discussing students' reading proficiency and needs with their next year's teachers. They can then be passed on to those teachers so that they can profit from the assessment and continue the record of students' growth in reading.

As you and your students make decisions about the purposes of portfolios in your classroom, the contents of these portfolios, and the ways in which portfolios will be managed and stored, the following definition offered by Cindy Gillespie and others (1996) should be helpful: "Portfolio assessment is a purposeful, multidimensional process of collecting evidence that illustrates a student's accomplishments, efforts, and progress (utilizing a variety of authentic evidence) over time" (p. 487). According to these authors, this evidence should include content that is selected by the teacher, selected by the student, and jointly selected as well as both teacher- and student-generated criteria for the inclusion of materials and the evaluation of these materials. Thus, portfolio assessment is not just a mechanism for collecting work samples, it is a process of thinking about reading development that becomes an integral part of the instructional process.

In addition to individual student portfolios, it is helpful to keep a class chart for quick reference. By listing the names of your students down the left-hand column of the chart and the knowledge, skills, strategies, and attitudes that are of concern along the top, you can create a grid such as that shown in Figure 9–1. You might use the letter *S* to denote *satisfactory* and *N* to denote *needs improvement* in each of the categories. Or, you might simply use checks to indicate students' mastery in particular areas. Such a chart is particularly handy when making grouping decisions for specific assignments and is also a constant reminder of the skills, strategies, attitudes, and knowledge that you are trying to help your students develop.

Students	Attitudes				Skills & Strategies						Knowledge	
	Reads Frequently	Enjoys Reading	Shares Reading	Applies Reading	Comprehends Well	Self-Corrects	Reads Fluently	Rate Adequate	Uses Word-Recog Strategies	Uses Vocabulary-Building Skills	Adequate Vocabulary	Shows Phonemic Awareness

Figure 9–1.   Class Assessment Chart

Finally, note that students may demonstrate their strengths and weaknesses in a wide variety of ways. For example, you can learn a great deal about a student's comprehension of a story by his spontaneous drawings, play, or other responses to the story.

COMPETENCIES AND ATTITUDES TO ASSESS

Here, we consider the specific knowledge, skills, strategies, and attitudes that need to be assessed and discuss specific ways in which each of these can be assessed. We begin with more global concerns, such as, *Does the student read and appear to enjoy reading?* and move toward increasingly specific concerns such as *Has the student learned the basic letter-sound correspondences of English?* We have chosen this organization for two reasons. First, the organization reinforces the point that learning to read is not a rigid linear process in which students first learn to recognize letters, then their sounds, then words, and so on. Instead, learning to read is a much more holistic and synergistic process, a process in which students learn to use their background knowledge, the text itself, the context in which they are reading, and their purposes for reading to construct appropriate meanings for what they read. Second, it makes sense to assess more global matters first because, if students are proficient at the global tasks, you may not need to assess their proficiency at some of the more specific tasks.

Does the Student Read and Enjoy Reading?

This is one of the most important questions to ask and one of the easiest to answer. It can be answered by observing students and talking informally to them. We suggest that you watch students when they have assigned reading to see if they appear to be doing it, observe them when they have free time to see if they choose to read some of the time, and talk to them about their reading. Then, record some brief notes on each student; a few sentences will do.

Does the Student Understand What He Reads?

This question is most easily answered by letting students read something and answer some questions on it. Usually, the text should be available to students as they are answering the questions. However, in some cases you may want to check both students' understanding and their memory, and in these cases they will need to answer the questions without checking the text. The reading for this type of assessment can typically be done silently, and, for the sake of efficiency, the assessment can be a group activity. Also for the sake of efficiency, multiple-choice items can be used for initial screening. In fact, commercially produced tests can be used. Then, for students who appear to have some problems in understanding what they read, you probably need individual sessions in which you have the student read, ask questions and prompt responses, and probe for further information when you are unsure of what the student is and is not understanding from what he reads. For students with good understanding, your record here can be a short one—for example, the percentile rank from a standardized test or a note that the student read these sorts of passages and competently answered questions on them. For students who show poor understanding, your record will need to be more complex and should include some specifics on both the sorts of problems they had and the strengths they showed.

Does the Student Share His Reading and Apply Ideas Gleaned from Reading to the Real World?

Students who enjoy what they read and are excited about it will want to share their pleasure and excitement with others. Similarly, students who are really learning something from their reading—students for whom reading reveals new ideas, new possibilities, and new ways of viewing the world—will naturally look for ways in which what they discover from reading applies to their world. Both of these outcomes of reading are ones that you want to nurture and encourage, and keeping track of how often students share and apply ideas from reading will prompt you to do so.

Both outcomes can be assessed through observation and by talking to students. Look for and record each student's spontaneous sharing of what he reads and his willingness to share when you or other students prompt him to do so. Similarly, look for and record each student's attempts to apply ideas from reading. For example, does he talk about how Fudge's pestering of his brother in Judy Blume's *Fudge-a-Mania* reminds him that a pest is not something he aspires to be? Does his reading *The Star Fisher* by Lawrence Yep prompt him to learn more about his own ancestors? Or, does his reading an article about trick-or-treating for UNICEF inspire him to organize a class trick-or-treat for UNICEF?

To What Extent Does the Student Self-Check and Self-Correct?

There are two general ways of finding out if students monitor their reading and do something to remedy problems when they occur, one of which is appropriate for younger and less proficient readers and the other of which is appropriate for older and more proficient readers. With younger and less proficient readers, assessment can be done as part of the type of informal reading inventory we already discussed. In this case, you are assessing oral reading, and the assessment deals largely with the students' checking and correcting their reading of relatively small units. For example, do they correct mispronunciations of words, and do they pause after a sentence that apparently does not make sense and reread it?

With older and more proficient readers, the concern shifts to evaluating their checking and correcting behaviors during silent reading, and the checking and correcting is often of larger units of meaning. For example, after reading an expository piece about how hurricanes are formed, do students check themselves to see if they understand the process and perhaps reread, ask other students, or ask the teacher for clarification if they do not?

Assessing the extent to which students self-check and self-correct involves several steps. First, look for signs in students' oral and written work that they are not self-checking and self-correcting; that is, look for statements and answers showing that they have misinterpreted parts of what they have read. Second, talk to students; try to determine whether they understand the general notion of self-checking and self-correcting. In some cases, you will find out that they simply do not. Finally, ask those students you are still uncertain of to be aware of points in their reading that cause them confusion and what they do about it. Ask them to jot down notes about their confusions and attempts to remedy them, and ask them to bring these notes to your attention. That students do not recognize and bring such points of confusion to your attention certainly does not guarantee that they are incapable of monitoring their reading and self-correcting when necessary. However, that information, coupled with the information you get from talking to students and the evidence you have from the lack of understanding you have observed, can give you a good clue that students need assistance here.

Recording the fact that students do monitor their reading and self-correct when necessary is simple. Recording the fact that students do not monitor and self-correct, or do so only in certain situations, is more involved. Initially, all you need to record is the fact that students require some help in this area. Later, as you work with students, you will be able to identify the specific areas of self-monitoring and self-correcting in which students need assistance. Quite probably, your assessment will reveal that many students need help in this area, and you will probably want to form short-term groups to work on developing these skills. Your assessment is also likely to reveal students who do monitor and self-correct, and you can use this knowledge when forming heterogeneous groups to work with challenging selections. That is, when groups of students are dealing with selections that are likely to require self-checking and self-correcting, ensure that some of the group members have these skills.

How Fluently Does the Student Read?

As discussed in the section on informal reading inventories, fluent oral reading is usually an indication of understanding, while lack of fluent reading can indicate a variety of difficulties that may be interfering with understanding. With older and more able students, a check on fluency is not absolutely necessary, but if you do choose to do a fluency check it is easy to do. Simply have students read a paragraph or so in a grade-appropriate text and jot down a one-sentence descriptive comment, such as, "Orally reads grade level material fluently and with few miscues." It is worth pointing out here that a few miscues is not a cause for concern. Even competent adults occasionally produce a miscue when they read orally.

With younger or less able readers, a fluency check is a definite must, and an informal reading inventory is an appropriate tool for this purpose. Such matters as omitting sounds or words, adding sounds or words, mispronouncing or substituting words, repetitions, self-corrections, and responses to prompts need to be noted and recorded. To learn more about analyzing miscues to identify the word recognition strategies that students do and do not use when they read, refer to Yetta Goodman and her colleagues' *Reading Miscue Inventory* (1987) or the section on running records in Marie Clay's *An Observation Survey of Early Literacy Achievement* (1993).

What Are the Students' Silent Reading Rates?

This question is easy to answer but important. It is important because how much reading you assign both in class and for homework needs to be dictated by students' reading rate. In particular, you want to be sure that you do not assign reading that would take much more time than you allot in class or much more time than can reasonably be expected for homework. The question is also important because very low rates may suggest a general lack of reading proficiency. Checking silent reading rates can be done as a class. We suggest that you choose two selections that students typically read in your class, one of which is fairly easy and one a bit challenging, and both of which are long enough that students will *not* complete them in five minutes. Next, make up three or four simple comprehension questions on each selection. After this, tell students that you want to get an idea of their reading rate, tell them that it is not a race and they should read as they usually do, and let them know that they will be asked to answer a few questions after they read the passage. Then, start them all reading at the beginning of the selection at the same time, and stop them at the end of five minutes and ask them to put a pencil mark where they finished. As soon as students have marked their finishing points, ask your three or four questions and let students jot down their answers. After students have completed both the easier and the more challenging selections, either you or the students can then tally the words read per minute, and this is what goes in your record. The comprehension questions were included just to let students know that they did need to read for understanding, and students' scores on these do not need to be recorded. Of course, checking their rates several times will increase the accuracy of your estimates.

How Large Is the Student's Vocabulary and What Sort of Vocabulary-Building Skills Does He Have?

Four matters, each of which is assessed in a somewhat different way, are worth considering—oral vocabulary, reading vocabulary, use of context cues, and knowledge of word parts. First, you can classify students' oral vocabularies as average, smaller than average, or larger than average simply on the basis of the oral language you hear them use. Second, you can classify students' reading vocabularies as average, smaller than average, or larger than average based on the vocabulary section of a norm-referenced test they have taken considered in conjunction with the word knowledge they display as they read in class. Estimates of both oral and reading vocabulary are particularly important for ESL students, who may have relatively small English vocabularies and who may need extensive opportunities to build their oral or reading vocabularies. At the same time, it is crucial that you avoid deeming a student incapable of increasing his standard English vocabulary or of below average intelligence because his vocabulary consists largely of words from another language or from a nonstandard dialect of English.

Third, you can check students' abilities to use context cues to determine the meanings of unknown words by having them read orally from a text containing some challenging words. When they come across a word they do not know, ask them to try and use context to figure out its meaning. The data you record here can be a simple statement about students' proficiencies. For example, you might note that a particular student is "Generally able to use context cues when reading easy materials but can make almost no use of them when reading difficult material." Assessing students' knowledge of word parts can be done in the same way.

How Well Does the Student Use Word-Recognition Strategies?

As is the case with fluency, word-recognition strategies—phonics, syllabication, blending, and structural analysis—are primarily of concern with younger and less able readers. For assessing phonics, we would again use the informal reading inventory. Also, your careful observation of what students do when they come to unknown words as they are reading orally—either as part of an informal reading inventory or simply as an oral reading activity—will reveal some information about their proficiency with the other word-recognition strategies. Additionally, for assessing blending and structural analysis, we recommend you construct simple and straightforward tests.

To assess blending, you can present students with letters representing part of a word—for example, *ee*—and have students pronounce them. Next, add another letter or letters—for example, *cree*—and have students pronounce that combination of letters. After that, add another letter or letters so that the letter string is actually a word—for example, *creep*—and have students pronounce the word.

For assessing structural analysis of compound words, prefixed words, or suffixed words, you need only present students with these types of words and have them separate the words into their component parts. Thus, you might write the words *houseboat, predetermine,* and *wanted* on the board and ask students to write down the two parts of each word, leaving some space between each part.

How much information you record about students' proficiency with word-recognition strategies will depend on how proficient they are. If students are adept at using phonics, blending, and word parts, then a brief sentence recording this fact is sufficient. If, on the other hand, they are not proficient with one or more of these strategies, then your record needs to reflect what they can do and what they cannot. For example, with respect to phonics, you might record that one student "Has learned virtually all the consonant letter-sound correspondences, but shows little knowledge of the sounds represented by the vowels." Or, with respect to word parts, you might note that a student "Recognizes the components of compound words, but generally does not recognize prefixes or suffixes when they appear in words."

For students who experience quite a bit of difficulty with word-recognition strategies, your assessment record may become quite lengthy. However, we want to emphasize that having a lengthy record of students' difficulties with word-recognition strategies does not mean that you should spend the majority of your time teaching these strategies. The detailed record simply focuses the time you do spend on those aspects of word recognition of greatest benefit to the student.

How Developed Is the Student's Phonemic Awareness?

As we noted in Chapter 4 in discussing phonemic awareness, realizing that words are made up of several sounds and hearing those sounds is a prerequisite to learning to use many word-recognition strategies. This is the most rudimentary area for which we suggest assessment. It is something you need to be concerned about only for beginning readers, those who have not learned to use word-recognition strategies. Furthermore, many students—particularly students who have had numerous experiences following along in books as they were read to—will enter school with well developed phonemic awareness. Other students—particularly students who have not had much experience with English or in following along in books as someone read to them—may not be skilled at recognizing the individual sounds that make up words. In fact, some students will not realize that words are made up of individual sounds. Luckily, this skill is easily assessed. Simply pronounce a word very slowly, and ask the student to tap once for each sound he hears in the word. For students who do not succeed at or perhaps even understand this task, Marie Clay (1985) has suggested presenting words with the letter or letters representing each sound boxed in, and then letting the student move markers from box to box as you slowly say the sounds. This procedure, of course, provides some instruction along with the assessment, and your notes on the student's phonemic awareness should reflect this. For example, you might record that the student "Cannot recognize individual sounds when simply hearing the word, but can recognize individual sounds when given clues to how many sounds there are in a word." When students are thoroughly skilled in phonemic awareness, they will be able to recognize most of the individual sounds in words without a prompt other than hearing the word.

The assessment pyramid shown in Figure 9–2 summarizes this section and emphasizes the importance of assessing both general and specific competencies and attitudes.

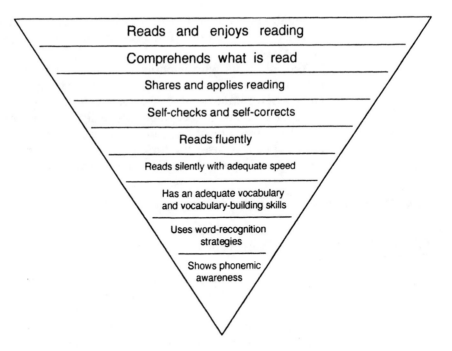

Figure 9–2. Assessment Pyramid

STUDENT SELF-ASSESSMENT

As we mentioned in our discussion of portfolio assessment, student self-assessment is an important piece of the assessment puzzle. As we first noted in Chapter 2 and explained further in Chapter 8, students need to become metacognitive about their reading. They need to realize when they are understanding what they are reading and when they are not understanding it so that they can do something to foster understanding. They also need to recognize other strengths and weaknesses that they have so that they can build on their strengths and try to remedy their weaknesses. If, for example, a student realizes that he is not very adept at using context to glean word meanings but is adept at using the dictionary, then he can make a conscious decision to get out the dictionary when encountering an unknown word. Similarly, if a student knows that a single reading of a science chapter is not likely to leave him with enough information to complete the experiment the chapter describes, then he can make a conscious choice to read the chapter two times, taking notes during the second reading.

Your role in helping students become increasingly metacognitive is threefold. First, let them know the importance of their becoming metacognitive, of becoming better and better at realizing which reading tasks they do well at and which ones they need to become more proficient at. Second, share the assessment information you gather with students frequently and in a way that indicates that you and your students are joint participants in fostering their literacy. Praise them for what they do well, point out areas in which they can improve, and congratulate them when they do improve. Finally, let students know that each of them is capable of becoming an independent and metacognitive reader who can assess his own proficiency and improve his skills, knowledge, and strategies where necessary. As part of doing this, make students active participants in creating their portfolios. Students should have access to their portfolios and should select some of the material that goes in them. They might, for example, include logs listing the books they have read, writing in response to some of their favorite readings, and comments on some of their reading goals.

TEACHER SELF-ASSESSMENT

In addition to teachers assessing students' performance and students' assessing their own performance, another kind of assessment is important to your conducting an effective reading program. To be maximally effective, you need to continually assess your own performance as a reading teacher—to engage in reflective teaching. That is, you need to repeatedly reflect on your instruction, students' responses to your instruction, and how you can improve your instruction to, in turn, improve students' performance. This is the continuing challenge and excitement of teaching. The classroom is an ever-changing mosaic of students, activities, goals, attitudes, and texts that you arrange and rearrange in order to constantly increase each student's success at becoming an able and avid reader. There is no perfect blend of comprehension instruction, small group work, independent reading, discussion, and instruction in word-recognition strategies that you eventually arrive at and can then continue to use throughout your career. Instead, each day, each week, and each new class present new opportunities for reflecting on what went well, what did not go as well, and what can be done to make your classroom an increasingly effective environment in which each student can develop his reading proficiency to the greatest extent possible.

CONCLUDING REMARKS

Here we present some guidelines for assessment that emphasize many of the major points made throughout this chapter and also reflect Kibby's (1995) thoughts on the topic.

- Assessment is an ongoing process.

- The primary purpose of classroom assessment is to support and give direction to instruction. The assessment you use needs to be appropriate for your curriculum and your goals.

- Assessment is really the process of answering questions. Your question determines the type of assessment that should be done. For example, if you wish to know whether a student can apply various word-recognition strategies, a test of silent reading will not be helpful. If, on the other hand, you are most interested in comprehension, a test of silent reading followed by questions is probably more appropriate than a test of oral reading followed by questions. Further, if you can already answer the question that you are posing, then you need not waste your time on assessment in this area.

- Assessment should reveal strengths as well as weaknesses. As you assess, look not only for what it is that causes students problems, but for what it is that they can do. Knowing what students can do puts you in the position to build on their strengths.

- Multiple sources of information, gathered over time and representative of authentic reading experiences, lead to the most accurate assessments.

- Information gathered for purposes of assessment should be considered collectively and holistically in order to provide the most useful information.

- Students should take an active part in assessing their strengths and weaknesses, and they should take an active part in planning how to build their proficiency in reading.

- Teachers should continually assess the efficacy of their instruction and look for ways to strengthen it.

SELF-CHECK

1. Distinguish between norm-referenced tests and criterion-referenced tests, and note some of the uses and values of norm-referenced and criterion-referenced tests.

2. Describe the informal reading inventory discussed in this chapter and explain some of its uses.

3. Describe some approaches to assessment other than tests and informal reading inventories.

4. Explain the purposes of reading portfolios and list several ways in which they can be used.

5. Name and briefly explain the reading skills, competencies, and attitudes that should probably be assessed and recorded in students' portfolios.

6. Briefly describe at least one procedure for assessing a reading skill and one procedure for assessing attitudes toward reading.

7. Discuss the sorts of self-assessment students should undertake.

8. Explain what *teacher self-assessment* is.

9. Define *reflective teaching*.

10. State several general guidelines to follow when assessing students.

11. Select a grade level that you might like to teach. Consider the reading competencies and attitudes you might assess at this grade level and write a prioritized list in which you identify those you consider most important to assess and those of lesser importance. Then write a brief rationale for the importance of each competency and attitude you have listed. Also, make a note of other sources you would like to consult before finalizing your list.

12. List a representative set of items that you and your students are likely to include in their portfolios. Then consider which of these items might be useful to share with parents at conferences and which might be useful to share with the teacher or teachers your students will have next year.

13. Assessment takes time, something that there is a limited supply of. Assuming you were going to spend two hours a day on reading, how much of that time might you devote to assessment? How would students' age and ability influence the amount of time you spent on assessment?

REFERENCES

Calfee, R. C. and Hiebert, E. H. (1991). Classroom assessment of literacy. In Barr, R., Kamil, M., Mosenthal, P. and Pearson, P. D. (eds.), *Handbook of reading research* (Vol. 2). New York: Longman, pp. 281–309. A detailed review of the research on assessing reading and writing.

Clay, M. (1985). *The early detection of reading difficulties* (3rd ed.). Portsmouth, NH: Heinemann-Boynton/Cook. A classic, insightful, and thought-provoking book.

Clay, M. (1993). *An observation survey of early literacy achievement*. Portsmouth, NH: Heinemann. Another though-provoking book focusing on the nature of early literacy acquisition.

Educational Assessment. (1993–present). Hillsdale, NJ: Erlbaum. This journal, which began publication in 1993, has become one of the leading sources of research on assessment.

Farr, R. (1992). Putting it all together: Solving the reading assessment puzzle. *The Reading Teacher, 46*, 26–37. This article looks at the assessment needs of students, teachers, administrators, and the public, and proposes a multifaceted approach that meets the needs of various audiences.

Flood, J., Lapp, D. and Nagel, G. (1993). Assessing student action beyond reflection and response. *Journal of Reading*, 36, 420–422. Discusses four ways of assessing changes in students' attitudes and behavior, focusing specifically on behavior and beliefs prompted by multicultural literature.

Gillespie, C. S., Ford, K. L., Gillespie, R. D. and Leavell, A. G. (1996). Portfolio assessment: Some questions, some answers, some recommendations. *Journal of Adolescent and Adult Literacy*, 39, 480–491. A synthesis of current thinking related to portfolio assessment.

Goodman, Y. (1991). Evaluating language growth: Informal methods of evaluation. In Flood, J., Jensen, J., Lapp, D. and Squire, J. (eds.), *Handbook for research on teaching the English language arts*. New York: Macmillan, pp. 502–509. A review of the research on informal methods of evaluating students' literacy.

Goodman, Y. M., Watson, D. J. and Burke, C. E. (1987). *Reading miscue inventory: Alternative procedures*. New York: R. C. Owens. An updated version of this well-known text on miscue analysis.

International Reading Association and National Council of Teachers of English. (1996). *Standards for the English language arts*. Newark, DE: International Reading Association. This volume defines each of the standards in detail, explains how they were constructed, and provides examples of how they might be implemented in classrooms.

Johnson, M. S., Kress, R. A. and Pikulski, J. J. (1987). *Informal reading inventories* (2nd ed.). Newark, DE: International Reading Association. A comprehensive description of conventional IRIs and how to use them.

Johnston, P. H. (1992). *Constructive evaluation of literate activity*. New York: Longman. A detailed account of alternative forms of assessment by one of the critics of traditional assessment practices.

Kibby, M. W. (1995). *Practical steps for informing literacy instruction: A diagnostic decision-making model*. Newark, DE: International Reading Association. A brief book providing guidelines for assessment, especially in relation to students experiencing difficulty with reading.

Leslie, L. and Caldwell, J. (1995). *Qualitative Reading Inventory—II*. New York: HarperCollins. One of the most thorough IRIs available.

National Council of Teachers of English. (1996). *Standards for the English language arts*. Urbana, IL: National Council of Teachers of English. Widely read proposed standards in English and reading.

Tierney, R. J., Carter, M. A. and Desai, L. E. (1991). *Portfolio assessment in the reading-writing classroom*. Norwood, MA: Christopher-Gordon. A close look at the thinking behind portfolio assessment and ways of implementing portfolio assessment in the classroom.

Valencia, S. W., Hiebert, E. H. and Afflerbach, P. (Eds.) (1994). *Authentic reading assessment: Practices and possibilities*. Newark, DE: International Reading Association. Presents several examples of district- and school-wide efforts to make literacy assessment more authentic.

CHILDREN'S BOOKS CITED

Blume, J. (1990). *Fudge-a-mania*. New York: Dutton.

Yep, L. (1991). *The star fisher*. New York: Morrow.

10 A Day in a Fourth-Grade Classroom

The day finally arrives when you get your teaching assignment—Edgebrook Middle School, fourth grade. You are both excited and apprehensive. All that you have learned about children and how you can best help them become competent, avid lifelong readers will be put into motion. So how do you take the bits and pieces you have learned over your years of study and practice and transform these, amalgamate them into an exciting and workable reading program for your fourth graders?

As you know, or will soon discover, as you begin planning your reading program, there are certain factors already in place that will, to a large degree, influence the make-up of your reading program: your school district and the school to which you have been assigned; its philosophy, policies, expectations, curriculum; the resources at your disposal—number and kind of computers, library volumes, audiovisual material; resource staff and teacher aides; your classroom, its size, shape, character; and, most of all, your students, their needs, interests, and abilities. These considerations combined with your knowledge and experience will help you to mold and shape your own reading program, from the general contours of the year's broad goals to the smallest details of individual lessons. What might those broad contours and small details look like? In this chapter, we present **one** possibility.

A DAY IN THE LIFE OF MS. PAVAROTTI AND HER FOURTH-GRADE STUDENTS AT EDGEBROOK MIDDLE SCHOOL

Our fictitious teacher, Ms. Pavarotti, views reading instruction as an integral part of every aspect of her fourth graders' day. Beginning with the morning meeting and continuing to the afternoon wrap-up, reading, along with its instructional twin, writing, is an integral part of her classroom activities.

Although Ms. P. allots a specific amount of time each day to what she designates as "reading"—a time in which students are actively engaged in reading activities aimed directly at improving the reading skills, strategies, and behaviors that we have discussed in previous chapters—she also realizes that reading and teaching reading cannot and should not be limited to a specified hour in the day. Because she and her students use language, and very often are reading it, throughout the school day—and beyond, for that matter—there are literacy opportunities from the moment students step into the classroom to the moment they leave.

Here is Ms. Pavarotti's *usual* daily schedule:

  9:00   Journal Writing and Sustained Silent Reading

  9:15   Morning Meeting and News Reports

  9:30   Reading, Language Arts, Social Studies, Art, Music

10:30   Recess

10:45   Reading, Language Arts, Social Studies, Art, Music

11:45   Lunch

12:15   Read-Aloud, Listening Time

12:35   Mathematics

  1:25   Physical Education

  2:15   Science and Health

  2:50   Wrap Up Day

  3:00   School Day Ends

Let's join Ms. Pavarotti for a day with her fourth graders. The day is January 11. It's a Monday.

9:00 Journal Writing

As students arrive, they take out their journals and write their entries for the day. Ms. P., who believes in modeling the behavior she expects of her students, writes in her journal as well. Here is her entry for January 11.

> Today we begin our unit on courage. I've been excited about this unit ever since I wrote the idea on my school calendar back in August. And I'm even more excited now because of the successful unit we had in the fall that revolved around the concept of "thankfulness." What I had written on the yearly calendar was "courage"—the unifying theme for January–February. Courage to my way of thinking is a concept worth spending some time on, and January and February seem the perfect time to do it—since Martin Luther King Jr.'s birthday is in January and February is Black history month and a month to remember and honor past

presidents. I'm looking forward to seeing how the kids will respond to this idea and what we will learn together.

As you can see from Ms. P.'s journal entry, much thought and planning occurred well before this day arrived. The idea for building activities around the central concept of *courage* had sprouted many months earlier. In fact, she had written it on her yearly planner back in August. Shortly after the winter holiday, Ms. P. formulated a general goal for her literacy activities.

General Goal for Unit on Courage: To learn more about the concept of courage as displayed in the lives of people past and present from a variety of cultures as it is expressed in literature, music, art, science, and in the community, school, and families.

After formulating a general goal, she started to do some brainstorming as the second step in planning the unit's activities. She thought about her curriculum and how she could incorporate literacy activities and the theme of courage into each subject area.

Some Thoughts and Ideas for Courage Unit

Reading, Language Arts, and Social Studies: Read and write biographies. Biography as a literary form or genre. Discuss various genres. Present opportunities for listening and viewing also—tapes and films, a guest speaker. Choral reading and dramatics? Time lines? Graphic display showing what parts of the world courageous people have come from. Work on strategies of summarizing and determining what is important. Figurative language—simile and metaphor?

Science: We will be reading about the plant and animal kingdoms. Think about where courage might come in here—can plants be courageous? Animals? (Food for thought!) Present some biographies of courageous scientists, particularly those representing diverse cultures. George Washington Carver? East Indian physicist Subrahmanyan Chandrasekher? First woman doctor, Elizabeth Blackwell? Others? Read aloud: *Kid Heroes of the Environment*—true stories about kids protecting the earth. Work on strategies for gleaning information from informational books.

Technology

Mathematics: Students are working individually, but we will work as a class on word problems. This takes courage! Peer tutoring a success. Doing a lot more of it this month. Bring in biographies of mathematicians. How about engineer Mary Ross? This Cherokee woman helped launch Sally Ride into space! Continue working on strategies for solving story problems. Have students write story problems. Make books containing story problems? Put story problems on computer?

Music: Songs about courage. Have students share contemporary songs that talk about courage. Bring in biographies of courageous musicians. What about Stevie Wonder and Ray Charles? Discuss when and why composers might write songs that instill or celebrate courage. Gospel music is very illustrative of this theme. Learn a gospel song that illustrates aspects of courage (ask Danika for suggestion).

Physical Education: We will be learning how to play volleyball. For many students, this takes a lot of courage. Discuss courage for doing sports. Biographies of courageous sports figures. How about Native American long-distance runner Billy Mills? One-armed baseball player, Jim Abbott, who became Olympic gold medalist? Book illustrator Ted Lewin's experiences as a teenage professional wrestler (combines both art and sports!)? Have students read rules, directions, and daily reminders written on board. Use context cues. How about a "courage" box or "good sportsperson" box for students to write about evidences of courage or good sportsmanship?

Health: We will be reading about diseases in the health text. People who have diseases need courage as well as the people who are trying to find cures. Read about Ryan White and his battle with AIDS? Christopher Reeves? Biographies of physicians and researchers. What about Constance Tom Noguichi who works on sickle cell anemia? Work on summarizing strategy and other strategies for gleaning information from chapters in textbooks.

Art: How is courage expressed in art? Visit art museum to view selected paintings illustrating this theme? Create a classroom mural depicting our most courageous heroes? Are artists themselves courageous? What about Hopi potter, Al Quoawayma, who switched from being a successful engineer to pursue his culture's ancient art? Children's book illustrator Filopino José Aruego. Chinese artist Maya Lin, who designed Vietnam War Memorial. Does it take courage to pursue your artistic dreams? Let students pursue individual art projects if they are so inspired. Pottery? Sculpture? Weaving? Jewelry making? (Senator Ben Nighthorse Campbell is also a Native American jewelry maker. Students could write to him to find out more about his art.)

After this brainstorming, Ms. P. plotted her ideas on her monthly calendars, outlining her general plans for the weeks to come. After she did this, she could focus on the individual weeks and days, make more detailed plans, order books and films, and line up field trips and guest speakers. Her overall plan is shown in Figure 10–1. Her weekly plans, shown in Figure 10–2, provide a bit more detail.

	WEEK 1	WEEK 2
Morning Meeting	Intro concept of courage, courage unit, and news reports on courage	Daily concerns Preview of week News reports
Reading and Language Arts Social Studies Music Art	Review skimming Begin "determining what is important" strategy Silent and oral reading Discuss biographies (culturally diverse) Figurative Language Response journals Courage in gospel music: Learn Black National Anthem Film on Harriet Tubman	Practice "determining what is important" w/ bios Review focusing; start silent reading in bios Discuss vocab work Response journals Read aloud Maya Lin bio and "The Wall" by Eve Bunting Students plan memorial sculpture or other project Make time lines representing people in bios Research major event of time periods represented
Reading Aloud	Martin Luther King, Jr. biography	MLK
Math	Independent and peer tutoring Group word problems Mystery word: *product*	Writing word problems Mary Ross bio Mystery word: *mathematician*
P.E. (Display bios of sports figures throughout unit)	Volleyball Context cues in directions, rules, etc.; "Courage" box	Volleyball Students write and read evaluation of group progress
Science or Health	Plants and animal kingdoms Strategies for gleaning info from informational books Ask question: Do plants and animals display courage? George W. Carver bio	Plant & animal kingdoms Strategies for remembering info (graphic organizers) Answer question: Do plants and animals display courage? Bio of monkey lady (get name)
Wrap-up	Discuss concerns and highlights of day	Discuss concerns and highlights of day

Figure 10–1. Five-Week "Courage" Unit

WEEK 3	WEEK 4	WEEK 5
Daily concerns Preview of week News reports	Concerns; preview of week Reports on courage of presidents	Concerns; preview of week Reports on courage of presidents
Finish reading bios Motivate, explain, and model bio writing Strategy (a writing strategy to be determined) Students do pre-writing for bios Guest speaker: Native American Gary Cavanaugh Students interview him for possible bio Begin courage mural Native American songs and drumming	Continue adding to time lines Students write rough drafts of bios Students read bios aloud to groups Critique groups; revise bios Continue mural and individual projects Individual conferences to hear students read bios Final draft of bio due Monday Listen to Asian guest musician	Make books or produce radio shows of bios Finish mural projects and time lines Read and perform bios to other classes and at nursing home Trip to art museum to view portraits Perform songs and dances Invite parents and others to class Compare and contrast Native American and Asian music
MLK and Comanche Chief, Quanah Parker	Quanah Parker	Quanah Parker
Students find bios of mathematicians, especially those from other cultures Mystery word: *dividend*	Independent skills work and peer tutoring Einstein bio Mystery word: *base*	Work w/ other numeric bases Bio of An Wang Compose and read chart of possible careers in math
Dance Read Billy Mills bio Learn Native American dance	Dance Learn Asian dance Read Diagrams	Dance Review Native American and Asian dances
Diseases Review approaches to chapter reading Read chapter using reading guide Group work	Diseases Reread chapter to complete chart Group work Read aloud bio on Constance Tom Noguichi	Review science and health units Evaluations and reports
Discuss concerns and highlights of day	Discuss concerns and highlights of day	Make drums for dances and songs

	MONDAY	TUESDAY
Morning Meeting	Semantic map on courage Explain and model news reports on courage Read and discuss daily schedule	Read and discuss daily concerns and schedule Explain and model second example of courage for news report
Reading and Language Arts Social Studies Music Art	Intro bios as genre Read snippets from bios to motivate Review skimming strategy Students skim at least three books to select bio to read SSR	Motivate, explain, and model "determining what's important" strategy Group work practicing strategies w/ bios Evaluate skills work and group functioning
Recess		
Reading and Language Arts Social Studies Music Art	Motivate, explain, and model response journals Distribute journals Silent reading bios Write responses in journals	Intro MLK and his colorful language—simile and metaphor Read excerpts Students write and illustrate own examples
Read Aloud	MLK—*I Have a Dream* Ch 1	Chapt 2
Math (Mystery word for week: *product*)	Group work—Review steps to solve story problems (see Collier and Redmond article) Mystery word clue 1 Independent work	Answer math question from previous day Mystery word clue 2 Skills group—long division
P.E.—Volleyball	Review context cues while reading conduct reminders	Introduce "Courage" or "Sportsmanship" box
Science or Health	Review info vs fiction Review features of info books Pose courage theme—Students skim and begin reading in trade books Plant and animal kingdoms	Meet with groups that want to do extra projects Groups meet to share what they learned yesterday
Wrap-up	As needed	As needed

Figure 10–2.   Week One of "Courage" Unit

WEDNESDAY	THURSDAY	FRIDAY
Daily concerns and schedule Form news report groups and review report model	Daily concerns and schedule Have one member from each group present news report in one category	Daily concerns and schedule Have one member from each group present news report in one category
Skills group on blending	Reading guide for practicing "determining what is important" w/ bios Evaluate activity and discuss as a class	See film on Harriet Tubman Discuss courage Make chart a slave brave smart spiritual (Harriet Tubman)
Students share responses from journals Silent reading in bios Write in journals	Courage as expressed in music Listen to recording of Black National Anthem; read lyrics; look for courage and examples of metaphor and simile; sing anthem	SSR in bios; meet individually with students Students and teacher make portfolio entries
Chapt 3	Chapt 4	Chapt 5
Whole class—word problems Skill group—word problems Math word clue 3	Students write story problems Skills group—long division Math word clue 4	Solve student story problems Skills group? Reveal mystery word Treat—new math game for class
Review rules—use context cues	"Sportsmanship" box	Read "Sportsmanship" entries Choose sport
Film strip on classifying plants and animals Group reading and recording in journals	Read from George Washington Carver bio	Whole class shares journal responses Classify plants and animals as a whole-class activity Make chart
As needed	As needed	As needed

By looking at Ms. Pavarotti's plans, it is obvious—there are more ideas than it will be possible to implement. However, the activities that best fit her students and their mutual goals will come into focus as the days progress and her plan becomes more precise and detailed. Also, the ongoing needs and interests of her students will dictate which activities to implement. Plans for Tuesday will need to be altered to reflect what occurred on Monday. Ms. P.'s plans are merely guidelines that she knows will be shaped and reshaped minute by minute and day by day.

Let's return now to January 11, and see how Ms. Pavarotti incorporates reading activities into every aspect of her student's day. After they finish writing in their journals, they begin Sustained Silent Reading.

9:05   Sustained Silent Reading

Background Information: Each morning, students read silently from material of their choosing.

While the students are reading this morning, Ms. P. is reading also—an article from *The Reading Teacher*.

9:15   Morning Meeting

Background Information: The morning meeting is a time to discuss daily concerns and to read and discuss the schedule for the day.

Today, before the schedule is even discussed, Ms. P. puts the outline for a *courage* map (Figure 10–3) on the chalkboard and has students brainstorm to suggest examples of three aspects of courage—courageous people, courageous deeds, and other words for courage.

After students have given their responses, Ms. P. explains that they will be focusing on the concept of courage for the next several weeks, thinking about how courage relates to many things they learn about and do in school and out. "By the end of the time, we'll all probably have a different view of this complicated and abstract idea," she tells them.

Ms. P. asks a volunteer to transfer the responses she has written on the board onto a chart. The chart will be kept on display and new ideas added to it as the month progresses.

Figure 10–3.   Courage Map

9:25   News Reports

Background Information: This portion of the day Ms. P. has allocated to "current events." Ms. P's class has been working on giving "news reports," which involves answering the questions Who? What? When? Where? Why? and/or How? Today Ms. P. will also use this time to introduce the courage theme using a semantic map in order to motivate students and get them thinking about the concept "courage."

Ms. P. begins by telling students she is going to read a newspaper article that she thinks illustrates the concept *courage* and asks students to listen to see whether they agree with her. The article focuses on a single mother of five getting her college degree. After reading the article, Ms. P. tells students why *she* thinks the woman shows courage and then encourages students to give their opinions.

Next Ms. P. displays the News Report Chart and shows students how she would complete it, sharing with them her thought processes as she does so.

NEWS REPORT

What is the report about? A woman getting her college degree

Who is the report about? Janet Crow, single mother of five

Where did the event take place? State University, Middletown USA

When did the event take place? December 23

How does this event show courage? I think it takes courage to go back to school when you're older because there may not be many people your age at school and it's probably been a long time since you've had to study and take tests. Also, Janet had to give up some things for herself and her kids. She was taking a chance that getting a college education would allow her to get a better job so her kids might have more opportunities. I think that takes courage.

Ms. P. explains to students that their news reports for the next several weeks will focus on courage. They can select articles from newspapers or magazines to read to the class, or they can write up a short report from TV or radio news. They can also report courageous events that take place in school or at home. As a class they will do two things to help remember the people and events they report—complete a *what, who, where, when* and *how* chart and record all courageous events reported on a large sheet of butcher paper on a "Courage All Over the World" chart.

COURAGE ALL OVER THE WORLD

Family: On Feb. 9, Billy's little brother took three steps by himself.

School: On Feb. 11, Marta read a paragraph aloud in English.

City: On Feb. 3, Byron Slone . . .

State:

Country:

World:

The Reading, Language Arts, Social Studies, Music, and Art Block

After the Morning Meeting and News Reports, Ms. P. begins the Reading, Language Arts, Social Studies, Music, and Art block of activities, which usually runs from 9:30 to 11:45 with a fifteen minute recess in the middle. Today, Ms. P. is not following her usual time schedule. The activities for the morning meeting and news reports demanded extra time. Also, since the activities Ms. P. has planned for Reading and Language Arts require a sustained block of time, music and art will not be included today. However, if you look on her weekly planner, music and art activities are slated for later in the week. For "reading" this morning, Ms. P. and her students will discuss biographies as a specialized genre, review skimming as a reading strategy for selecting a biography to read in depth, and read silently for fifteen minutes. Beginning tomorrow, Ms. P. will also work with a selected group of students who need help with various skills. Language arts activities revolve around journal writing, and social studies activities include investigating courage as displayed in real people's lives. All of these subjects —reading, language arts, and social studies—are interrelated, a mirror of the real world.

9:45   Reading: Motivating and Suggesting Strategies

Background Information: To motivate her students, Ms. P. has spent some time beforehand selecting biographies (with the help of the school librarian and several bibliographies) that reflect the varying interests and abilities of her students. Because one of her goals is to expose students to individuals of many different cultures, her selection of biographies reflects this.

On the chalkboard ledge and table, she has displayed numerous trade books, biographies of culturally diverse individuals. These books range from picture books to lengthy chapter books.

Ms. P. begins by telling students that all the books on display have one thing in common—each of them focuses on the life and deeds of one individual. After that, she has students think about and discuss why these people might have had a book written about them and writes students' suggestions on the board.

Next, she reads a paragraph or two from several of the biographies that she has preselected and that she knows will pique her students' interests. After reading, she tells students that these books are called biographies—written accounts of a person's life. She writes *biography* on the board and explains to students how biographies differ from other types of books. She asks students to tell about biographies they have read, note if they liked them, and explain why. She poses the question, "Why do you think people are interested in writing about and reading about other peoples' lives?" but doesn't ask for a response now. She tells students to keep that question in mind as they explore the contents of "these wonderful biographies."

Ms. P. explains to students that during the next five weeks they will be reading and writing biographies and will get to choose which biographies they want to read and whom they want to write a biography about. She discusses with them what they might expect to gain from biographies, why biographies are interesting and informative, and how the ideas revealed in biographies might be helpful in their own lives.

To help students decide which biography they want to read, Ms. P. suggests that a good strategy to use is skimming. She models the strategy with several of the biographies—reading the title and the table of contents, scanning the chapters from beginning to end, commenting on illustrations and photographs, and maybe reading a few selected passages aloud. Then she models the thinking she went through in trying to decide whether or not *Beyond the Myth: The Story of Joan of Arc* by Polly Schoyer Brooks was the biography she wanted to read. "Hmm. This might be an interesting book. I like reading about heroic women. But I see that Joan of Arc lived in the 15th century, and I think I'd like to read about someone a little more modern. Also, it's kind of long and has a lot of words I don't know. I like learning knew words, but it may take me too long to read if I have to stop and look up a lot of words. I think this is a book Tara would like—and I'm going to recommend it to her—but I think I'll see what some of the other books are about."

Ms. P. then models skimming and considering a few more books before letting students choose their own books to skim. Finally, she tells students to skim at least three books and then choose one of those to read. They will have until recess to skim and read.

10:45   Language Arts—Response Journals

Background Information: The next activity—which Ms. P. has labeled in her plans under the subject "Language Arts"—is a continuation of the previous "reading" activity and is one the students are familiar with, having kept reading journals of various sorts since the beginning of the school year. It is also an activity students will be involved in daily until they finish reading their selected biographies.

Ms. P.s' students have made dual entries in their journals before, but since they will be doing something slightly different in these journals, she spends a little time motivating, explaining, and modeling the procedure.

"You know," Ms. P. tells her students, "When I was reading through biographies to bring to class, I kept reading things that made me stop and think, 'Wow, that's neat,' or 'I know how she feels. I felt that way myself.' Things like that. I'll show you what I mean."

After that, Ms. P. reads a sentence or two from a biography about mathematician and computer genius An Wang to illustrate her point, and then writes on the board.

Response Journal

Idea from Biography	My Response
Page 8. Wang's new word processor made it easy to see your words and to correct your mistakes.	I love you, Wang!

As Ms. P. explains to her students, "When I read that Wang had invented the word processor, it really hit me how much this man had made my job so much easier and more enjoyable. I really feel grateful to him."

Ms. P. proceeds to describe several other types of responses she had—questions brought to mind, ideas that prompted her to make connections with her own experiences, strong feelings she had in response to certain events or ideas—and writes these on the board. After sufficient explanation and modeling, Ms. P. tells students she wants them to use their journals similarly while reading in their biographies—to write a quote, idea, word, whatever, on the left side of the journal page and their response to the quote, idea, word, whatever, next to it on the right side of the page.

Ms. P. distributes the journals but, before students begin reading and writing in them, she makes certain that they are clear on the purpose and procedure for this activity. She assigns "reading buddies" to students who might need extra help reading and writing. Buddies go to special locations designated as conference areas—places where students are free to interact with each other without disturbing others.

While students are reading silently and writing in their journals, Ms. P. is reading a biography and writing in her journal. Her classroom aide (who is available every day from 10:30 to 12:00) circulates among students to offer advice and encourage students to keep on task.

Before students leave for lunch, Ms. P. asks if any of them have something they would like to share from their journals. If not, she shares something from hers.

11:45   Lunch

12:15   Read-Aloud Time

Background Information: This is a routine that fosters quiet and rest after an active play period, and also provides students with an opportunity to hear good literature skillfully read. When Ms. P.'s students come in from lunch they can sit anywhere where they feel the most comfortable, at their desks with their heads down, on the rug, in the bean bag chairs—as long as they are quiet and polite and don't interfere with the rights of others. If there is disruption of the calm, which Ms. P. insists on for "read aloud" time, then students forgo their right to choose where to sit, and Ms. P. exercises her right to choose for them.

Today, Ms. P. begins reading aloud from *I Have a Dream, the Life of Martin Luther King, Jr.* by Margaret Davidson. To preserve the atmosphere of calm that prevails at this time of day, she begins reading with only a brief introduction in which she talks about courage and how students will see many examples of courage as they listen to the biography. Before she begins reading the first chapter, she encourages them to think about and remember one example of King's courage that is illustrated in the chapter.

At the end of the reading, she asks students if they noticed any courage illustrated. But instead of discussing their ideas, she asks them to keep their thoughts private, think about them, and maybe share them later with a friend or family member.

12:35   Mathematics

Technology

Background Information: Ms. Pavarotti's students typically work on math skills independently while she instructs a group of students on specific math concepts and procedures. The group and what is being taught changes as necessity dictates. Students spend ten minutes of their skills time tutoring and ten minutes being tutored. Highly skilled students are tutored by upper grade students, high school volunteers, and computers. Each student, no matter his or her ability, has a tutoring responsibility. Ms. P. has had good results with this approach, finding that even the most reluctant students can learn if they are expected to teach someone else.

Before students begin independent work, tutoring, or small group instruction on a specific skill, Ms. P. will conduct a 15 minute whole-class lesson which includes two topics: Reviewing how to solve story problems and presenting the new "mystery" math word for the week.

From prior lessons, Ms. P.'s students already know that math is a kind of language that requires a different approach than the language in a story or informational book. Today's lesson is a review of the steps to solve story problems. Ms. P. took the problem from one that had arisen in the previous week in which students were running laps in the gym and trying to keep track of their progress.

At the beginning of the lesson, Ms. P. writes this problem on the board:

The gym floor is 100' × 50'. How far did Matt run if he ran 10 lengths of the gym?

"Does this problem sound familiar?" she asks her students.

The students recognize what Ms. P is talking about. The week before they had been keeping track of how many lengths they ran across the gym, but didn't calculate how *far* they had run.

Ms. P. refers her class to the questions for solving word problems on the chart shown below, and together they come up with the equation: $100' \times 10' = 1,000'$.

QUESTIONS TO ASK FOR SOLVING STORY PROBLEMS

1. What is the situation being described?

2. What is it you're trying to find out?

3. Is all the necessary information included?

4. Is any *unnecessary* information included?

5. What mathematical procedures do you need to apply? Adding? Subtracting? Multiplying? Dividing?

6. Does the answer you get make sense?

Ms. P. challenges students with this question: "Did Matt run more than a mile or less than a mile? How much more than a mile or less than a mile? Try and find out, and we'll discuss the answer tomorrow."

Before students begin their tutoring and group sessions, Ms. P. shows them the first clue for the "mystery" math word for the week—$A \times B = C$. Students are not to say the word out loud, but put their written guesses with their name and the date on them in the "mystery word box." Each day Ms. P. reports how many have correctly guessed the word, and gives a new clue. At the end of the week, she reveals the mystery word, and if

90% of the class has guessed it, the class gets a special reward. The "mystery" word this week is *product*.

1:25 Physical Education

Background Information: For the next few weeks, Ms. P.'s students will be learning how to play volleyball. This will involve both learning a set of game rules and abiding by the rules of conduct in the gym and traveling to and from the gym. Both activities will require some reading. Ms. P. has decided to focus on using context cues to figure out unknown words as an appropriate and useful reading skill to concentrate on. The concept *courage* will also be reinforced as an attribute of those who participate in sports. To encourage sportsmanlike behavior and to provide a concrete way for students to use writing skills, Ms. P. has developed a "Sports Person of the Day" box. Similar to a "suggestion" box, students write the name of someone they think demonstrated good sportsmanlike behavior or courage. On the paper, students answer the questions who, what, when, and why. Who did the sportsmanlike or courageous behavior? What was it? When was it done? Why is it sportsmanlike? Ms. P. will introduce this idea on Tuesday or Wednesday.

Before students go to the gym to play volleyball, Ms. P. writes these sentences on the board:

When we walk to the gym we need to remember other classes are working. If we are noisy, we might disturb them. Let's try and remember to be *unobtrusive*.

Ms. P. encourages her students to use context cues to figure out the meaning of *unobtrusive*. She asks students who can guess what the word means to raise their hands and tells them she will know if they had the right meaning if they do as the sentences tell them on their walk to the gym.

After students return from the gym, Ms. P. praises their excellent behavior, then discusses the meaning of *unobtrusive*, encouraging students to explain how they used the context she had provided to discover its meaning.

2:15 Science

Background Information: Last week Ms. P. began motivating students for their unit of study on the plant and animal kingdoms. She decided that reading and research in these topics would best be accomplished with both group and individual work. When planning goals and activities for the unit, she also made provisions for those with special needs and interests. Additionally, the books Ms. P. selected for the unit reflect the varied reading abilities of her students.

To begin, Ms. P. reviews the special features of informational books, reminding students that informational books are written and organized differently from novels and short stories because their main purpose is to provide the reader with information, while stories are primarily meant to entertain. (Of course, both can do either. Good informational books are often entertaining; and good stories can also give us information and get us thinking about ideas.) To illustrate what she means about communicating information being the main goal of informational books, she reads a few book titles aloud and asks students to tell what sort of information they think the book will disclose. Next, she explains that informational books often have a number of special features. Some of these include a Table of Contents, headings and subheadings, introductory paragraphs and summaries, graphs, illustrations, labels, charts, maps, indexes, and glossaries. Ms. P. points out these features in several books she has preselected for this purpose.

After Ms. P. has reviewed these features, she asks students why the author might have included them. After a brief discussion, Ms. P. offers students the "bottom line." "The author includes these features to make information more memorable and understandable for readers. They're put there for us—the reader. That's why we want to take advantage of these things when we read."

Next, Ms. P. divides the class into two groups—those who want to learn more about plants and those who want to learn more about animals. The students are to each select at least three books to skim. Paying attention to the various features of the books—table of contents, headings and subheadings, introductory paragraphs and summaries, graphs, illustrations, labels, charts, maps, indexes, glossaries—they are to record one piece of information they find interesting in their Informational Books journals. (These are binders students have kept from the beginning of the year to jot down various responses while reading informational books.) The next day they will meet again with their groups to share what they found. To tie in the courage theme, Ms. P. also asks students to think about the question of whether or not plants or animals are capable of courage. They will discuss this idea as they get further into their study of the plant and animal kingdoms.

Students gather with their groups and select and skim through their books, recording the title and one piece of information from each in their journals. Since students have differing interests and abilities, and work at varying rates, Ms. P. has provided for these individual needs: Students who need special assistance—for example, her ESL students and her visually-challenged students—will be assigned to reading buddies.

Technology

Additional activities will challenge students talented in various areas. Students can create a graph either on graph paper or on the computer indicating the number and kind of features found in the various books on their selected topic; or write glossaries for those books without them and include student glossary pages in the books for other readers to use; or draw additional illustrations, charts, or maps for the various books.

These will be on-going projects for students to work on at their own pace. Ms. P. will meet with students interested in pursuing these projects to explain how to do them. Any student in the class has the option of working on these projects. Students can work on them individually or in groups. Also, students might chose to work on these projects at other times of the day when their other work is completed.

2:50   Wrap-up

Background Information: Although days are busy and sometimes a bit hectic, Ms. P. strives to include time at the end of each day to bring closure to the day's activities. The daily "wrap-up" usually includes some sort of review and discussion of the special delights or problems the day held.

Ms. P. calls students' attention to the schedule for the day, which is written on the chalkboard. Together they read and briefly talk about each subject or activity. During this time students ask questions, or share something they enjoyed or learned, or bring up problems they had. Problems that can't be resolved easily are "tabled" for the moment until there is a better time for resolution, perhaps during the next day's morning meeting.

3:00   School Day Ends

After the students have gone, and while the day's events are still fresh in her mind, Ms. P. begins her planning for the next day. As she reviews the day's activities, and looks at what she had planned for Tuesday, she realizes she will have to make some changes. In math, some students had a difficult time solving the word problem. Instead of taking whole-class time for another problem, she decides she will group these students for a mini-lesson. Other students then will have longer time to work independently and to do their tutoring. Since her parent volunteer comes on Tuesdays from 12:25 to 1:25, the volunteer can help monitor these students while Ms. P. works with the group that needs some more assistance on word problems.

AFTERWORD

This day in the life of Ms. Pavarotti illustrates, of course, only one of the many possible ways reading and reading instruction might be implemented in the elementary school classroom.

There is a song from a Broadway musical with lines that go something like this, "bit by bit, putting it together, we can make a work of art." Here the lyricist is alluding to a musical production, but in many ways a teacher, along with his or her students, plays every role in the on-going production of classroom instruction—playwright, producer, actor, audience, and critic. What the teacher and students produce together, with the help of many stage hands, and with hard work, energy, commitment, laughter and sometimes tears, is a work of art whose value is measured by the degree to which the lives of those who had a hand in its creation are enriched and empowered.

Author Index

Subject Index